Milton's
HOUSE
of GOD

Milton's
HOUSE of GOD

The Invisible and Visible Church

Stephen R. Honeygosky

UNIVERSITY OF MISSOURI PRESS
Columbia and London

Copyright © 1993 by
The Curators of the University of Missouri
University of Missouri Press, Columbia, Missouri 65201
Printed and bound in the United States of America
All rights reserved

5   4   3   2   1   97   96   95   94   93

Library of Congress Cataloging-in-Publication Data

Honeygosky, Stephen R., 1948–
    Milton's house of God : the invisible and visible
church / Stephen R. Honeygosky.
        p.   cm.
    Includes bibliographical references and index.
    ISBN 0-8262-0876-2 (alk. paper)
    1. Milton, John, 1608–1674—Religion. 2. Christianity
and literature—England—History—17th century.
3. Christian poetry, English—History and criticism.
4. Church—History of doctrines—17th century.
5. Church in literature. I. Title.
PR3592.R4H66   1993   92-38869
821'.4—dc20   CIP

∞™ This paper meets the requirements of the
American National Standard for Permanence of Paper
for Printed Library Materials, Z39.48, 1984.

Designer: Kristie Lee
Typesetter: Connell-Zeko Type & Graphics
Printer and Binder: Thomson-Shore, Inc.
Typefaces: Palatino, Caxton Book, Engravers Text

"Some people have entertained angels without knowing it."

(Hebrews 13:2)

To my brother Kevin and to my family—
special angelic visitor and special
unwitting hosts.

CONTENTS

ACKNOWLEDGMENTS

Without certain academic preparation, professional direction, and personal support, this book would not have been written. I am grateful for the theological and scriptural training received at Saint Vincent Archabbey and Seminary in Latrobe, Pennsylvania. The knowledge I gained there provided me with two pillars without which my literary claims would have stood much less solidly.

I owe unrepayable thanks to a few individuals. Rene Kollar referred me to the most recent scholarship in history and historiography, which taught me much about Milton's relationship to the Radical Puritan Tradition.

At the dissertation stage of this study, at the University of Wisconsin-Madison, Alexander Chambers provided measures of professional and personal assistance that surpassed the call of duty. His twin lamps of fastidious criticism and hearty encouragement lit the way through some shadowy valleys. Leah Marcus and Andrew Weiner suggested emphases and organizational strategies that enhanced the shape of a number of ideas and helped me keep my intended focus.

Joseph Wittreich, who introduced me to Milton in my very first graduate course, read portions of this manuscript and encouraged me to pursue publication. I especially thank him for believing in this book. More recently, John King—in his seminar at The Ohio State University on "The Protestant Imagination," funded by the National Endowment for the Humanities—greatly supported me in the sculpting of most of this text out of my dissertation. I am deeply thankful for his response to the restructuring, his close reading of Parts II and III, and his enormous encouragement. Additionally, I benefited there from the critical suggestions, wide-ranging excellences, and enthusiasm of all eleven other colleagues. And as the manuscript neared its last stage, Albert Labriola offered valuable commentary and endorsement.

I am indebted to the editors of *Milton Quarterly* and *Studia Mystica* for granting permission to reprint, with changes, two of my articles written for their journals: All of "*License* Reconsidered: Ecclesial Nuances," *Milton Quarterly* 25 (1991): 59–66, appears with changes in a section of the introduction and in chapter 7. Sections 2 and 4 of "The Mystical in Milton: A Radical Protestant View," *Studia Mystica* 14 (1991): 45–59, are reprinted with changes in a portion of chapter 2 and a portion of chapter 15, respectively. And I am most grateful to William B. Hunter who promptly and generously shared a copy of his paper, "The Provenance of the *Christian Doctrine*," with me before its publication, along with responses, in *SEL* 32 (1992): 129–66. I should also like to thank Peter F. M. Koehler, dean of the College of Arts and Sciences, and Dr. Alberta Sbragia, director of the West European Studies Program, at the University of Pittsburgh, for subsidizing publication costs.

Without other major practical generosities and favorable conditions in which to work, however, my ideas would have had no opportunity to be made, no shops in which to be forged and refined, and no smiths to help with the various steps in the production. Saint Vincent College granted me time off for a portion of this study; Saint Vincent Archabbey contributed financially; and the NEH awarded the 1990 Summer Seminar grant, which greatly helped me get this into book form. The hideaway at St. Vincent's Library and the woodsy hermitage at the St. Benedict Center fostered the stillness and energy necessary for my right and left hands to manage what I wanted to say about Milton's house of God.

Standing out among generous souls are Chrysostom Schlimm, director of libraries, for his many exceptions to regulations; Shirley Dorazio for book loans; Candace Henry, a devoted student and research assistant, for gathering material with unwavering care; Gloria Lutz for proofreading; and my confreres Archabbot Douglas Nowicki and Clarence Karawsky for crucial time and magnanimity. In preparing the manuscript, Ruth Kelnhofer and all her personnel at "The Office" in Madison demonstrated unusual and consistent speed, precision, and kindness. And in producing this book, I will always be grateful to Beverly Jarrett, Jane Lago, Karen Caplinger, and my editor, Polly Law, at the University of Missouri Press.

Most of all, I recognize my family, whose cheers and charity were "deeds / Above heroic"; the darker side of my solitude never lessened the constancy of their patience and love.

A NOTE ON TEXTS
AND ABBREVIATIONS

Biblical citations are to the King James Version, known also as the Authorized Version.

The following editions have been used for the works of Milton: *The Complete Prose Works of John Milton*, gen. ed. Don M. Wolfe (New Haven: Yale University Press, 1953–1982), 8 vols., cited parenthetically within the text by volume and page number(s) and abbreviated only in the notes as *CPW* for editorial referencing. There are two editions of volume seven, and I am quoting from the earlier 1974. *John Milton: Complete Poems and Major Prose*, ed. Merritt Y. Hughes (Indianapolis: Odyssey-Bobbs-Merrill, 1957), abbreviated only in the notes as *CPMP*.

The following abbreviations will be used parenthetically in the text to identify oft-cited primary texts by other writers:

MT	William Ames, *The Marrow of Theology*
ICR	Jean Calvin, *Institutes of the Christian Religion*
NRC	Jean Calvin, *The Necessity of Reforming the Church*
LW	Martin Luther, *Works*, vol. 53, *Liturgy and Hymns*
WWP	William Perkins, *The Work of William Perkins*
WHZ	Huldreich Zwingli, *The Works of Huldreich Zwingli*
ZW	Huldrych Zwingli, *Writings*

Milton's
HOUSE
of GOD

It is certain . . . that it is not the visible church but the hearts of believers which, since Christ's ascension, have continually constituted the *pillar* and *ground of truth*. They are the real *house and church of the living God*, 1 Tim. 3:15.

Christian Doctrine (CPW 6:589)

INTRODUCTION

t is usually believed that the writing of *Lycidas* in 1637 marked Milton's break with the established Church of England and, thus, became the definitive turning point in his ministerial development from priestly to prophetic service.[1] With this received understanding, moreover, comes the presumption that Milton rejected church and liturgy. If, however, one examines the prose texts that Milton begins writing shortly after this period of formal institutional renunciation, one discovers clear and systematic treatment of church doctrine, church membership, and church worship. Someone so committed to keeping covenant and contact with God, as Milton had been, would not—indeed, could not—relinquish spiritual responsibility to feed God's flock or ignore ecclesiastical Reformation, since both pressing tasks stemmed from a deep continuous need and desire to bond with Christ and his members in a mystic, though not entirely invisible, relationship. Just as William Kerrigan talks of Milton's "prophetic impulse" or Michael Lieb of Milton's "consecratory impulse" and "cultic impulse," so also is it reasonable to speak of Milton's ecclesial impulse—an urge so basic to Milton that without it his ecclesiastical, political, and theological treatises, as a whole, make little single-minded sense and his later poems have much less ideological purpose.[2]

Michael Fixler maintains that *Paradise Lost* "was originally conceived as a church, designed, that is, for a unique act of public or liturgical worship."[3] But if *Paradise Lost* is a church about which it is important to know something of its building, it is just as important

---

1. See Margo Anne Kent, "Poetry as Liturgy: Poet as Priest in Some of Milton's Early Poetry."

2. Kerrigan, *The Prophetic Milton,* 12; Lieb, *Poetics of the Holy: A Reading of* Paradise Lost, 64, 224.

3. Fixler, "The Apocalypse within *Paradise Lost,*" 174.

1

to know something about the assembled congregation and about the texts that bring and bind these church members together. Following his ecclesial impulse, Milton provides this information throughout his prose, but encases the substance of his teaching specifically in his *Christian Doctrine* when discussing the invisible church and the visible church (bk. 1, chaps. 24, 29, and 31) and when explaining internal and external worship (bk. 2, chaps. 3 and 4).

For now, a summary of that teaching is sufficient and necessary. Of the invisible church Milton writes: "The body of Christ is mystically one, so it follows that the communion of his members must be mystic. It need not be subject to spatial considerations; it includes people from many remote countries, and from all ages since the creation of the world" (6:500). The visible church is "THE ASSEMBLY OF THOSE WHO ARE CALLED" (6:563), and it "is either UNIVERSAL OR PARTICULAR" (6:568). Milton proceeds to describe each kind of visible church in separate chapters: "THE UNIVERSAL VISIBLE CHURCH IS THE WHOLE MULTITUDE OF THOSE WHO ARE CALLED FROM ANY PART OF THE WHOLE WORLD, AND WHO OPENLY WORSHIP GOD THE FATHER IN CHRIST EITHER INDIVIDUALLY OR IN CONJUNCTION WITH OTHERS" (6:568); "A PARTICULAR CHURCH" is a society of persons professing the faith, united by a special bond of brotherhood, and chiefly organized for the purpose of promoting mutual edification and the communion of the saints" (6:594). I will argue that for Milton the two major dimensions of church (the invisible and the visible) have an inextricable, ongoing, intersecting-though-not-equivalent relationship. It is the dynamic interaction between these two faces of the Church out of which Milton's entire ecclesiology proceeds.

But because a church's doctrine is tangibly and measurably evident in the way it relates to the God it teaches about, it is also important to consider worship—the other focal point for providing information about Milton's church. He explains that "OUR DUTY TOWARDS GOD IS IMMEDIATE WORSHIP, which may be either internal or external," and then delineates that "internal worship means . . . acknowledgement of the one true God and devout affection for him" (6:656). In the next chapter, although he announces that he is turning to external worship, Milton's obvious preoccupation is with what he regards as the primary and more preeminent of the two. External worship is what "is usually called RELIGION: not that internal worship is not religion, but it is not usually called so unless it shows itself in externals. External worship, moreover, though it may be distinguished from internal for the sake of argument, should in practice go hand in hand with it" (6:666). Milton can conclude, therefore, that "internal worship, provided that it is sincere, is acceptable to God even if the external forms are not strictly observed" (6:668).

Milton's treatment of church and worship manifests, in small, his ecclesial penchant, and the ecclesiology that pervades the rest of this treatise and most of his prose crystallizes in these two specific places of *Christian Doctrine.*

Readers of Milton range widely in their acknowledgment, articulation, and application of Milton's doctrine on the Church. Some ignore it; others minimize it; still others, who may recognize it, read Milton's work less than adequately—even wrongly in certain instances—either by omission of pertinent parts of his ecclesiology or by overemphasis of certain ones. There are no thorough discussions of Milton's ecclesiology or of the leftist ecclesial identity deriving from it. Critical references to the doctrine of the Church in Milton are spotty and brief, dealing frequently with political, topical, or structural issues, or with translations of a doctrinal point into political faction, poetic personage, or poetic schema. Nonetheless, ecclesial comments lacing these studies can provide points of reference—positive and negative. Since the critical literature on Milton's church doctrine is without a tradition, to begin, I wish to gather the valuable trace commentary to establish a critical forum for this particular topic and to show where this study is and is not heading; hence, the following rather extensive critical exchange.

To elucidate the ecclesiastically political business of Milton's *Mask,* Leah S. Marcus uses Milton's unusual application of the Matins pericope of Michaelmas (Mark 2:23–28) on the debate between the Pharisees and Christ over the (un)lawfulness of his disciples' picking corn on the Sabbath: While strict Sabbatarian Puritans *obviously* resembled the Pharisees, the Laudians distorted Christ's teaching no less "in the opposite direction." "By building tight ecclesiastical structures, requiring rigid adherence to canon law, royal proclamations, and the traditions of the church," the Prelates "were molding believers to fit the demands of the church and not the church for believers." According to Marcus, both parties rejected the inner freedom that undergirds Milton's and his patron's religious and political beliefs, symbolized by Sabrina, who—like Comus—"is associated with the ritual functions of the church but in freer and less centralized form." In Sabrina's victory over Comus, "Milton sym-

bolically disarms the Laudian Church in its challenge to secular ju-
dicial authority," since "a church which would rather tolerate spiritual indolence than cope with the unsettling ferment of genuine
spiritual freedom is not the institution best qualified to police public
morals and improve the spiritual health of the community."[4]

Clearly, Marcus's political reading depends on Milton's idea of the
Church, however generalized and implicit it exists there. Correctly
subordinating the external operation of the Church (with the hierarchy's structures and strictures) to the internal or spiritual (with
the individual's open deliberation and free choice), Marcus asserts
and applies only the upshot of Milton's ecclesial teaching. While the
importance of the invisible church lurks just beneath the surface of
her reading, Marcus never names this primacy or foregrounds the
distinction and interaction between the invisible church and the visible church, much less delineate Milton's pertinent ecclesiology.

Assisting her symbolic reading of the Lady in *A Mask*, Alice Lyle-
Scoufos, to the contrary, emphasizes the Protestant importance of
the "division of the church into visible and invisible," which gave
Milton and other Protestants "a way of condemning the material
church of Rome and of commending the spiritual or mystical church
of the reformers." Lyle-Scoufos argues that, as an alternative to "the
worldly state of the Church of England in its early prelatical period," Milton, in the "virginal" Lady, creates "a pure symbol of 'the
visible church of true believers'"; she argues further that "believ-
[ing] the individual soul *was* the church, alone or in communion,"
Milton has his Lady signify "both Psyche and Ecclesia in one figure." Scoufos succumbs to a split between the dimensions of the
Church and to an emphasis on the invisible church, idealized visible
church, and individual soul to the detriment of the *actual* visible
church, both universal and particular. As I will argue, this dichotomy and this emphasis are off target for Milton.[5]

Michael Lieb also draws upon Milton's "view of the church, both
invisible and visible," as background for understanding "Milton's
use of the body as polemical device" in his prose and Renaissance

4. Marcus, *The Politics of Mirth: Jonson, Herrick, Milton, Marvel, and the Defense of
Old Holiday Pastimes*, 202–3, 207–8.

5. Lyle-Scoufos, "The Mysteries in Milton's *Masque*," 121–22, 120–21, 134 (cf. John
Foxe, who in his *Christus Triumphans* [1556] "distinguishes between the individual
soul [Psyche] and the community of souls in the church [Ecclesia]" by "mak[ing]
them sisters, both daughters of Eve" [Lyle-Scoufos, 134]).

"organicist polemic in general." With the source for the invisible entity of the Church located in the idea of the *corpus mysticum*, Lieb notes that the visible church for Milton is "decidedly inferior" in importance to the invisible since Milton "associated the visible church with the Old Dispensation, the invisible church with the New." Pointing to the antiprelatical tracts to illustrate Milton's polemical exploitation of "the bodily associations of the invisible and visible churches," Lieb cites Milton's contrast of the deformed body of Prelatism with the pure, spiritualized, mystical body of the elect in *Of Reformation* as one example of the "movement in Milton from the corporeal to the mystical, the external to the internal, the visible to the invisible." Lieb errs in presuming this movement is final. What is permanent and necessary, in Milton's view of the Church, is a dynamic intercoursing between these poles—with the mystical, internal, invisible being primary but not sole.[6]

Scoufos and Lieb typify the assumption that the *actual* visible church, for Milton and his contemporaries, was always and automatically contaminated in this life and, consequently, had to be metaphorized (positively or negatively), spiritualized, or internalized away—a *virtuous* visible church deferred until the end of time when the invisible would be revealed. This is the sort of error that leads Malcolm M. Ross to lament: "The old lines of communication between the visible and invisible are discarded. The Mystical Body is retained in a thoroughly bodiless concept." Ross notes, "The church is *utterly* invisible, as is the fellowship it is said to contain"—an observation cited by Lieb to support a Miltonic ecclesiology that privileges the invisible dimension.[7] On the contrary, Ross regards ecclesial invisibility—indeed, primary for Milton—pejoratively. (*"Utterly* invisible," for Ross, means a regrettable void of the visible.) Ross, like so many, distorts Milton's teaching on the Church by ignoring Milton's careful, positive attention to the visible church: charity is the signal for the truth of the visible church (6:565); Christ is the head of the visible church (6:566); belief in the scriptures in a general way comes first to one often through the authority of the visible church (6:589–90); everyone has the duty to join a correctly instituted church, if possible (6:568); in joining this visible particular

---

6. Lieb, *The Sinews of Ulysses: Form and Convention in Milton's Works*, 22–23, 24–25.
7. Ross, *Poetry and Dogma: The Transfiguration of Eucharistic Symbols in Seventeenth-Century English Poetry*, 189; Lieb, *Sinews of Ulysses*, 24.

church, one is to make "a solemn promise to God and to this Church to carry out every office" (6:608); and so on. Thus, while Milton's church doctrine depends on a corrective against a luxurious, over-ritualized, and tyrannical visible church, it nonetheless depends on the visible church's establishing and maintaining a vital and healthy intersection with the invisible mystical church.

Maurice Kelley and Gordon Campbell deal with the heart of Milton's doctrine on the visible church—the sixth of the ten-part *Christian Doctrine* (pt. 1, chaps. 29–33), which includes, among other topics, the "Visible Church" ("Universal" and "Particular"), "Ministers" ("Extraordinary" and "Ordinary"), "Particular Churches," and "Church Discipline." But these two scholars attend mainly to the framework of this sixth part in relation to its structural context, in order to describe Milton's final product. Continuing their debate, now for over a decade, as to whether or not Milton completed the re-organization of the whole, most recently Kelley takes Campbell's criterion and conclusion to task.[8]

On the basis of the organizational method and the use of formal transitions (both perfect and imperfect) stipulated in Milton's own *Artis Logicae*—and scrupulously followed, according to Campbell, in the rest of the *Christian Doctrine*—Campbell finds these last five chapters of the first book "chaotic." At a loss to explain "why the organization crumbles" from the misplaced chapter on Scripture along with the unplaced transitions, Campbell avers: "The only tenable explanation of why *De Doctrina* was not published is that the work was not ready for publication, and that Milton never completed it."[9]

Admitting the presence of "some organizational difficulties," the primary one arising from the placement of chapter 30, "Of the Holy Scripture," Kelley supplies this chapter with a transition, and repositions it after chapter 32, "Of Church Discipline." In this revised form, Kelley believes that chapters 29–33 "present clearly Milton's beliefs concerning the five topics treated therein and do not deserve to be condemned as 'internally confused' and 'chaotic.'" Kelley further observes that, while Campbell bases his description of Milton's

8. See Kelley, *This Great Argument: A Study of Milton's* De Doctrina Christiana *as a Gloss Upon* Paradise Lost, 22 n. 27; and *CPW*, vol. 6, ed. Maurice Kelley, 103–4. Campbell, in "*De Doctrina Christiana:* Its Structural Principles and Its Unfinished State," challenges Kelley's position that it is complete; Kelley responds, thirteen years later, with "On the State of Milton's *De Doctrina Christiana.*"
9. Campbell, "Its Structural Principles," 250, 252–54.

text "on the presence of transitions," he has miscalculated them in chapters 1–28. Kelley's recount (only eleven with perfect ones, four with imperfect, and twelve with none) challenges Campbell's conclusion of a disrupted organization—a conclusion whose critical scaffolding is what collapses. "To comprehend more clearly the state of the *De Doctrina*," Kelley recommends distinguishing between a work that is "complete" (that is, having all its parts and covering its subject) and a work that is "finished" (that is, published, with its contents in form presentable to the public). With that, he describes the work as "unfinished," but "complete."[10]

Yet in spite of their attention to the structure and state of these pertinent chapters, neither Campbell nor Kelley deals with Milton's actual church teaching, which consists in the given structure of this sixth part and others—especially the relationship of the invisible church to the visible (both universal and particular); or with the doctrinally and thematically perfect placement of chapter 30, "Of the Holy Scripture," immediately after the chapter, "Of the Visible Church." Chapter 30, I would argue, functions integrally where it is since much of the teaching contained therein specifies what the *visible* church is not, and what it may not do; and since the teaching deals with believers—more specifically, reading believers—who, as the new visible church, are entitled, enabled, and encouraged to read and interpret Scripture in order to maintain vital and virtuous ecclesial membership in a radically Reformed church.

Two other literary critics who make use of Milton's notion of the invisible and visible church (though in contexts designed to serve their discussion of Milton's later poetry) are Howard Schultz and Mother Mary Christopher Pecheux. While some of the information they provide is useful, more noteworthy is the fact that they diverge not only in the conclusions that they reach, but also in the premises beneath their critical investigations and in the processes used to yield their vastly differing respective positions.[11]

Schultz paraphrases Milton, in considering those who are to be counted within each aspect of the Church, and then elaborates on the special function(s) unique to each of those aspects:

10. Kelley, "On the State," 44, 45, 46–47.
11. Schultz, "A Fairer Paradise? Some Recent Studies of *Paradise Regained*"; and Pecheux, O.S.U., "The Second Adam and the Church in *Paradise Lost*." For another translation of poetic personages into church concepts, see Rupin W. Desai, "Adam's Fall as a Prefiguration of Christ's Sacrificing Himself for the Church."

> The entire body of professing believers, the visible church, inev-
> itably includes hypocrites. It distinctively concerns itself therefore
> with cult, with worship and the externals of church government.
> The invisible church, the body known only to Christ, obviously
> contains no hypocrites. It therefore concerns itself more distinc-
> tively with doctrine, matters of true belief, the teaching of which is
> Christ's function as Prophet.

While his paraphrase of Milton's definitions of the aspects of the
Church is not disputable, his working of those terms is. Schultz carries Milton's opposition between "visible" and "invisible" for the purpose of theological distinction too far—to the point of separation, as
evinced in the special concerns that he presumes are designated for
each segment of the church. By so extrapolating, Schultz distorts Milton, presuming a rupture between world and spirit, the profane and
the holy that Milton does not intend. Schultz's dichotomizing premises have made their way into his Miltonic ecclesiology and theology
and caused camps (one of church business, including worship; the
other of God's truth). Seeing division between the visible and invisible church, Schultz has therefore continued the bifurcation into worship and truth. His sense of worship is mainly this worldly, and so it
is concerned with regulation, rubric, and ceremony. As will soon become evident, this split is simply not true for Milton.[12]

Pecheux provides a different reading on the visible church, one
that allows for invisible worship among the visibly churched and
serves for a historically more accurate understanding of a visible
church required and delighted to express "acknowledgement of the
one true God and devout affection for him" (6:656). Showing the importance of the elect and their transportation from the kingdom of
grace to the kingdom of glory for Milton's ecclesiology, Pecheux writes:

> The logical counterpart of the Holy Spirit, who in traditional thought
> is the fruit of the mutual love of the Father and the Son . . . should
> be members of that visible church of which Milton speaks in the
> Christian Doctrine, . . . the elect who, forming the kingdom of
> grace on earth, will one day come into the kingdom of glory. For
> the spiritual progeny borne by the invisible Church of Christ, the
> marriage supper of the Lamb is the supreme event, the final justi-
> fication of God's ways.[13]

12. Schultz, "A Fairer Paradise?" 288.
13. Pecheux, "Second Adam," 179. The four corresponding trinities, in Pecheux's
view, are the following: God, Son, and Spirit; Satan, Sin, and Death; Adam, Eve,
and their Promised Seed; and the Second Adam, the Church, and the elect.

Absent from Pecheux is that overemphasized separation between the invisible and visible church, between spirit and redeemed flesh—a separation fueled by assuming (as Schultz does) that concerns over doctrine belong at one pole and those over worship at the other. She minimizes the distinction between the two aspects of church, instead of exaggerating it, and prevents the separation that would have been regarded by Milton as untrue and unwholesome. She does so by focusing on the elect as the point of connection between this earth and the new earth. Thus, she accurately adheres to Milton's concept of the visible universal church as that "whole multitude of those who are called from any part of the whole world" (6:568) and to his concept of the invisible church as that "mystic body" which has come into being "from [the] union and communion with the Father and with Christ" (6:499), that body which "includes people from many remote countries, and from all ages since the creation of the world" (6:500). I would insist that, as the cohering device between the visible and invisible church, these elect are both sign and proof of the consubstantial unity of only *apparently separate* memberships in the Church, which is in truth, to Milton's and others' way of thinking, the one Bride of Christ.

Milton's church teaching does not abide the mutually exclusive dichotomizing assumed by most Miltonists. His explanation of spiritual union with the Father and communion with Christ and all the members of his body as the foundation of the invisible church means that Christ is always present to all (including the visible living) who share in this continuous mystic incorporation. Looking at this interrelating from the other side, one is to recall Milton's doctrine of ingrafting, whereby "the Father plants believers in Christ" (6:477), who is responsible for a certain perfecting and incomplete glorifying of believers even while they exist in their yet visible, flawed state. Thus, dwelling simultaneously below and above, Christ is at once restoring those to whom he is ever-present *and* transporting them into transcendent glory. Milton has Christ bridge the too-often-presumed separation of church into the seeming disconnected segments of visible church here and now and invisible church there and then—dimensions of the one church that correspond to the *Miltonically untrue scheme* of the impure, temporary, and immediate gathering as opposed to the pure, permanent, and mystical final one.

Recently, William B. Hunter, in a great effort to have a Milton who "stands closer to the great traditions of Christianity, no longer associated with a merely eccentric fringe," and to have a poem unencumbered with and undisturbed by the heretical bothers of the *Christian Doctrine*, has argued that the theological treatise is not even Milton's. While his observations are titillating and his claims forceful, I am unconvinced. Arduously working to banish Milton's leftism does not yield the actual Milton of history, whose ideas in late *and* early treatises—the *Christian Doctrine* aside—are clearly, firmly, and often vehemently Nonconformist (on church governance and discipline, the primacy of conscience, scriptural literacy, antipredestinarianism, antihierarchism, ordinary ministers, the inward man, sacraments, diversity, discussion, and so forth), as the following chapters will examine in detail. Relying on the internal evidence of Milton's radically Nonconformist church teaching—derivable throughout the prose, significantly enough, *exclusive* of the *Christian Doctrine* (which nonetheless perfectly expresses it)—and relying on Milton's notion of heresy (that is, "choise only of one opinion before another" [7:250]), which is never a bother but a boon contributing to the vital diversity needed in the progress to Truth, I stand with those who believe Milton to have authored the *Christian Doctrine*.[14]

The ecclesial dimension, as a major force unifying the prose to a single purpose and as a valuable tool for making sense out of that body of work in and of itself (rather than as a means to get at Milton's larger and later poems), deserves systematic, thorough attention. One of the eventual advantages of pursuing this task is that one will have available the information needed for understanding Milton's later poetry as liturgical (in the broadest, loosest, most revolutionary sense), expressing his renewed ecclesiology and serving his radically reformed ecclesia. The rationale at work here differs from one, like Kelley's, which uses the prose only as an appetizer to get to the main dish—or, in Hunter's case, to fast from, so as not to have the entree spoiled.[15] To the contrary, the church doctrine con-

14. Hunter's position was presented in a paper, "The Provenance of the *Christian Doctrine*," at the Fourth International Milton Symposium. This paper, along with responses from Barbara Lewalski and John T. Shawcross (given there) and the follow-up from Hunter (given later) appears in *SEL* as "Forum: Milton's *Christian Doctrine*." I am grateful to Professor Hunter for having shared a copy of his papers with me before their publication and for having challenged me with his thesis. Hunter's reply (166).

15. Maurice Kelley has been criticized for using the *Christian Doctrine* to gloss *Paradise Lost*. Hunter, in "Forum: Milton's *Christian Doctrine*," does the reverse. He uses his preferred orthodox poem—with its wished-for beautifully expressed cen-

tained in the prose is not preliminary, but prerequisite for and pertinent to all of Milton's writing. In fact, I would argue that the final poetry has the most complete meaning intended by Milton only if it is understood in its ecclesiological context along with all the others—political, sociological, theological, hermeneutical, philosophical, generic, rhetorical, and so on.

Serious investigations into the Radical Puritan mind and Milton's ties to it were virtually nonexistent until the last twenty years or so. Historians like Christopher Hill, J. F. McGregor, and B. Reay have considerably advanced scholarship on pre-Revolutionary and Revolutionary England.[16] They and others have probed into the Radicals and have dealt thoroughly with the implications of their *entire* religious range, to produce a more accurate and complete sense of the period. Most importantly, they have argued a bond that this Radical element and Milton shared. Hill argues Milton was "in dialogue with the [Radical] culture," his ideas holding a position in between "the ideas of traditional Puritanism" and "those of the radical milieu." Andrew Milner takes issue with Hill's "surprisingly depoliticized" view for having made the conflict cultural rather than political by a "substitution of two *cultures* [Puritan and Radical] for three *parties* [Presbyterian, Independent, and Leveller]." Milner scolds Hill for his "failure to distinguish with any real clarity between Independents and radicals" and for his consequent "insistence on 'cultural' as opposed to 'political' explanations." With a resurrec-

---

tral theology—to fail, by design, to match the unorthodox theological treatise. But, as we shall see, instead of enforced predictable and repeated orthodoxies, Milton always privileges originality, diversity, and discussion that are prompted by the indwelling Spirit and conscience. If we are not to read the poem by the treatise, it makes even less sense to read the treatise according to the poem and then unauthor the treatise as Milton's by using the *sometime* orthodoxy in the poem. Hunter's argument buckles beneath his vested interest to have neo-orthodoxy in a poem whose subordinationism, antitrinitarianism, creationism, mortalism, interiority, and anti-institutionalism will always prevent the delivery of mainline, orthodox Christianity exclusively. Though one might prefer otherwise, the poem is simply not orthodox enough for the orthodox of Milton's day, nor the treatise radical enough for the leftists either. The two works tellingly reveal common ground rather than continental divide.

16. See the following by Hill: *The Experience of Defeat: Milton and Some Contemporaries;* "Irreligion in the 'Puritan' Revolution," in McGregor and Reay, eds., *Radical Religion in the English Revolution;* and *Milton and the English Revolution.* In *Radical Religion,* see also McGregor, "The Baptists: Fount of All Heresy," and "Seekers and Ranters"; Reay, "Radicalism and Religion in the English Revolution: An Introduction," and "Quakerism and Society." See also Richard L. Greaves, "The Puritan-Nonconformist Tradition in England, 1500–1700: Historiographical Reflections."

tion of bourgeois Independents and a distinction between them and petty bourgeois Levellers, Milner avers that Milton "is, in fact, an Independent pure and simple." Milner erroneously omits the ecclesial factor, thereby depreciating the *actual* historico-political conflict he desires to assess.[17]

Literary scholars have likewise considered the writing of the English Revolution. Long after Merritt Hughes's 1943 pioneer article, "Milton as a Revolutionary," critics like Boyd Berry, John T. Shawcross, and Michael Wilding have read the historical signs of Milton's time to enable them to make greater sense of the literary ones. Berry, believing "Milton is much more nearly a Radical reforming Puritan than conservative establishmentarian," locates him "at the radical end of the liberal reformist-radical continuum." Shawcross distinguishes Milton from other, less extreme Reformists for his unrelenting, self-sacrificing, conscientious push: "Some harm the cause by drawing back to compromise." Milton and others, he finds, "break with the past, cut the roots, as it were, and begin anew with the wisdom that the past has afforded." Michael Wilding claims that Milton has been "dehistoricized" and therefore "distorted," concluding that "the rediscovery of Milton's radicalism requires not any new evidence, but a rereading of the material we already have."[18] Thus, on the grounds of recent historical scholarship and Milton's ecclesiology (stated explicitly in his *Christian Doctrine* and throughout much else of his prose), I would argue that one must acknowledge this emerging Radical ecclesial identity to and for which Milton spoke.[19]

Using his prose, this investigation will attempt to distill and deliver Milton's radically Reformist ecclesiology and to define the ecclesia with whom Milton's writing suggests he perceived a certain invisible and visible affiliation on the basis of a shared ecclesial identity. Having formulated an ideology and found a renovated spiritual

17. Hill, *Milton and the English Revolution*, 19–21, 115, 336–37; Andrew Milner, *John Milton and the English Revolution: A Study in the Sociology of Literature*, 198–99; see chap. 7, " 'When They Cry Liberty' " in this volume.

18. Berry, *The Process of Speech: Puritan Religion, Writings and* Paradise Lost, 68, 270; Shawcross, "The Higher Wisdom of *The Tenure of Kings and Magistrates*," in Michael Lieb and John T. Shawcross, eds., *Achievements of the Left Hand: Essays on the Prose of John Milton*, 147; and Wilding, "Regaining the Radical Milton," 141.

19. The preceding two paragraphs are reprinted with changes from my *"License Reconsidered: Ecclesial Nuances,"* in *Milton Quarterly* with permission of Roy C. Flannagan, editor.

congregation, Milton was able to satisfy his overwhelming ecclesial drive; he was at the same time also able to serve his liturgical purpose (eventually to be conjoined with his poetic one) to cherish and celebrate that impulse and its ultimate mystical, marital consummation with Christ and the other members of his body. Through redefinition of a variety of words and concepts, notably, *church, worship, separation, schism, license, heresy, holiness, clergy, learning, trade, Sacrament, Scripture,* and *house of God*—redefinitions accomplished by a single verbal pattern—Milton strove to change ecclesial doctrine and ecclesial life. These were the means used to establish and foster his church identity and ideology.

Part I lays a Reformational foundation by linking Milton to major reforming predecessors, like Luther, Calvin, Zwingli, Perkins, and Ames, without denying Milton scope to trace the origin of the Reformation to Wyclif in fourteenth-century England or to observe affiliation, to some degree, with extreme Nonconformists like Winstanley, Saltmarsh, Everard, Reeve, and Muggleton. This first part is not intended to be a source study, but only to establish the environment and spectrum of Reform and to provide points of reference from which one can observe similarity and divergence in Milton and his Revolutionary England. This section also considers Milton's definitions of the invisible church, the visible universal church, and visible particular churches. The foundation for these interrelated doctrinal aspects is the simultaneously vertical and horizontal mystical relationship that the Church has with Christ and that particular churches have with one another in him. Chapter 1 also examines the ideas of internal worship and external worship. This discussion of worship is ultimately useful in understanding Milton's ecclesiology since worship serves as a concrete index for grasping his Reformational church theory and for gauging and more accurately evaluating the religious progress of an otherwise elusive subject.

Part II considers Milton's treatises on the twofold process of election: the "separatist" and "ecclesial" mandates stipulated by Scripture.

The *separating* nature of election is the scripturally founded call to come away from whatever or whoever endangers believers' predestined sacred spiritual union with God. This antiseptic "separatist spirit" is emphasized to preserve the cleanliness and health of the spiritual life of the Church—whether that church be a congregation, a few believers, a family, or even an individual. The language of the period attributed this insidious, deadly infecting to Antichrist, believed to be a genuine, influential, and personal force.[20] In the seventeenth century, Christ and Antichrist are the cosmic and spiritual antipodes—not only ideas, for those in Milton's age, but personalities. If the person of Christ is the focus from whom the unvirtuous separate themselves and to whom the virtuous join themselves, then the person of Antichrist is the antifocus with whom the wicked affiliate and from whom the just flee.

In tracing the development of the people's belief as to where Antichrist resided in the progression of the seventeenth century, Christopher Hill explains the adversarial context that drove Milton and many of his contemporaries to alienate themselves from Antichrist— that is, from Pope, state, bishops, King, or eventually even from whatever oppressive or self-serving pernicious tendencies within their own hearts threatened their spiritual purity and union with God.[21]

The point and result of this discussion on the Antichrist for Milton is to demonstrate that septic conditions in the mid-seventeenth century were rife in a new way: universal external enemy—perceived variously in the Roman church, the English church hierarchy, and the King—had become universal internal enemy. This sort of religious thinking contributed to the accent Milton's doctrine places on the mystical relationship between Christ and the various levels of Church (world, assembly, household, individual) and paved the way for the identity of the primary and preeminent concept of church to be individual, invisible, and interior before it could hope to break forth and be anything visible and overtly communal. The saints' necessary separation is the prelude to their desired spiritual union and ecclesial fellowship.

If the "separatist spirit" required keeping clear of what infects one, the "ecclesial spirit" demanded keeping close to what restores one, by relying on conscience, which is informed through Scripture and the Spirit. The individual becomes the basic ecclesial unit upon which a new corporate ecclesial identity of church is formed. Chapters in this second part trace the development of this emerging church identity in Milton. Primarily spiritual, it consists of being always spiritually gathered into mystic, saintly communion; and it

20. Christopher Hill, *The Antichrist in Seventeenth-Century England*, 2.
21. Ibid., 130.

results only gradually through conflict—first with Prelates, then Presbyterians, next Independents, and finally, Restored Anglicans. The progression of Milton's responses to the various forces of opposition reveals an ecclesia that Milton believed he shared with many others in England and throughout the world—an ecclesia he spoke for and preached to through his prose. In this church, reverence for conscience and appreciation for diversity and disagreement became honorable means for arriving at Truth and, hence, for preserving the True Church.

Part III points out the place Milton gave to things visible and external, once they were reexamined and redefined, so long as they were not forced or rigid, and so long as they were always subordinated to the invisible and internal realm. Here, then, I consider how Milton's invisible church makes itself clearly visible and how this manifestation affiliated Milton quite definitely with the aggregate of believers known as "the Radical church." Links with this communion are evident early on in Milton's thought, expressed in *The Reason of Church Government,* and later, too, flowering in his *Christian Doctrine* and other tracts less explicitly theological. Most important for the success of this new visibility was an evangelization about the renovated dignity of the individual as the basis for thorough Reformation and for the making of a true Protestant church. Once this was done, real Reformation had its foundation, and other new external signs of the further Reformed church could naturally follow. There would be a dissolution of the distinction between the lay and clerical states and a war on clericalism, which meant, practically speaking, on the university system, tithes, and church-state-relatedness used to perpetuate that self-serving elitism. There would then be the establishment of a lay ministry; a consequent shift in the meaning, custody, and performance of the sacraments; and a focus on the household church and on the individual as the most basic unit of any church. This new sense of ministry, Sacrament, and church would flourish from an emphasis on Saint James's exhortation to perform good works; that is, this thorough Reformation would promote a religious posture whose signature was outwardness and activity, rather than privatism and pacifism, as an alternate radical religious posture. Finally, there would be a shift in the meaning of holiness back to the gospel-intended valuing of that sanctity that is internal and available to everyone. The ecclesia that Milton purported to have found was visible and vibrant in these specific signs. While the formulation of his radical theological doctrine grew more systematic and more vocalized throughout his life, most of it was there all along because the experiences inciting him to leave the still impure established church and reunite with the thoroughly reformed one were present all along as well. Over time, Milton learned disillusionment, not new doctrine; and his medium changed—as did his forum—but not the message he heard or preached.

The third part concludes by considering the sacramental status of the Word written externally and internally in such a way that Church, Scripture, and Sacrament are transmuted to a new external form. Milton provided for his radically Reformed church a scripturally founded seventeenth-century cultural expression that consolidated Church, Scripture, and Sacrament into *the sacred individual believer as a single mythic form* taking its place within that larger myth of the mystical, marital relationship between Christ and the communion of saints through him.

One can conclude that Milton accomplished this myth-making process by reforming and reappropriating certain important terms— namely, *church, worship, separation, schism, license, heresy, holiness, clergy, learning, trade, righteous works, Sacrament,* and *Scripture*—and also by reclaiming certain forgotten concepts—notably, the universal dignity of all believers, their universal right to read and interpret the scriptures for themselves, and their universal privilege to regard themselves corporately and individually as the House of God.

Thus, this book proposes that Milton's writing has an ecclesial foundation, that Milton formulated a church doctrine beyond what is ostensibly ecclesiological in the *Christian Doctrine,* and that there is an ecclesial system of belief, the discovery and discussion of which makes available yet another important center out of which Milton's literary works come into being and from which they operate.

I

Church Interrelationships in Reformational Context

Things Invisible and Visible

PREFACE TO PART I

ecause Milton surely considered himself to stand among "true" Protestant Divines, he placed himself within a long line of Reformers and a distinct tradition beginning, practically speaking, with Luther. The ultimate purpose of this part is to see Milton in Reformational context—to see how Luther's teaching about an evangelical church and its correspondent spiritual worship anticipated what Milton's doctrine actually fulfilled, and how Milton professed and attempted to promulgate a style of worship that would agree with a multifaceted concept of church that was normative in England during the Revolutionary period. One can consequently acknowledge that Milton's model of devotion, appropriate for spiritually ever-gathered worshipers—who may visibly assemble as church or not—climaxes and concludes what is usually and formally regarded as the Reformation.

1

Luther's Reform

A View to "Christians in Earnest" and Their "Truly Evangelical Order"

ad it not bin the obstinat perversnes of our Prelats against the divine and admirable spirit of *Wicklef,* to suppresse him as a schismatic and *innovator,"* Milton laments in *Areopagitica* (1644), "perhaps neither the *Bohemian* Husse and *Jerom,* no, nor the name of *Luther,* or of *Calvin* had bin ever known." But the Prelates had truncated the Reform, robbing England of its privileged election to have "sounded forth the first tidings and trumpet of reformation to all *Europ"* (2:552–53). The mission devolved on Luther to reinitiate Reform and reinvigorate the church a century after Wyclif. Thus, in *The Tenure of Kings and Magistrates,* Milton gives first place to Luther in the catalog of continental and native Reformist authorities cited for their theory of the divine right of the people covenanting with their ruler. Crediting Luther with being the necessary impetus that reawakened Reform, Milton recommends Luther as a model of Reformist teaching in citing him *first* among those "famous and religious men, who first reformed the Church," establishing a standard "that men may yet more fully know the difference between Protestant Divines, and . . . Pulpit-firebrands" (3:242–43). Thus, Luther serves as an important reference point for Milton himself and, consequently, as a very useful one for our examining the extent of Reform.

The concept of church shared by John Milton and other seventeenth-century Reformers is a partial fulfillment of the Reformed

21

church as envisioned by Luther to occur someday. While Luther may not have arrived at the position of holding that the individual is Scripture (as expressed by William Dell)[1] or that the individual can be considered as "a church" (as believed by Milton),[2] he had realized that the church is more than institution or building and that worship is more than nationally uniform words and rubrics. Furthermore, while he may have worried about enthusiastic, undisciplined misleading of the commoners, he had evidently anticipated and trusted the consequences of Reform in years to come, in spite of the risks. Reform, Luther knew, was dangerous business since the power, once unleashed and passed on, would be difficult, if not impossible, to control, much less reclaim and contain. Still, he trusted. Luther gave the Reformation scope such that printing press, education, accessibility of God's Word in the vernacular, and inspired preaching on that Word might ultimately take form in an evangelical gathering that worships in the spirit. Luther may never have expected some of the bitter fruit that grew in England during the seventeenth century on that tree of Christian Liberty which he himself had helped to cultivate, yet that likely surprise should in no way detract from our assurance of his readiness for and welcome of communities more evangelically advanced than those comprising the ostensible audience of his Orders of Worship. From the start, Luther's concern was, indeed, not to disrupt but to provide calm and stability in doctrine, liturgy, and ecclesial self-concept—both for the mainstream, too easily confused by diversity, and for the "weaker" brethren, too easily frightened by the independence of church communities. Nonetheless, his own words clearly reveal vision and tolerance that could accept the "stronger" and that would await eventual fulfillment. Thus, Johann Bugenhagen, sermonizing on the text of Revelation 14:6 in 1546 at Wittenberg for Luther's funeral, hailed Luther as that apocalyptic angel flying about heaven, preaching the everlasting gospel to those on earth. In so doing, this colleague and friend initiated a tradition of the prophetic, apocalyptic Luther that continued into the twentieth century.[3]

1. Dell, *Trial of Spirits* (1653), quoted in Christopher Hill, *The World Turned Upside Down: Radical Ideas during the English Revolution*, 259.

2. See *CPW* 6:568. See also Arthur Barker, *Milton and the Puritan Dilemma: 1641–1660*, 38.

3. Jaroslav Pelikan, "Some Uses of Apocalypse in the Magisterial Reformers," 74–75.

I would like to begin by examining some of Luther's statements about worship. The advantage in beginning a discussion of the Reformed church by speaking about worship is that while many other references in Luther's canon might provide greater ideational information (which must eventually be considered), these provide valuable tonal information. Attitudes evident in his directives for worship, because they reveal and particularize the spiritual, assist one in glossing definitions of church and creeds about church—information whose abstractness can leave any reader, especially a twentieth-century one, wanting more in order to arrive at precise connotations and to establish the most accurate context. So naturally and closely linked to the church's reason for being, worship acts as a concrete index for grasping church theory as well as for measuring and evaluating the progress of an otherwise ethereal, elusive subject. Furthermore, Luther's communications with church leaders about their congregations, implying a popular scope rather than an elitist one, give a fairly vivid vignette of the desired effects of Reform on the general body of believers. Because Milton's increasingly populist orientation (especially documented in his *Christian Doctrine* as well as evinced through his own ecclesial sympathies and ministry) reveals the same sort of breadth and universality found in Luther, these two Reformers invite comparison as markers of the origin and climax of Reformation during the Renaissance. Let us first turn to the prophesying of this German "angel," whose excerpted texts are so ample and unbroken both because the selections are unfamiliar to Miltonists and because they are cited to convey the attitudes and tone of the Reformation as much as its teaching. As the repeated phrase "for the time being" signifies in his *Concerning the Order of Public Worship* (1523), Luther's directives both for orders of worship and for churches are unmistakably transitional:

> The daily masses should be completely discontinued; for the Word is important and not the mass. But if any should desire the sacrament during the week, let mass be held as inclination and time dictate; for in this matter one cannot make hard and fast rules.
> Let the chants in the Sunday masses and Vespers be retained; they are quite good and are taken from Scripture. However, one may lessen or increase their number. But to select the chants and Psalms for the daily morning and evening service shall be the duty of the pastor and preacher. For every morning he shall appoint a fitting responsory or antiphon with a collect, likewise for the eve-

ning. . . . But for the time being we can shelve the antiphons, responsories, and collects, as well as the legends of the saints and the cross, until they have been purged, for there is a horrible lot of filth in them.

All the festivals of the saints are to be discontinued. . . . The festivals of the Purification and Annunciation of Mary may be continued, and for the time being also her Assumption and Nativity, although the songs in them are not pure.

Other matters will adjust themselves as the need arises. And this is the sum of the matter: Let everything be done so that the Word may have free course instead of the prattling and rattling that has been the rule up to now. We can spare everything except the Word. (*LW*, 13–14)

The Reformist way in its sixteenth-century flowering is open and fluid. Its strength lies in its adaptability as the purifying process continues.

In *An Order of Mass and Communion for the Church of Wittenberg* (1523), Luther writes to Nicholas Hausmann, bishop of the church in Zwickau, that he can no longer refrain from innovating merely out of fear of association with the frivolous faddism of the enthusiasts. The hour has come for providing an evangelical form of saying mass and administering communion, yet with explicit awareness that such a form is neither absolute nor permanent. Luther is "not wishing . . . to prejudice others against adopting and following a different order. Indeed, we heartily beg in the name of Christ that if in time something better should be revealed to them, they would tell us to be silent, so that by a common effort we may aid the common cause" (*LW*, 19). The tentativeness emphasizes a church whose reform calls for constant progress.

Getting more specific about the forms of prayer, while conveying once again the usual liberality and transitionality, Luther acknowledges wholesome diversity by not condemning the preferences of other local churches:

First, we approve and retain the introits for the Lord's days and the festivals of Christ, such as Easter, Pentecost, and the Nativity, although we prefer the Psalms from which they were taken as of old. But for the time being we permit the accepted use. And if any desire to approve the introits (inasmuch as they have been taken from the Psalms or other passages of Scripture) for apostles' days, for feasts of the Virgin and of other saints, we do not condemn them. But we in Wittenberg intend to observe only the Lord's days and the festivals of the Lord. (*LW*, 23)

A church from which the burden of enforcing uniform worship has been lifted prepares for and fosters a church that will be imbued with tolerance in other areas as well, such as doctrine, discipline, church government, and scriptural interpretation, to name a few.

While beginning with his usual Pauline concern lest the people be dragged by innovation and variety, rather than governed by unity, Luther, in his 1526 *German Mass and Order of Service*, ironically gives even more explicit reverence to all local churches in their variety and equality:

> Where the people are perplexed and offended by these differences in liturgical usage, however, we are certainly bound to forego our freedom and seek, if possible, to better rather than to offend them by what we do or leave undone. Seeing then that this external order, while it cannot affect the conscience before God, may yet serve the neighbor, we should seek to be of one mind in Christian love, as St. Paul teaches [Rom. 15:5-6; 1 Cor. 1:10; Phil. 2:2]. As far as possible we should observe the same rites and ceremonies, just as all Christians have the same baptism and the same sacrament [of the altar] and no one has received a special one of his own from God.
>
> That is not to say that those who already have good orders, or by the grace of God could make better ones, should discard theirs and adopt ours. For I do not propose that all of Germany should uniformly follow our Wittenberg order. Even heretofore the chapters, monasteries, and parishes were not alike in every rite. But it would be well if the service in every principality would be held in the same manner and if the order observed in a given city would also be followed by the surrounding towns and villages; whether those in other principalities hold the same order or add to it ought to be a matter of free choice and not of restraint. . . . In short, we prepare such orders not for those who already are Christians for they need none of them. . . . Their worship is in the spirit. But such orders are needed for those who are still becoming Christians or need to be strengthened. . . . They are essential especially for the immature and the young who must be trained and educated in the Scripture and God's Word. (*LW*, 61-62)

Here Luther—while pressing for some degree of similarity of form, mainly for purposes of instruction—anticipates the freedom, trust, and tolerance desired by seventeenth-century English Nonconformists as represented in the writings of many, but especially in those of Milton. Luther acknowledges already at the outset of Reformation the existence of "those who already are Christians" and who "need none of [such orders of worship]" since "their worship is in the spirit." In England during the 1640s and 1650s the evangelism warranting this freedom and fluidity was perceived to be not the exception, but the rule. Even during the Restoration—when majority and minority reversed themselves, making professed evangelicals into undesirables who were differentiated from their admirable, spiritually elite German forebears—these Christians remained Radical in persisting to conceive of church and its worship as being "in the spirit," thereby requiring neither structures nor fixed formulae.

It is in this same document that we find Luther's vision of how the Reformation may proceed and take shape as he discusses the three kinds of divine service or mass. With the first two forms Luther deals with the church as it now is and with the Reformation to date:

> The first is the one in Latin which we published earlier under the title *Formula Missae* [*An Order of Mass and Communion for the Church of Wittenberg*]. It is not now my intention to abrogate or to change this service. It shall not be affected in the form which we have followed so far, but we shall continue to use it when or where we are pleased or prompted to do so.
>
> The second is the *German Mass and Order of Service,* which should be arranged for the sake of the unlearned lay folk and with which we are now concerned. These two orders of service must be used publicly, in the churches, for all the people, among whom are many who do not believe and are not yet Christians. (*LW,* 62–63)

With the third form, Luther looks beyond the moment to the increase of gatherings of saints that resemble the conventicles of sixteenth- and seventeenth-century England with their domestic flavor of congregational discipline, direction, charity, and rather loosely structured, simple worship. At the same time, Luther's prescription is aimed also at those current rare congregations that he must have observed, having admitted (as we have seen above) the superfluity of orders of worship for certain believers. In the process of reform, concerns over worship are closely tied to those of church, so Luther's discussion of this third kind of service provides quite an elaborate description of a corresponding kind of church, which serves as a keystone for the sort of church that gains prominence throughout the next century and a half and that forms the foundation for the idea of church expressed throughout Milton's prose:

> The third kind of service should be a truly evangelical order and should not be held in a public place for all sorts of people. But those who want to be Christians in earnest and who profess the

gospel with hand and mouth should sign their names and meet
alone in a house somewhere to pray, to read, to baptize, to receive
the Sacrament and to do other Christian works. According to this
order, those who do not lead Christian lives could be known,
reproved, corrected, cast out or excommunicated, according to the
rule of Christ, Matthew 18:15–17. Here one could also solicit benevolent gifts to be willingly given and distributed to the poor. . . .
Here would be no need of much and elaborate singing. Here one
could set up a brief and neat order for baptism and the sacrament
and center everything on the Word, prayer, and love. Here one
would need a good short catechism [catechization] on the Creed,
the Ten Commandments, and the Our Father. (*LW*, 63–64)

Our hindsight confirms that such a description is quite realizable.
However much Luther denies the arrival of such a church in his day,
he nonetheless reveals an idealism about regenerate, spiritual humanity that sounds very Miltonic:

In short, if one had the kind of people and persons who wanted to
be Christians in earnest, the rules and regulations would soon be
ready. But as yet I neither can nor desire to begin such a congregation or assembly or to make rules for it. For *I have not yet the people
or persons for it,* nor do I see many who want. But if I should be
requested to do it and could not refuse with a good conscience, I
should gladly do my part and help as best I can. *In the meanwhile*
the two above-mentioned orders of service must suffice. And to
train the young and attract others to faith, I shall—besides preaching—help to further such public service for the people *until Christians who earnestly love the Word find each other and join together.* (*LW*,
64; emphasis added)

While Luther may not have provided any political or ecclesiastical
blueprints, he dreamed awhile, thereby providing an expression of
that possibility and giving that possibility his blessing. The seventeenth century received all of this as its heritage.

At what is normally regarded as the outset of the Reformation,
then, Martin Luther dreamed of those gathered assemblies and domestic churches that were forever to mark religious nonconformity
even while he directed his own traditional German churches in very
practical ways. Whether or not he would have liked all the ramifications of Reform that he instigated, the fact is that he foresaw the
logical completion of Reformation in church and worship. He gave
possibilities room where people soon came to dwell. More than anything else, perhaps, to Milton and others like him Luther passed on
a style and attitude essential for "true" Reform. What characterized

the Radical or Nonconformist church from Luther's day through the next century and into England was a commitment—authorized by the primal and preeminent Word of God—to transitionality, adaptability, openness, diversity, freedom and autonomy for the local church, and a tendency toward domestic gatherings of simplified evangelical worship. The Radical church parted from the remainder in its belief that these features were permanent; the non-Radical church, on the other hand, believed in closure when Reform had gone far enough.

While others, like Calvin and Zwingli, could see what Luther pointed to, it was only the Independents and others more extremist than they who actually pitched their tents and dwelt in that promised land which Luther envisioned, but which he himself could not (or would not) inhabit. Still, there it was: a land flowing with unlimited concepts of church and worship.

With the ambience of Reform understood through many of Luther's remarks about worship, we can now turn to his definitional statement on the church as expressed in his discussion of "The Third Article" of the creed found in *The Greater Catechism*. ("I BELIEVE IN THE HOLY GHOST, THE HOLY CHRISTIAN CHURCH, THE COMMUNION OF SAINTS, THE FORGIVENESS OF SINS, THE RESURRECTION OF THE FLESH, AND THE LIFE EVERLASTING. AMEN.") His definition is a thorough, etymological one:

> The Creed calls the holy Christian Church *Communionem Sanctorum*, a communion (*Gemeinschaft*) of saints, for both mean one and the same thing. But formerly the latter phrase was not added, and it has been ill and incorrectly translated a communion (*Gemeinschaft*) of saints. In order to explain it clearly a different expression must be used in German, for the word *ecclesia* signifies no more than an assembly. Now we are accustomed to use the little word *Church* otherwise, and simple folk take it to mean, not the assembled congregation, but the consecrated house or building: although the building should not be called a Church unless because of the congregation assembled there. For we who assemble make or take a special place for ourselves, and give the house the name of the congregation.
>
> So the word *Church* really signifies nothing but a congregation, and is a word of Greek origin (like the word *ecclesia*), for in their language they call it *Kyria*, and in Latin it is also called *Curia*. Therefore in good German and our mother tongue it should be translated a Christian community (*Gemeine*) or congregation, or best of all and most clearly, a holy Christendom. So likewise the

word *Communio,* which is attached to it, should not be translated *communion (Gemeinschaft),* but *community (Gemeine).* It is merely a definition or explanation to indicate what the Christian Church is.[4]

In England by the mid-seventeenth century, as Luther had envisioned to occur one day somewhere, Christians who earnestly loved the Word had, in fact, found each other and joined together. And they awaited "a truly evangelical order." It was incumbent on one so ecclesially educated and ecclesially enthusiastic as Milton to formulate doctrine for this church. In his *Christian Doctrine,* then, Milton articulated a Radical ecclesial identity and a fitting order of worship in the spirit.

4. *Luther's Primary Works: Together with His Shorter and Larger Catechisms,* 103. The contemporary biblical scholar Lewis Berkhof notes the meaning of *church* that derives from its biblical usage: "[The] New Testament word *ekklesia,* derived from *ek* and *kalein.* It is a designation of the Church, both in the Septuagint and in the New Testament, and points to the fact that this consists of a people that is 'called out,' i.e. out of the world in special devotion to God" (*Principles of Biblical Interpretation,* 68).

2

Milton's Ecclesiology

"The Real House and Church of the Living God"

 n his *Christian Doctrine,* Milton, making the same distinction between church as building and church as gathered believers, follows the Reformist emphasis as expressed by Luther above that the church is an "assembly of believers" on the basis of God's own Word:

It is true that Paul says, I Tim. iii. 15: *the church of the living God is the pillar and ground of the truth.* Some people turn these words into a claim that the visible church, however defined, has the supreme authority of interpretation and of arbitration in controversy. However, once we examine this and the previous verse, it becomes evident that such people are very far from the truth. Paul wrote these words to Timothy, and for him they were meant to have the force of Holy Scripture. The intention was *that he might know,* through these words, *how he ought to behave in the house of God, which is the church*—that is, in any assembly of believers.

The church is not a building or a governing structure or an arbitrating body. It does not give a rule but follows one:

Therefore it was not the house of God, or the church, which was to be a rule to [Timothy] *that he might know,* but the Holy Scripture which he had received from Paul. . . . It does not follow that [the church] is the rule or arbiter of truth and scripture. For the house of God is not a rule to itself; it receives its rule from the word of God, and it ought, at any rate, to keep very close to this. Besides,

30

the writings of the prophets and of the apostles, which constitute
the scriptures, are the foundations of the church. Eph. ii. 20: *built
on*, etc. (6:585)

Milton begins his ecclesiology by considering, first, the invisible
church: "It is from this union and communion with the Father and
with Christ, and among the members of Christ's body themselves,
that there comes into being that mystic body, THE INVISIBLE CHURCH,
the head of which is Christ" (6:499). His proof text for this doctrine
is Ephesians 2:19—a passage that marks his definition of church as
ecclesial rather than *ecclesiastical*, that is, having to do with people
rather than with hierarchy or structures:

> *No longer are you strangers and lodgers but fellow citizens of the saints,
> and the household of God: built on the foundation of the apostles and
> prophets, Jesus Christ himself being its corner-stone. In him the whole
> building duly put together, grows to be a holy temple to the Lord: you,
> too, are built together in him to be the home of God through the Spirit.*
> (6:500)

He then turns to the visible church: "THE VISIBLE CHURCH is either
UNIVERSAL or PARTICULAR. THE UNIVERSAL VISIBLE CHURCH IS THE
WHOLE MULTITUDE OF THOSE WHO ARE CALLED FROM ANY PART OF
THE WHOLE WORLD, AND WHO OPENLY WORSHIP GOD THE FATHER IN
CHRIST EITHER INDIVIDUALLY OR IN CONJUNCTION WITH OTHERS"
(6:568). The particular church is "a society of persons professing the
faith, united by a special bond of brotherhood, and chiefly organized for the purpose of promoting mutual edification and the communion of saints" (6:593). The components for a particular church
are ministers (that is, presbyters and deacons) and people:

> Any church which is composed of these parts, although it may
> have only a few members, is to be a self-contained and complete
> church, in that it has supreme right in matters of religion. It has no
> man, no assembly, and no convention on earth set over it. For it
> can hope . . . that it will enjoy the scriptures and promises, the
> presence of Christ and the guidance of the Spirit, and the favor of
> those gifts which are to be obtained by communal prayer. Matt.
> xviii. 20: *where two or three are gathered together in my name, there I am
> in their midst.* (6:601)

The primary essential in determining a church, however, is the people, that "society of persons professing the faith, united by a special
bond of brotherhood." So, as Richard Mather wrote in the then anon-

ymous pamphlet *Church Government and Church Covenant Discussed,*
"The Church is before the Ministers." So, too, Thomas Hooker in his
Survey: "There must be a Church of believers to choose a Minister
lawfully. . . . Therefore here is a Church before a Minister." And even
though, as John Owen posthumously publicized, it is the gift of Christ
in the Ministry "which renders a Church completely Organical," they
may nonetheless "become a Church essentially before they have any
ordinary Pastor or Teacher."[1] The gradual shift in emphasis for the
Reformed church in general and for Milton in particular is away from
institution, hierarchical structure, and ministerial caste and toward
believers who come together and bond with each other in faith.

As Horton Davies points out, this development has an extended
Reformational history which dates back at least to the "Privye Church"
that met in London during Queen Mary's time. The meeting "was
organized worship under persecution and provided later separatists with a precedent for gathering secretly to worship in defiance of
the rules of the land, according to their own conscience."[2] The Elizabethan, Jacobean, and Caroline worlds did not force private religious gatherings underground to the degree that Mary's reign did.
But, the smaller, privately gathered model of church was part of the
living and unrepressed historical memory, which the most advanced
sects were quick to recall as they formed what they called "gathered
churches." A. L. Morton, in his classic study of the Ranters, explains
the procedure for establishing a gathered church—a procedure that
began, perhaps, with the most radical sects, but before long spread
throughout the seventeenth century to include many not on the fringe:

> Setting aside the old parochial organization, which by now was
> mostly in the hands of the Presbyterians, they declared that any
> group of believers in any place could constitute themselves as a
> church with full liberty to act and believe as they pleased. And
> when such a church was set up, all its members signed a covenant,
> an agreement binding themselves to unity and laying down of all
> the rights and duties of all.[3]

This description of the gathered church holds to the doctrine on the
church evident in Luther, Calvin, and Ames and fulfills the dream

1. Geoffrey F. Nuttall, *Visible Saints,* 85.
2. Davies, *The Worship of the English Puritans,* 95.
3. Morton, *The World of the Ranters: Religious Radicalism in the English Revolution,*
14.

for an evangelical church embedded within their teaching. This Reformist concept of church culminates and concludes in the ecclesiology of Milton's *Christian Doctrine*, which stresses the "society of persons professing the faith, united by a special bond of brotherhood." Elaborating on this bond in his next chapter, "Of Church Discipline," Milton exemplifies the central ingredient of the gathered church evident in Morton's characterization above, namely, willful and mutual covenanting: "The uniting bond of any particular church is CHURCH DISCIPLINE. . . . What this means is the common consent of the church to order its life correctly, according to Christian doctrine, and to perform everything in a decent and orderly way at its meetings" (6:607).

The concept of the gathered church became so ubiquitous that the historian Michael Walzer claims that it even carried over into the way the New Model Army fought.[4] Clearly, subscribing to a gathered church could eventually be considered extremist only if one's perspective were identified with one of the establishments (Bishops, Presbyterians, later Independents, Army Grandees, or Restoration Anglicans) threatened by the absence of uniformity and centralized control.

Thus, any such gathered assembly would be regarded as "a self-contained and complete church," having "supreme right in matters of religion." In *A Treatise of Civil Power* (1659) Milton makes the same point about a church's integrity: "The settlement of religion belongs only to each particular church by perswasive and spiritual means within it self" (7:271). Having stressed the completeness and autonomy of any church in both his theological and civil treatises, Milton held this tenet to be very important. To illustrate and legitimate this autonomy that each church enjoys (however small), Milton distinguishes in his *Christian Doctrine* between a particular church and a Jewish synagogue by regarding each one's acceptability for worship:

> The synagogue was a particular assembly, and a religious one, but it was not a particular church, because the total and entire worship of God could not properly be performed in the synagogue. Sacrifices and ceremonies were to be carried out only in the temple. But now everything that has to do with the worship of God and the

4. Walzer, *The Revolution of the Saints: A Study in the Origins of Radical Politics*, 270–97.

salvation of believers, everything, in fact, that is necessary to constitute a church may be performed in a correct and properly ordered way in a particular church, within the walls of a private
house where no great number of believers are assembled. (6:602)

Milton's scriptural support for calling those societies "churches . . .
even when each has only a few members," obtains from biblical
passages that convey the domestic church as the primary and model
church: "Rom. xvi. 5: *the church which is in their house,* similarly 1
Cor. xvi. 19; Col. iv. 15: *the church which is in his house;* Philem. 2: *the
church which is at your house*" (6:602).

In contrast to the first century, Jews and proselytes had to travel
to Jerusalem because there was "only one national or universal Jewish church, and no particular churches. . . . Now there is no national
church and a great number of particular churches, each absolute in
itself and equal to the others in divine right, and power. These, like
similar and homogenous components, joined together by a bond of
mutual equality, form a single, catholic church" (6:602–3).

With such emphasis on the community of believers, it follows for
Milton that it is "the duty of every believer to join himself, if possible, to a correctly instituted church" (6:568). Ideally, then, belonging
to the church meant bonding with a particular congregation: "Similarly, when any individual joins a particular church he should, as if
he were entering into a covenant, make a solemn promise to God
and to this church that he will insofar as he is able, carry out every
office, both toward God and toward that Church, which may concern either his own edification or that of his fellows" (6:608).

Milton, in *Areopagitica,* chastises those professed Christians who
"stumble and are impatient at the least dividing of one visible congregation from another, though it be not in fundamentalls" (2:564).
What appears to be a contradiction here—backing legitimate self-
removal and reestablishment as visible church elsewhere, so long as
departure is from place but not from *essential* doctrine—is clearly
not. While Milton, in this earlier treatise, acknowledges some degree of difference that would cause and justify people to dissociate
themselves in good faith from one assemblage in order to associate
with another, he is quite consistent about the importance of belonging to a particular community. But he is neither sanguine nor naive
about its building and blossoming. Since church harmony does not
arrive or continue without flaw and tension, Milton cannot but look
askance at separating without good reason:

Not that I can think well of every light separation, or that all in a
church is to be expected gold and silver and precious stones: it is
not possible for man to sever the wheat from the tares, the good
fish from the other frie; that must be the Angels' Ministry at the
end of mortall things. Yet it all cannot be of one mind, as who
looks they should be?—this doubtless is more wholsome, more
prudent, and more Christian, that many be tolerated, rather than
all compell'd. I mean not tolerated popery, and open supersti-
tions, which as it extirpats all religious and civill supremacies, so it
self should be extirpat, provided first that all charitable and compassionat means be used to win and regain the weak and the
misled. (2:564–65)

The doctrine of toleration, which is present here and which will
assume a more prominent role in the later prose, is Milton's device
for achieving the balance necessary for any wholesome Christian
community. Tolerance requests deliberative charity—both from those
who would bolt at the first signs of hardship and disagreement as
well as from those who would insist on rigid uniform doctrine at the
first signs of disputation and diversity. These criticize too hastily;
the others disunite too hastily. But both are at fault for the same
imbalance: they lack the trust and toleration that enable a visible
church to cohere in peace.

The gentle demeanor ("charitable and compassionat") with which
Milton recommends that even Papists, the epitome of enemies, be
treated stands out amidst this exhortation for unity in *Areopagitica*.
With their inclusion one grasps, through Milton, true biblical charity that dispenses with delineations and margins. All that matters is
to be that new man

which is renewed in knowledge after the image of him that created
him: Where there is neither Greek nor Jew, circumcision nor un-
circumcision, Barbarian, Scythian, bond *nor* free: but Christ *is* all,
and in all. Put on therefore, as the elect of God, holy and beloved,
bowels of mercies, kindness, humbleness of mind, meekness,
longsuffering; Forbearing one another, and forgiving one another,
if any man have a quarrel against any even as Christ forgave you,
so also *do* ye. (Col. 3:10)

Having gotten excited over the wrong things, many, Milton claims,
have missed the larger issue, namely, truth, and in so doing, have
caused exactly what they have wanted to prevent: splintering, since
they "care not to keep truth separated from truth, which is the fierc-
est rent and disunion of all" (2:564). Their means is "a rigid externall

formality"; their end, a return to "a grosse conforming stupidity, a stark and dead congealment of *wood and hay and stubble* forc't and frozen together, which is more to the sudden degenerating of a Church than many subdichotomies of petty schisms" (2:564).

While Milton disputes with Puritans of the right, center, and left, he nonetheless stands within that tradition. It is important to note connections on the understanding of church between the acclaimed father of the English Puritan tradition, John Calvin, and Milton—regardless of other doctrinal disagreements (as, for example, predestination and trinitarianism)—especially since Milton regarded Calvin as one of "the most learned theologians" and "one of the great leaders of the church" (6:714, 4:453). Their similarity in delineation, expectations, tone, and ultimate goal suggests direct dependence of Puritan son on parent.

Calvin, in his *Institutes* (1536), writes on the universal and particular or, what he calls individual, dimensions of church:

> The church universal is a multitude gathered from all nations; it is divided and dispersed in separate places, but agrees on the one truth of divine doctrine, and is bound by the bond of the same religion. Under it are thus included individual churches, disposed in towns and villages according to human need, so that each rightly has the name and authority of the church. Individual men who, by their profession of religion, are reckoned within such churches, even though they may actually be strangers to the church, still in a sense belong to it until they have been rejected by public judgment.
>
> There is, however, a slightly different basis for judgment concerning individual men and churches. For it may happen that we ought to treat like brothers and count as believers those whom we think unworthy of the fellowship of the godly, because of the common agreement of the church by which they are borne and tolerated in the body of Christ. We do not by our vote approve of such persons as members of the church, but we leave to them such place as they occupy among the people of God until it is lawfully taken from them. (*ICR*, 1023)

Believers are exhorted to be tolerant and to refrain from judging, for to indulge the desire to judge with the absoluteness of God is to precipitate an untimely conclusion of the victory of goodness over evil as well as a presumptuous decision, according to human rather than divine approval as to who are to be gathered. The characteristic singleness of truth, full status and autonomy of the many individual assemblies, tolerance of differences, and patience while waiting for the end when only God will judge the many and varied approaches to him on the basis of his Son—all of these are evident in Calvin's teaching on the church no less than in Milton's.

As he continues, Calvin likewise stresses the importance of participating within a local assembly that has the marks of a true church: "Whenever we see the Word of God purely preached and heard, and the sacraments administered according to Christ's initiation, there is not to be doubted, a church of God exists" (cf. Eph. 2:20). For his promise cannot fail: "Wherever two or three are gathered in my name, there I am in the midst of them" (Matt. 18:20; *ICR*, 1023). He, too, cautions against anyone's lightly spurning a church's authority; in fact, doing so amounts to "the sin of schism":

> No one is permitted to spurn its authority, flout its warnings, resist its counsels, or make light of its chastisements—much less to desert it and break its unity. For the Lord esteems the communion of his church so highly that he counts as a traitor and apostate from Christianity anyone who arrogantly leaves any Christian society, provided it cherishes the true ministry of word and sacraments. He so esteems the authority of the church that when it is violated he believes his own diminished. (*ICR*, 1024)

Because Calvin, like Milton, realizes that God has not promised imminent success (that is, a perfect religious society), he counsels stability and patience. But amidst advice for such restraint stands the enormous IF: "provided it cherishes the true ministry of Word and sacraments."

Clearly, one must be able to excuse weakness in the church: "The errors which ought to be pardoned are those which do not harm the chief doctrine of religion, which do not destroy the articles of religion . . . and with regard to the sacraments, those which do not abolish or throw down the lawful institution of the Author" (*ICR*, 1041). Calvin's immediate disjunctive in the very next sentence underscores, through syntactical balance, the importance of *judicious* belonging, thereby signaling a kinship of conscience-preeminence shared with Milton on the point: "But as soon as falsehood breaks into the citadel of religion and the sum of necessary doctrine is overturned and the use of the sacraments is destroyed, surely the death of the church follows—just as a man's life is ended when his throat is pierced or his heart mortally wounded" (*ICR*, 1041). Removal of oneself from such perdition is not removal from a church since a church without right doctrine and sacraments is without spirit and is, therefore, no living church at all. In Milton's words, this "dividing," precisely because it is "in fundamentalls" spiritual, is not only allowed but required.

In his comparison of a false and a true church, Calvin uses the same scriptural authority of Ephesians and 1 Timothy and the same interpretation that Milton later does to explain in greater detail and with greater force the disintegration of a church because of falsehood:

> And that [the death of the church] is clearly evident from Paul's words when he teaches that the church is founded upon the teaching of the apostles and prophets, with Christ himself as the chief cornerstone [Eph. 2:20]. If the foundation of the church is the teaching of the prophets and apostles, which bids believers entrust their salvation to Christ alone—then take away that teaching, and how will the building continue to stand? Therefore, the church must tumble down when that sum of religion dies which alone can sustain it. Again if the true church is the pillar and foundation of truth [I Tim. 3:15], it is certain that no church can exist where lying and falsehood have gained sway. (*ICR*, 1041)[5]

William Perkins, one of the leading English divines of the 1590s who was responsible for giving Puritanism one systematic theology, emphasized, in *A Warning Against the Idolatry of the Last Times*, the importance of the visible worshiping church: "The church of God upon earth is, as it were, the suburbs of the city of God and the gate of heaven; and therefore entrance must be made into heaven in and by the church" (*WWP*, 314–15). Yet, in spite of echoing Calvin's ideal of belonging to a distinct group of believers and his injunction against separating from a church, Perkins, too, in *An Exposition of the Symbols*, allows separation for either of two aberrations, neither of which exists in England at this time:

> So long as a church makes no separation from Christ we must make no separation from it and therefore in two cases there is warrant of separation. The one is when the worship of God is corrupt in substance. . . . The second is when the doctrine of religion is corrupt in substance. . . . As for the corruptions that be in the manners of men that be of the church they are no sufficient warrant of separation, unless it be from private company. . . . It appears that the practice of such as make separation from us is very bad and schismatical, considering our churches fail not in the

5. See *CPW* 6:585.

substance of doctrine, or in the substance of the true worship of
God. (*WWP*, 273–74)

A generation later William Ames, renowned Reformed systematic theologian, in *The Marrow of Theology* (1623), likewise requires
joining a particular congregation of the believer and expresses a
severe sanction against anyone who, though able, refrains from
joining a church: "Therefore, those who have the opportunity to
join the church and neglect it most grievously sin against God because of his ordinance, and also against their own souls because of
the blessing joined to it. And if they obstinately persist in their care-
lessness, whatever they otherwise profess, they can scarcely be
counted believers truly seeking the kingdom of God" (*MT*, 181). But
absent here is that exemptive proviso found in Calvin, Perkins, and
Milton: excused self-extrication from a church for its falsehood and
potential infection of the saint. Instead, one finds just the reverse
emphasis expressed through covenant language, and one detects a
latent angst in Ames that the logical and potential infinite splintering into churches of several or even into those of single individuals,
which could easily result from rampant multiplication of free and
willful gathered assemblies, was more than theological speculation.
One detects a nightmare that was becoming real:

> Believers do not make a particular church, even though by chance
> many may meet and live together in the same place, unless they
> are joined together by a special bond among themselves. Other-
> wise, any one church would often be dissolved into many, and
> many merged into one.
> This bond is a covenant, expressed or implicit, by which be-
> lievers bind themselves individually to perform all those duties
> toward God and toward one another which relate to the purpose
> [ratio] of the church and its edification. (*MT*, 180)

Ames's "special[-]bond" believers sounds much like Milton's "special bond of brotherhood . . . organized for the purpose of promoting mutual edification and the communion of saints." Milton describes such belonging as "entering into a covenant" whereby the
church member would, "insofar as he is able, carry out every office,
both towards God and towards that Church, which may concern his
own edification or that of his fellows." But Ames's discussion lacks
the elasticity and adaptability of Milton's where considerations like
convenience in gathering, the completeness of church status however small the assemblage, and the approval of separation from the

false church weigh as heavily as the duty to join and remain with a congregation.

Regardless of whether one were looking to join or disjoin a church, however, one needed criteria by which to judge the true substance of a church. Milton, like Calvin, referred to such criteria as "marks"; Wolleb, as "notes."[6] Whereas for Calvin and Wolleb the marks or notes of a church are two (preaching of the Word and the lawful use of the sacraments), Ames adds a third: "Profession of the true faith is the most essential mark of the church"; in fact, "this profession may in some congregations precede the solemn preaching of the Word and the administration of the sacraments" (*MT,* 181). For Perkins, two of the three "things required to the good estate of the church" are "the preaching of the gospel" and "the administration of the sacraments"; but Perkins includes a third, "the due execution of discipline according to the word," distinct from Ames's. While Ames gives his innovative third mark (profession of faith) preeminence, Perkins relies on the ordering inherent in the Reformist tradition: "Yet if the two latter (administration of sacraments and execution of discipline) are wanting, sobeit there be preaching of the word with obedience in the people, there is for substance a true church of God" (*WWP,* 269). In an effort to give additional aid in distinguishing a true from a false church, Perkins explains that a true church can be identified by two "properties or qualities": holiness ("a created quality in every true member thereof, whereby the image of God which was lost by the fall of Adam is again renewed and restored") and largeness (as "noted in the word catholic, that is general or universal") (*WWP,* 274).

Milton enumerates four marks of the Church: "Pure doctrine, the true external worship of God, true evangelical charity, insofar as it can be distinguished by man, and the correct administration of the seals" (6:563). Since pure Reform taught and preached only that doctrine which derived from the scriptures, we can assume that Milton's mark, "pure doctrine," and the others' mark, preaching of the Word, are nearly coterminous. If so, then Milton agreed with the other Reformers on two of the marks that constitute a true church: scriptural doctrine and scripturally authorized sacramentality. The two marks that distinguish Milton from the others regularly and prominently appear as major concerns within the Radical church,

6. For Calvin, see *ICR,* 1023; Milton, *CPW* 6:563; Wolleb, *CPW* 6:563 n. 2.

namely, *purity of worship* and *true charity*. The spiritual company Milton keeps with others who likewise emphasize the two marks which distinguish him from the major reforming predecessors will reveal a church that, though deriving perhaps much from the larger, mainline Puritanic tradition, can nonetheless be regarded as set apart—as "true" at most or "tru*er*" at least.

Milton may have winced at Calvin's theology for how its system bound God as well as humanity, but he appears to have followed the structure of Calvin's ecclesiology and its suggested overall tone of patience and understanding. The preferred way to salvation was joining a church and remaining within it in spite of the flaws evident at both the universal and local levels. The organization, after all, was comprised of human beings who had not arrived yet but were only en route to their destiny of complete glorification. Both agreed on the absolute requirement that participation, however tolerant one had to be with fellow congregants' misbehavior, had to take place within a true church. Deciding what the grounds for such an entity were, and how one was to get along should one be unable to find any church except a false one were knotty issues, but grappling with them would mentally and spiritually awaken many Protestants to pragmatic new social structures like church governance and leadership in worship. Calvin and Perkins realized that the ideal might not always be possible. However, it was unlikely that Calvin or Perkins could ever have augured that the pernicious "overturning" of doctrine and what was perceived as the maladministration of the sacraments would splinter the church and scatter the saints into the tiniest of gatherings, much less into churches of one.

Milton, as shown above, speaks of "the duty of every believer to join himself, if possible, to a correctly instituted church" (6:568) and exhorts the believer, "as if he were entering into a covenant," to "make a solemn promise to God and to his church that he will, insofar as he is able, carry out every office, both toward God and toward that church, which may concern either his own edification or that of his fellows" (6:608). Yet, clearly Milton is not making incorporation into the Church contingent on being socially covenanted to particular believers. A socio-political gloss on the covenant figure is wrong. The purpose of the simile is spiritual. A literal compact or agreement—at least here in Milton's *Christian Doctrine*—is not primary or even essential for membership in Christ's Church. What *is* is that "union and communion with the Father and with Christ, and among the members of Christ's body themselves," which may or may not happen in a certain place with a fairly defined aggregate of Christians (6:499).

With mounting intolerance among the Puritan Grandees and then, after the Restoration, with persecution reinstated by the Royalist establishment, the church, however *visible* it had been in a Miltonic sense, "openly worship[ing] God through Christ individually or in conjunction with others," became much less visible. At such time, whatever congregating Milton had formerly condoned for the sake of giving direction and discipline became mainly mystical, and whatever covenanting transpired was likewise spiritual. It is easy to understand the stance of Colonel John Hutchinson, who Christopher Hill claims was "closest" to Milton's mature idea and expression of church. Hill recounts: "When asked after the Restoration where he [Hutchinson] went to church, he replied 'Nowhere.' To the question 'How he then did for his soul's comfort?' he replied 'Sir, I hope you leave me that to account between God and my own soul.'" Hill notes, "There is much evidence for failure to attend at the parish church after 1660."[7]

What Milton and those to the left of the Puritan establishment shared was a concept of church that was predominantly mystical, spiritual, invisible, and increasingly internal.[8] With such an emphasis, their union was less easily tampered with by enemies and much more easily celebrated by members. As Milton stated in *Areopagitica*, "Neighboring differences, or rather indifferences . . . whether in some point of doctrine or of discipline, which though they may be many, yet need not interrupt the *unity of Spirit*, if we could but find among us the bond of peace" (2:564–65).

7. Hill, *English Revolution*, 113 n. 3.

8. The last three paragraphs, reprinted with changes, appeared first in my *"License* Reconsidered." For a discussion of the term *mystic*, as used by Milton in its mid-seventeenth-century Protestant context, see my essay, "The Mystical in Milton: A Radical Protestant View." In Milton, the word has nothing to do with some gradated and chartable spiritual ascent. It "refers to the spiritual mode" and is "much less recipe for getting somewhere than it is splendid recognition and frequent remembrance of arrival at union with God through 'ingrafting' in Christ" (54). For a different view, which finds mystical incorporation into Christ missing from Milton's spirituality, see Ross, *Poetry and Dogma*, 183–204. Ross rewrites Milton in claiming: "The Mystical Body is retained in a thoroughly bodiless concept. Indeed, Milton's assertive individualism threatens the concept itself" (189). Quite the opposite, Milton makes the concept of the Mystical Body the very center of his doctrine on the church.

Incorporation in the True Church—in its invisible and visible dimensions—admits of no limitations that are geographic, political, or temporal: "The Christian church is universal; not ti'd to nation, dioces or parish, but consisting of many particular churches complete in themselves" (7:293). In the *Christian Doctrine* Milton acknowledges his union with all members of the Church: "The body of Christ is mystically one so it follows that the communion of his members must be mystic. It need not be subject to spatial considerations: it includes people from many remote countries, and from all ages since the creation of the world" (6:500). With this concept of church, Milton could believe in, commemorate, and celebrate that bond with God as well as with other believers of all times and places without the external structure, congregation, or hierarchy—in times of persecution, certainly, but even in times of peace. For the invisible, mystical, spiritual Church there would always be the conjoined saintly and angelic worshiping community gathered before the throne of God: the saints are those "people from many remote countries, and from all ages since the creation of the world," that is, both those still fighting the good fight and those who have already fought it (in traditional ecclesial language, the church militant and the church triumphant); and the angels, continuous adorers of Christ, "stand around the throne of God as ministers, . . . praising God" (6:344–45).

It is this Church in which believers find union and communion, and it is to this Church that Milton joins his poetic voice in concert with the angels who sing of the Son's triumph in defeating Satan and of his power in giving shape to chaos,[9] confident that others, in his poem's words or in their own, will be able to concelebrate these and other instances of God's providence. As True Church, both the onward-moving militant dimension and the already rewarded triumphant dimension are spiritually one in their new state as "invisible and immaculate church of [Christ]," thereby allowing, Milton reasons, "Christ's love for [it] to be figured as the love of husband for wife" (6:500). In light of their supranatural condition, then, both the militant and triumphant saints have, in a sense, already arrived. And as True Church, these united saints share, along with the an-

9. *CPMP*, 268 n. 413. See also Michael Fixler, "Milton's Passionate Epic," 172–75; Fixler, "Apocalypse"; and Francis C. Blessington, " 'That Undisturbed Song of Pure Concent': *Paradise Lost* and the Epic-Hymn," 494–95.

gels, a worshipful function. This True Church, the invisible, spiritual, mystical church—not exclusive of the visible, but not equatable with it either—is always invisibly gathered with every group of believers (or with the individual believer, as we shall see) carrying out the Church's worshipful function.

3

"That Mystic Body" and "Societ[ies] of Persons" within "The Whole Multitude"

Vertical and Horizontal Mystical Union

he major ecclesiological issue of the Reformation increasingly became the correspondence (or lack thereof) between the church that we see and the Church that only Christ and the triumphant see. In considering this relationship, one needs to be aware of a twofold mystic union between humanity and Christ—a union that is not only vertical, but horizontal simultaneously. In Milton's words, "The body of Christ is mystically one so it follows that the communion of his members must be mystic" (6:500). They are gathered together into particular churches to be united to one another as well as to him, for "these, like similar and homogenous components, joined together by a bond of mutual equality, form a single, catholic church" (6:603). To appreciate how close and confusing the concept of this dual, overlapping union was for the English Reformist mind of the mid-seventeenth century, one might use phrasing that emphasizes the dissimilar similarity: besides the *Church's* mystical union with Christ there is also the *churches'* mystical union with him. Each union posed a problem: with the former came the difficulty of deciding how to, or even whether to, incorporate hypocrites; with the latter came the more practical, hence pressing, problem of explaining and executing the churches' mystic "union and communion" not only "with the Father and with Christ," but "among the members of Christ's body themselves" (6:499). This latter issue became one of the main political

45

and theological problems of the age. It was so central that the two new basic establishments during the Revolutionary period, the Presbyterian and the Congregational, aimed to address it, but from opposite positions. Milton, I believe, posited a synthesis of the two.

Let us first look at the relationship within the visible church—at that relationship between "the whole multitude" and its parts in its historico-political context.

Perry Miller explains the controversy between Presbyterian and Congregational thinking on the church as arising from the dispute over whether the Church was a "totum integrale," in which the whole gives meaning to the parts, or a "totum universale," in which the parts give meaning to the whole. Samuel Hudson argued the Presbyterian view, that churches were *given* "being" as individual churches; Thomas Hooker and Samuel Stone argued the Congregationalist, that churches were *giving* "being to the whole."[1]

Milton appears to be somewhere in between. Frequently he begins discussion on this or that point of his church doctrine (as evident above in his treatment of the invisible church) by emphasizing the Church's universal mystical entity that, through Christ, gives essence and meaning to all parts. Yet before he has finished his sentence on "THE INVISIBLE CHURCH" (6:499), Milton mentions the parts in such a way ("among the members of Christ's body themselves") that their cohesiveness seems to inform the whole catholic, mystically united Church. Milton's doctrine and the vehicle for its expression are not self-begot but rather derive from the Apostles' authoritative Creed, a fact that Milton documents in the immediately preceding paragraph: "From this communion which we have with Christ there arises the mutual communion of his members which, in the Apostles' Creed, is called THE COMMUNION OF SAINTS" (6:499). Here, too, appears that ambi-directional mode, fostering the synthesis and balance that Milton typically tries to achieve. Finally, Scripture, which binds his doctrine to that of the Apostles, becomes the literary mortar of the treatise's text which juxtaposes the brick of "THE COMMUNION OF SAINTS" with the brick of "THE INVISIBLE CHURCH." And this substance that Milton chooses to mix is very much in keeping with that of his bricks, for the scriptural selections rhythmically shift the reader's attention between the parts and the whole and back again, until a doctrine about seemingly

1. Miller, *The New England Mind: The Seventeenth Century*, 438–39.

irreconcilable opposites is almost incantationally achieved, again, by swinging the reader's focus to and fro:

> Rom. xii. 4, 5: *for as we have many members in one body, and all members do not have the same function; so we, being many, are one body in Christ, and each of us members one of the other;* I Cor. xii. 12, 13: *as the body is one, and has many members; and as all those members of the body; so it is with Christ. For through one spirit we are all baptized into one body, which one, are many, but it is still one body; so it is with Christ. For through one spirit we are all baptized into one body, both Jews and Greeks, both slaves and freemen: and we have all drunk into one spirit,* and xii. 27: *you are the body of Christ, and each of you a member.* (6:499)

The almost lyrical result of having our attention directed between the church's unity and its diversity produces, as part of this chain reaction, an experience (the psychological effect) of completeness, balance, and equanimity that, in turn, together assist Milton in expressing a doctrinal synthesis between opposing statements.[2]

At the other end of the spectrum, when Milton talks "OF PARTICU-LAR CHURCHES," both in his definition as well as in his description that differentiates them from their Hebraic counterpart, the Jewish synagogues (both of which I have dealt with above), he employs the same ambi-directionality. The particular congregation, however few its members, receives meaning and being by its profession of faith in a union with someone and a communion with something greater than itself, even while it returns meaning and being to the universal Church in an ongoing reciprocal way. This seeming theological fluidity translated into contemporary history for Milton. While being unable to yield to measures of repression and forced uniformity that the Presbyterians aimed at, he could not wholly give up the dream of a united England which would accompany a complete Reformation; just so, while being unable to yield to the elitism of saintly Congregationalists, who could efficiently remove themselves from the ungodly and remove the ungodly from among themselves,

---

2. If Milton in *Animadversions* and *Of Reformation*, with his visions and songs of praise, is "the unclassical Puritan who turns tract into an eschatological poem" (as Thomas Kranidas maintains in "Style and Rectitude in Seventeenth-Century Prose: Hall, Smectymnuus, and Milton," 261), then here and elsewhere in *Christian Doctrine*, particularly when talking of the intimacy between Christ and the members of his Church, Milton—through his own phrasing as well as through his proof texts—periodically escapes from the *mode* of theological treatise and into the *mode* of mystical poem.

Milton dreamed of that perfect saintly society in spite of his doctrinal pronouncements that the church included reprobates as well as the regenerated until the end of the world. The reciprocity of parts both *getting meaning from* as well as *giving meaning to* doubtless caused tension within Milton, but it encouraged and yielded ecclesiastical and spiritual poise in a man whose compassion and patience, once preached, would need to be practiced with Ranters, Fifth Monarchists, Levellers, and extreme Presbyterians and Congregationalists who tried to tip the scale either to one side or the other, or to remove it altogether.

Having discussed the relationship between the universal visible church and its visible parts, we can now turn to the related problems of determining the membership of a church and of explaining the existence of weakness and sin among saintly elect church members.

The Presbyterian or the Independent version of totality on its own is inadequate in addressing either of these problems in a less than absolutist, simplistic way. If the universal Church, visible or invisible, derives its meaning only from the parts that comprise it (a *totum universale,* as Independents maintained), then the covenanted visible gatherings of believers require a purging of the unholy so that these churches, singly and collectively, will consist only of the thoroughly converted, perfect saints.[3] (Of course, hard-core Puritans were uneasy about this desire to purify the group so that only the fit remain, because of the nefarious traps of self-righteousness and pride that, if left unchecked, could damn the soul.) If, on the other hand, the whole communion gives meaning to the individual churches (a *totum integrale,* as Presbyterians maintained), then even the insincere could be regarded as participating within that fellowship without any slur against its integrity, since the whole was considered to be mysteriously and mystically greater not only than any one or several of the parts, but also than their sum. (This automatic incorporation only instigated and fueled the danger of spiritual complacency, according to the ideal of Milton and other spiritual extrem-

---

3. See Nuttall, *Visible Saints,* chap. 4, "Be Ye Holy: The Principle of Fitness," in which he shows the Principle of Fellowship—the strength of the Congregationalist movement—gone obsessive-compulsive, washing their communities of all but "saints" who were perfect. Hill in *Antichrist* notes: "The question of the possibility of identifying the godly remnant split the Calvinist movement. The sects held that the godly should organize themselves voluntarily in their own churches, distinct from the Antichristian institutions of the English church" (168).

ists. "Saints" without the ongoing conversion and the sincerity of heart required to become "truly perfect" were, to Milton and his breed, no saints at all.)

Calvin, in attempting to untangle the theological knot often caused by conflicting concepts of church, refers to Scripture that, he notes, speaks of the church in two ways:

> Sometimes by the term "church" it means that which is actually in God's presence, into which no persons are received but those who are children of God by grace of adoption and true members of Christ by sanctification of the Holy Spirit. Then, indeed, the church includes not only the saints presently living on earth, but all the elect from the beginning of the world. Often, however, the name "church" designates the whole multitude of men spread over the earth who profess to worship one God and Christ. . . . In this church are mingled many hypocrites who have nothing of Christ but the name and outward appearance. There are very many ambitious, greedy, envious persons, evil speakers, and some of quite unclean life. . . .
>
> Just as we must believe, therefore, that the former church, invisible to us, is visible to the eyes of God alone, so are we commanded to revere and keep communion with the latter, which is called "church" in respect to men. (ICR, 1021)

This dual usage of the term *church*, which Calvin finds in Scripture, we see in Perkins as his spiritual and ecclesial heir.

William Perkins defines the church as a "peculiar company of men predestined to life everlasting, and made one in Christ" (*WWP*, 263). This chosen group may reside "in heaven or earth"; hence, his distinguishing "the church triumphant in heaven and church militant on earth" (*WWP*, 266). According to Perkins, the parts of the militant church are the "particular churches" according "to regions and countries"—churches that either "lie hid in persecution" or "are visible, carrying before the eyes of the world an open profession of the name of Christ" (*WWP*, 268). Mirroring Calvin and adumbrating Milton, Perkins describes the visible church as *"a mixed company of men professing the faith, assembled together by the preaching of the word. . . . I call it a mixed company, because in it there be true believers and hypocrites, elect and reprobate, good and bad"* (*WWP*, 268–69).

According to Christopher Hill, this "dual conception of the church" (that is, referring sometimes only to the saints, living and deceased, and at other times to the whole "mingled," or "mixed," multitude who claim to worship one God and Christ) is an "essential feature of Calvinist thought," which marks "the real breach with medieval Catholicism." I would point out that it additionally marks the major breach *within* seventeenth-century English Protestantism.[4]

The English Presbyterian church (like churches in Germany and Switzerland) relied upon a national call to be separate. What distinguishes the Congregationalist idea of church from other contemporary ideas of church—as found in Switzerland, Germany, and England—is the refusal to allow the corporate call to and consent by the national church to replace or exhaust the call to the family and to the individual. Milton shares this view in that responsiveness at these levels is important in Milton's theology, ecclesiology, and sense of worship. It was mainly the increasing perfectionism and elitism, requisite for judging others' consciences to keep the society of persons "fit," that distanced Milton from the Congregationalists. Geoffrey Nuttall explains that Congregationalists differed from their contemporaries in "their admission . . . of none but the saints to church membership." This restricting "was to assure the congregation of those whose regeneration was real."[5] Countering this perfectionistic, judgmental, nearly Pelagian position is Milton's more inclusive one, adherent to Calvin and Perkins: "THE ASSEMBLY OF THOSE WHO ARE CALLED IS THE VISIBLE CHURCH. I say *of those who are called* so as to refer to them all, whether regenerate or otherwise" (6:563).

Milton had virtually no disagreement with this Congregationalist check against new tyranny, though he had great objection, as has already been stated, with the increasing Congregationalist insistence on a perfectionistic scrutinizing of members. For him, excluding the unregenerate to depict the visible church as a spotless bride (or, from the opposite point of view, to know that the mystic, invisible church was enfleshed in the church one could see) was indefensible.

Seeing the link between "the whole multitude" (that is, the universal visible church), called and worshiping, and any "society of persons" professing faith and brotherhood for edification and saintly communion (that is, any particular visible church) was difficult enough for Reformers. But comprehending the intersection of both visible aspects of church with the "mystic body" (the invisible and immaculate church) seemed impossible, especially since the visible church—

4. Hill, *Puritanism and Revolution: Studies in Interpretation of the English Revolution of the Seventeenth Century,* 288–89; see esp. chap. 7, "William Perkins and the Poor."
5. Nuttall, *Visible Saints,* 160, 161.

universal and particular—was flawed and sinful, and the invisible church, immaculate.

The question of how a maculate, visible church squares with an immaculate, invisible church and the question of how a church's relating to Christ vertically corresponds to the churches' relating to him horizontally are related. Considering the churches' spiritual union can address these questions and provide further insight, if not an answer, into understanding the seeming contradictory "perfect" status of a sometime sinful living church—an issue of enormous importance for thoroughly appreciating Milton's teaching on the church.

Let us turn then to the relationship between the visible church (the whole and its parts) and the invisible church.

Amidst much typical Reformist ecclesiology, Ulrich Zwingli in his *Sixty-seven Articles* (publicized in 1523) and in his "The Church: A Reply to Jerome Emser" (dated August 20, 1524) provides additional information on the components of church, information that by contrast can be useful in grasping the link between the invisible and visible church for Milton.

Zwingli's "Eighth Article" states: "That all who live in the head are members and children of God. And this is the church or communion of saints, a bride of Christ, ecclesia catholica" (ZW, 41). Here, Zwingli cites three distinct uses of the term *church*. First, the church can refer to "the total gathering of all those who are founded upon the one faith in the Lord Jesus Christ" (ZW, 42). Second, the church can refer to "special gatherings which we call parishes or ecclesiastical communities" (ZW, 43) (also called "individual churches" in the Reply to Emser discussed below). Finally, the church can refer to the "ecclesia catholica," that is, "the universal gathering which in the Spirit of God is gathered together in one body to be a wedded daughter and bride of Christ and he to be her husband and head" (ZW, 44). These three notions of church in Milton are referred to, respectively, as the universal visible church, particular visible churches, and the invisible church or "the mystic body."

Zwingli's "The Church: A Reply to Jerome Emser" contains the identical three components of church doctrine as his discussion of the "Eighth Article," though without the identical ordering. Here Zwingli talks again, first, of "the whole multitude of Christians that counts itself faithful" but "is not yet the church undefiled" (WHZ, 367). He switches the other two, however, discussing next "the church unknown to men," "the spouse of Christ, without any "spot or wrinkle"—"the church that cannot err" (*WHZ*, 374, 368, 371). Finally, Zwingli discusses what he calls "individual churches," but immediately qualifies as "one church," before identifying *them and it* as "Christ's spouse" and "a communion of all the saints" (*WHZ*, 375). The rearrangement, so far as I can tell, appears arbitrary and inconsequential. Not so his argument.

The crucial difference between Milton's ecclesiology and Zwingli's lies in their renditions of the spousal relationship of the church to Christ. Milton forgoes any explicit or implicit mention of particular churches while discussing the church's invisible and immaculate relationship to her Spouse; Zwingli, on the other hand, spiritualizes and purifies as he amalgamates his visible individual churches into a bride right before our eyes. There is no such sleight of hand by Milton. While some members of the visible particular church(es) on earth are included among that invisible, immaculate spiritual company, all are certainly not. In other words, for Milton it is a principle of intersection, not one of identity, which helps to explain the relationship between the invisible, immaculate church and the visible particular church(es).

To appreciate the issue beneath Milton's and Zwingli's doctrinal discrepancy on this point, one needs to consider the issue of whether or not hypocrites or those not truly converted in heart—though claiming to be Christian and to belong to a church—can, in truth, be considered as belonging to the Church.

As we have already seen, Milton explicitly states that he chose the phrase *"those who are called"* for defining the "ASSEMBLY" of his "VISIBLE CHURCH," precisely "to refer to them all, whether regenerate or otherwise" (6:563). In his reply to Emser, Zwingli—sounding like Luther, Calvin, and the English Reformers—*claims* to include both faithful and unfaithful in the visible church:

> "Ecclesia" is used not only for the pious, holy, and faithful, but also for the impious, wicked, and unfaithful, provided only they were of the seed of Abraham according to the flesh and were intermingled with the pious. . . .
> In like manner in the New Testament also we see that "ecclesia" is used for all those who have named the name of Christ and who walk and live within the company of Christians, even though in reality they are not very faithful. (*WHZ*, 366–67)

Crediting Christ with accomplishing the cleansing of the communion of saints (the invisible church), Zwingli even foreshadows Milton by anticipating theological objection and providing a strong, thorough explanation for how a real, human church can be without blemish: "Certain ones object: 'Such a church no more exists than does Plato's Republic because no one lives without fault, because all have sinned. . . . How, then, is it possible for there to be anywhere a church that has not spot or wrinkle?' These I satisfy in this way: What is without spot and wrinkle is not its own nature but thanks to Christ" (*WHZ*, 368–69).

Yet, for all the ostensibly neat, distinct segmenting within Zwingli's ecclesiology, on closer examination of the particular dimension of the church (especially the churches' spiritual relationship to Christ *intercommunally*), his teaching is not all that tidy or intelligible. Zwingli, in spite of all his doctrinal contribution, causes ambiguity at a key place in his ecclesiology. He maintains, on the one hand, and quite systematically, that the Old Testament and New Testament church "was composed of the faithful and those who were unfaithful but pretended faith, and therefore was not yet such that neither wrinkle nor spot attached to it," yet within the same document ("The Church: A Reply to Jerome Emser") he argues that all the individual churches are "one church, Christ's spouse, . . . a communion of all the saints, i.e. of all the faithful," and concludes that "it is the office of these churches, as is now clear, to reject one who is shamelessly delinquent" (*WHZ*, 367–75). Missing are both a clear definition as to who are "faithful" and "unfaithful" and a response that anticipates the question as to whether anyone incorporated into Christ can ever be regarded as "unfaithful" or "spotted" since all true believers have been perfected through Christ's justification. To equate visible churches with the spotless invisible church and view them as Christ's bride, as Zwingli does *here*, would necessarily mean the actual exclusion of the unfaithful, not to mention the hypocrites, thereby precluding the ongoing possibility of their full conversion through some sort of continuous relationship with Christ through his Church. Not to equate the two, but *to interrelate them*, as Milton does, could allow for contact with and conversion to Christ through his Church to which even the hypocrite could belong in this life.[6] Milton, after all, had not divided humanity into two basic groups—the saved and the

6. For a fuller treatment of the interrelationship between the invisible and visible church, see the explanation offered on Wyclif's *De Ecclesia* given by John T. McNeill in "Some Emphases in Wyclif's Teaching," esp. 452–55.

damned—as Reformist scholars often have, but into three. Michael Fixler finds included in this third group "the bulk of mankind, each individually possessing in some degree a sufficient measure of prevenient grace to save himself from the consequences of original sin." This is the group Milton aimed not to neglect. This "broad class of sinners who *might be saints,*" I would insist, increasingly holds the principal focus within Milton's broadening ecclesial community and radically Reformist doctrine.[7]

Zwingli, in the end, is unable to sustain the neat dialectic ideology because that ideology, like any, is ultimately incapable of delineating, measuring, and accurately conveying the whole and absolute truth about a relationship that is spiritual in all its facets (horizontal, vertical, invisible, and even visible). In other words, the most desired spiritual information cannot be quantified or comprehended through the categories of human knowledge. The truth of the unseen relationship between Christ and the unseen *and* seen church is the doctrine that has been ready to doff linguistic and systematic holds all along and that, defying *solely rational* controls, finally breaks through to announce itself as gospel to those with spiritual ears to hear.

In spite of being one of the great Puritan systematic theologians of the early seventeenth century, William Ames is much less categorical than Zwingli and others. Especially in his treatment of the invisible and visible church, Ames exhibits an approach that is distinctively qualitative; and his ecclesiology focuses on the spiritual relationship between the visible and invisible church. In considering Milton's concept of the church, one would want to consult Ames because his theological treatise, *The Marrow of Theology,* was the standard Puritan authority in the seventeenth century and because Milton himself acknowledges Ames's work in his *Christian Doctrine* for both its clear system and modest size. But for this study it is imperative to consult Ames because his qualitative distinction between the visible and invisible dimensions of church looks forward to Milton's in its ability to accommodate the truth of the spiritual relationship among the parts as well as between them and Christ. This emphasis is essential to thoroughly appreciating Milton's concept of church, Scripture, and Sacrament.

Ames divides the church "according to the degree of communion

7. Fixler, "Milton's Passionate Epic," 174.

it has with Christ." In this sense it is called either militant ("that which knows only of a communion begun and so still struggles with enemies in the battlefield of the world") or triumphant ("that which is already perfected"). Moving immediately to the militant church, he explains that this sort of church is "both invisible and visible" (*MT*, 177). His refinement of the distinction is striking:[8]

> 25. This distinction is not a division of genus into species, as if there were one church visible and another invisible, or of the whole into members, as if one part of the church were visible and another invisible. It relates to *phases of the same subject: Invisibility is a condition or mode of the church* having to do with its essential and internal form; *visibility is a condition or mode of the church* having to do with its accidental or outward form.
> 26. The essential form is invisible both because it is a relation which cannot be perceived by the senses and *also because it is spiritual. . . .*
> 27. The accidental form is visible because it is an outward profession of inward faith, easily perceived by sense. (*MT*, 177; emphasis added)

When Ames talks of spiritual things, his language and theological system are more successful than Zwingli's. Ames's distinction between the visible and invisible church is "not a division of genus into species, as if there were one church visible and another invisible." Zwingli's distinction, by contrast, appears to make such a division. And that division follows through to separate space into the here and the hereafter and time into the now and the then. In Zwingli, the respective pairs of "species" of church, space, and time remain unbridged, causing great confusion when he talks of ecclesial-spiritual realities like the individual churches—with faithful *and* unfaithful—as Christ's spouse. Ames's talk of modes or "phases" reveals an attempt to bridge a chasm so that the invisible is evident in the visible, the beyond in the here, and the end in the now.

In their discussions of the particular church, both Milton and Ames consider two basic ideas: the absolute power that every part shares from the whole *and* the mutual bonding with and responsible commitment of believers. While the two are in basic agreement on both, Milton is much less prohibitive on what will not constitute a particu-

---

8. For the importance of Ames's distinction "between the visible and the mystical churches" for Congregational theory and covenant theology, see Miller, *New England Mind*, 442.

lar congregation. The exhortation for duties in Milton notwithstanding, one feels an openness and a fluidity in him over the inception (or dissolution) of a congregation and over the individual's participation (or withdrawal) that one does not sense in Ames. Increased slipping into and out of congregations was very likely what induced the tough stand and legal cant with its quite unmetaphorical sound and use that we find in Ames.

Ames prefaces his discussion of the particular church by stating that there are "as many visible churches as there are distinct congregations" (*MT*, 179). For Ames, as for Milton, the particular congregation shares the substance and authority of the universal church, "but in respect of the catholic church, which has the nature [*ratio*] of a whole; it is a member made up of various individual members gathered together; and in respect of these members it is also a whole" (*MT*, 179). Ames proceeds, un-Miltonically, however, by restrictive, negative details about what and who constitute a church:

14. Believers do not make a particular church, even though by chance many may meet and live together in the same place unless they are joined by a special bond among themselves. Otherwise, any one church would often be dissolved into many, and many also merged into one.
15. This bond is a covenant, expressed or implicit, by which believers bind themselves individually to perform all those duties toward God and toward one another which relate to the purpose [*ratio*] of the church and its edification. . . .
21. No sudden coming together and exercise of holy communion suffices to make a church unless there is also that continuity, at least in intention, which gives the body and its members a certain spiritual polity. (*MT*, 180)

More evident here than in Milton is a social-political weave in his teaching on the church, and less evident are those original Reformist threads of gathered assembly, domesticity, respect for the local church, and mutual equality among these particular churches— things that return in Milton. While Ames's ecclesiology does not deny any of these, his constitutional flavor and socially conditional emphasis evince a different focus than appears in Luther, Calvin, Zwingli, Perkins, and Milton.[9]

9. For a standard comprehensive treatment of the interrelated aspects of covenant thinking throughout the seventeenth-century society, see Miller, *New England Mind*: chap. 13, "The Covenant of Grace"; chap. 14, "The Social Covenant"; and chap. 15,

Yet Ames, in describing the ineffable knot by which the invisible and visible church was joined, provided the core of church doctrine and key to a believer's spirituality. Ames's chapter 31 (bk. 1), entitled "The Church Mystically Considered," contains such moving expression of the passionate and procreative love between Christ and his Church that the idea seems to reach beyond the prose, for poetry, the only suitable dress for the sublime: "15. The relationship is so intimate that not only is Christ the church's and the church Christ's, Song of Sol. 2:16, but Christ is in the church and the church in him, John 15:4; 1 John 3:24. Therefore, the church is mystically called *Christ*, 1 Cor. 12:12, and the *Fullness of Christ*, Eph. 1:23" (*MT*, 176).

Ames's idea of the invisible church, which Milton appears to follow, allows for invisible worship even among the visibly churched. This historically more accurate ecclesiology prevents an over-emphasized separation between the invisible and visible church, between spirit and redeemed flesh. The distinction between the two aspects of church is to be minimized instead of exaggerated, for their separation is a condition that Ames and Milton would have regarded as untrue and unwholesome. The doctrinal solution for

---

"The Church Covenant." While "it is still impossible to decide the primary question, whether Perkins, Ames, and Preston deliberately extended the idea of compact from their social to their religious thinking, or whether they worked their way from theology to social theory" (412), "there can be no doubt that these theologians inserted the federal idea into the very substance of divinity, that they changed the relation even of God to man from necessity to contract, largely because contractualism was becoming increasingly congenial to the age and in particular to Puritans" (399).

For discussions on the growth of the concept of covenant (for example, the gradual shift in emphasis from the covenant of God's single substance of Grace common to the Old and New Testaments to the dichotomization of God's covenant into that of Works and that of Grace), see the following: Charles Lloyd Cohen, *God's Caress: The Psychology of Puritan Religious Experience,* esp. chap. 2, "Covenant Psychology"; Michael McGiffert, "God's Controversy with Jacobean England," esp. 1164; McGiffert, "Grace and Works: The Rise and Division of Covenant Divinity in Elizabethan Puritanism," which provides the most comprehensive and compact standard treatment of the foundation and development of the idea of covenant based on "the fact that covenant, unlike predestination, stirred no dispute between Zurich and Geneva but formed part of the broad common foundation of Reformed divinity" (469); and Jens G. Möller, "The Beginnings of Puritan Covenant Theology," who, realizing the sociological slant of scholarship on the covenant, initiated major redirection on the heretofore neglected aspects of "theology and history, before the meaning of puritan covenant theology [could] be clearly stated" (46). See especially John T. Shawcross's "Milton and Covenant: The Christian View of Old Testament Theology," in James H. Sims and Leland Ryken, eds., *Milton and Scriptural Tradition: The Bible into Poetry,* for a literary application of much of the historiography of covenant theology, especially for the Renaissance Christian view that what Old and New Testaments held in common was that both were "covenants of grace" (164).

preventing erroneous dichotomizing is focusing on the elect as the point of connection between this earth and the new earth. As noted in the introduction, Pecheux's informative discussion of the concept of the elect is useful in keeping one fixed to Milton and faithful to his Amesian source.[10] It is important to adhere to Milton's concept of the visible church as that "whole multitude of those who are called from any part of the whole world." These are the elect, that is, the "called" of the Letter to the Romans: "For whom he did foreknow, he also did predestinate to be conformed to the image of his Son, that he might be the firstborn among many brethren. Moreover whom he did predestinate, them he also called: and whom he called, them he also justified: and whom he justified, them he also glorified" (8:29–30).

In Milton's definition of the universal visible church, it is right to read Milton's "called" as elliptical, containing the entire Pauline anadiplosis of Romans that proclaims the steps to glory for the elect as they grow from visibly elect worshiping community to visibly glorified worshiping community. Pecheux summarizes this transaction from visibility to invisibility and ultimate revisibility:

> Hence the elect—the invisible church—are seen as the final victorious fruit of the union of Christ and his bride-church. . . . Thus it is the work of the third person of the first trinity [Father, Son, and Spirit] which ultimately destroys the power of Death, the third person of the second trinity [Satan, Sin, and Death], by elevating the descendants of Adam and Eve, who form the third trinity, to life in the eternal kingdom of glory as trophies of the second Adam and his Church [who with the elect form the fourth trinity].[11]

The justified call allows for a certain spotlessness even among the visible church and for the concomitant observance of "true religion"—worship aside from externally delineated rites, nations, congregations, and believers—but only because of this Body's Head. The elect are not flawless, and yet they are perfect because of their incorporation into Christ.

Milton explains the process of this union in book 1, chapter 21 of the treatise, "Of Ingrafting in Christ, and Its Effects":

> INGRAFTING IN CHRIST . . . is the process by which God the Father plants believers in Christ. That is to say, he makes them sharers in Christ, and renders them fit to join, eventually, in one body with

10. See Pecheux, "Second Adam," 179.
11. Ibid., 183.

Christ. Matt. xv. 13: *every plant which my heavenly Father has not planted will be rooted out;* John xv. 1. 2: *I am the true vine, and my Father is the farmer. Every branch in me which does not bear fruit, he removes.* (6:477)

However, union for the believers (i.e., the saints) does not banish all tension. As Mary Ann Radzinowicz reminds us: "Election is not the positive pole of a divine activity, of which the negative pole is reprobation. Nor is election the guarantee of perfect spiritual security."[12] Milton realistically admits, "Although it is not to be hoped for in this life, we ought nevertheless to struggle and strive towards perfection as our ultimate goal." Still, while he concludes, "There is a struggle between flesh and spirit in the regenerate man . . . and a struggle against the world and Satan" as well, he adds very pointedly, "So, too, there is a victory" (6:482).

This explanation of struggle for the ingrafted saints is significant in understanding Milton's ultimate purpose which he next addresses, namely, that of how the reality of imperfect, struggling beings intergrafted onto Christ fits with scriptural proclamations of believers' sinlessness:

As a result [of the victory], those who carry on this struggle with real vigor, and labor earnestly and tirelessly to attain perfection in Christ, are often, through God's mercy, described attributively in the Bible as "perfect" and "blameless" and "sinless." Of course they are not really perfect, but these titles are given to them because, although sin resides within them, it does not reign over them. Gen. vi. 9: *Noah, a just man, was perfect in his days,* and xvii. 1: *walk always in my sight and be perfect.* (6:483)

Additionally one might look to Milton's explanation of, and scriptural authority for, the sanctification of "THE WHOLE MAN, BOTH SOUL AND BODY" (6:461) for a text with particular Radical appeal, as it presents not the exhortation to perfection, but its accomplishment, along with the by-products of immunization against sin and of absolute freedom:

Whoever is born of God, does not sin, because God's seed remains in him: nor can he sin, because he is born of God, and v. 18: *whoever is born of God does not sin, but he who is begotten of God keeps himself, and the evil one does not touch him.* Thus regeneration is sometimes called sanc-

12. Radzinowicz, *Toward* Samson Agonistes: *The Growth of a Poet's Mind,* 340.

tification, and indeed this is the right name for it, *regeneration* itself being merely a metaphorical term. (6:463–64)

In chapter 24 ("Of Union and Communion with Christ and his Members; also of the Mystic or Invisible Church") and chapter 25 ("Of Incomplete Glorification: also of the Assurance of Salvation and the Perseverance of the Saints") of the first book, Milton continues his discussion of growth of the regenerate in "UNION or COMMUNION with the Father in Christ the Son" (6:498). Here he speaks in terms of glorification, which is either complete or incomplete. Incomplete glorification, which takes place "in this life" (6:614), is another way of talking about how human beings still in the process of living amidst personal and institutional flaws can be considered "perfect." Instead of the language of husbandry and horticulture, we have the language of *eschaton*. Milton uses the eschatological reference point (and its terminology) to note and measure humanity's distance from it, but not from the final effects already at work in people because of Christ: "INCOMPLETE GLORIFICATION means that WE ARE JUSTIFIED AND ADOPTED BY GOD THE FATHER AND ARE FILLED WITH A CERTAIN AWARENESS BOTH OF PRESENT GRACE AND DIGNITY AND OF FUTURE GLORY, SO THAT WE HAVE ALREADY BEGUN TO BE BLESSED. John xvii. 22: *and I have given them the glory which you gave me*" (6:502). The condition of incipient glorification instills confidence since both "regeneration and growth are accompanied by confirmation or preservation," which is "also the work of God" (6:503). While God is responsible for "regeneration, growth, and preservation," man is responsible for the effects, "*faith, charity,* and so on." The divine "proximate causes" and their human-based "effects" "combine to produce the ASSURANCE OF SALVATION and the PERSEVERANCE OF THE SAINTS":

> ASSURANCE OF SALVATION, then, is A CERTAIN DEGREE OF FAITH. IT MEANS THAT A MAN IS PERSUADED BY THE TESTIMONY OF THE SPIRIT, AND FIRMLY BELIEVES THAT IF HE BELIEVES AND PERSISTS IN FAITH AND CHARITY, HE WILL WITHOUT ANY DOUBT ATTAIN ETERNAL LIFE AND PERFECT GLORY, SINCE HE IS ALREADY JUSTIFIED, ADOPTED AND PARTIALLY GLORIFIED BY UNION AND COMMUNION WITH CHRIST AND THE FATHER. (6:503)

In all this treatment of the perfect condition of the not-yet-immaculate saints, one can detect an increasingly clearer statement with Radical-Reformist qualities. All along one has heard the sounds of primacy of faith; security and calm of saintliness already able to be enjoyed (however faintly); perfectibility of human nature; liberty because of union and communion with the Godhead; the importance of works, not of ceremony but of charity; and more. The sound of Radical Protestantism is loud and clear.

4

"Rites and Methods which [God] Himself Has Prescribed"

Solution to the Riddle of True Reform

hat was to take place in this "house and church of the living God"? How was this spiritual communion—horizontal and vertical—to be celebrated? Where and when? Questions like these lead to the closely related area of worship. For Milton, as for Luther, worship acts as a concrete index for grasping Reformation church theory and for gauging and more accurately evaluating the religious progress of an otherwise elusive subject. Furthermore, statements about the expression of believers' belonging to God and to one another *through devotion* reveal attitudes of a theologian or an ecclesiologist like Milton that might be at least as important as his denotative definitions and credal statements. I have reversed the order that I used in discussing Luther. Here, I take up worship only after having dealt with the church for two reasons: first, the focus of this book is on Milton's concept of the church, to which all other matters are subordinate; and second, this is Milton's own ordering for the *Christian Doctrine* where he discusses the church in book 1 whose focus is "FAITH AND KNOWLEDGE OF GOD" and then worship in book 2 whose focus is "THE WORSHIP OF GOD and CHARITY" (6:128, 638).

Milton's catechetical method is designed to work on the reader—not only informing him with distinctive content but rehearsing him for a spiritual, revolutionary sort of liturgy that directs devotion without regularizing, uniformalizing, or even requiring externals.

Examining the reading process will enlighten us about why Milton, who advocates spiritual worship, bothers with externals at all.

Following his predecessor Wolleb, Milton speaks first of internal worship, then of external. Internal worship means "acknowledgment of the one true God and devout affection for him" (6:656). Elaborating on the meaning of devout affection, Milton explains: "DEVOUT AFFECTION FOR GOD consists of OUR LOVE FOR HIM, CONFIDENCE AND HOPE IN HIM, GRATITUDE TO HIM, FEAR OF HIM, AND HUMILITY, PATIENCE AND OBEDIENCE TOWARDS HIM" (6:656, 657). External worship can be either acceptable or unacceptable. His criterion for its acceptability is God's pleasure:

> True religion exists when God is worshipped sincerely by rites and methods which he himself has prescribed. . . . Opposed to true religion is superstition, or a man-made form of worship. . . . Also opposed to true religion is hypocritical worship, where the external forms are duly observed, but without any internal or spiritual involvement. This is extremely offensive to God. (6:666–67)

Milton next discusses the external worship of God "which is usually called RELIGION: not that internal worship is not religion, but it is usually not called so unless it shows itself in externals" (6:666). But, typical of Milton, while distinguishing, he at once blurs the two basic types of worship so as to reconcile what must really never be disjoined: "External worship, moreover, though it may be distinguished from internal for the sake of argument, should in practice go hand in hand with it, and the two are never separated except by the viciousness of sinners" (6:666). Noting divorced worship to have occurred after the Fall as "one of the tragic signs of moral degeneration," Regina M. Schwartz quite rightly emphasizes that what Milton objects to is "a *separated* worship," not to the externals themselves.[1] Before continuing with "the parts and circumstances of true religion or the worship of God," he asserts which sort of worship is preeminent and essential: "But internal worship, provided that it is sincere, is acceptable to God *even if the external forms are not strictly observed*" (6:668; emphasis added). Ideally, then, there is to be a harmony between inward and outward devotion, but it is the external that must conform to the internal, not the reverse.

1. Schwartz, *Remembering and Repeating Biblical Creation in* Paradise Lost, 76; see 66–90 for Milton's statements on worship vis-à-vis apparent violations within the poetry.

Milton's final task in his treatment of worship is to consider the various external forms themselves, each of which is acceptable only because it is authorized by Scripture. For example, to consider spoken prayer and the formula of worship that should govern a church's service to God, Milton selects the Lord's Prayer, the epitome of how to pray since it was Christ himself who, in the Gospels, so instructed his followers: "Even the Lord's Prayer is a pattern or model, rather than a formula to be repeated verbatim either by the apostles or by the churches today. So it is clear that the church has no need of a liturgy: those who prompt and assist our prayers are divine helpers, not human" (6:670). Milton's Christ has given only a guideline for how to pray to the Father. There is nothing especially sacred, much less magical, about the very words Christ used. To hold such a position would be nothing less than that superstition decried by Milton. Or to put it another way, there is nothing less sacred about the wording that an individual believer finds suitable to himself or herself than there is about Christ's. If there is nothing mandatory or magical about Christ's words and form, there is even less about those prescribed as liturgy by men who presume "to prompt and assist our prayers" when such aid can be given only by "divine helpers, not human." In fact, words at times being so inadequate in conveying the most profound prayer, Milton acknowledges that "we do not always have to raise our voice. Private prayers may be silent: they may be uttered in whispers or even in groans" as was Moses' who in Exodus 14:15, Milton points out, "was crying only in his mind." Milton concludes that by making prayers "more private . . . we shall obey the injunction of Matt. vi. 6" to pray in secret (6:671). Thus, while Milton has raised the issue of spoken prayer, he has gently but firmly removed the spokenness of prayer as essential to prayer. And while he has cited the Lord's Prayer, he has just as gently but firmly erased it by having emptied it of its believed "repeated verbatim" power.

It might appear that Milton, on the basis of the gospel, believed that it was better to pray alone. Not so. He maintains that "we may pray either alone or with other people." Even though "Christ generally prayed alone and by himself, whether the disciples were with him or not, . . . when he told his disciples to pray he said nothing about whether they should do so alone or with other people" (6:672). It is difficult to get one's bearings again and know exactly the environment that affords better prayer. Yet even the disciples could provide no set conditions to be imitated, for "they sometimes prayed individually, though in the same place, each one thinking his prayers to himself and directing them towards some subject which they had previously agreed upon. . . . Or sometimes one of their number would speak aloud on behalf of the rest" (6:672).

When Milton considers the posture most conducive to prayer, he liberates the Christian who subscribes to his treatise from enslavement by removing the monolithic quality of any established pattern, thus leaving the responsibility for that dimension of worship with the believer. Consequently, "the positioning of the body during prayer was not strictly prescribed under the law" (6:672). Neither was there a hard and fast rule as to the proper place for prayer (room or sanctuary) or as to the preferred style of prayer respective to those places (private or public):

> As for the place for prayer, any place is suitable: I Tim. ii. 8: *I wish men to pray everywhere.*

> In private prayers, a place where we can be unobserved: Matt. vi. 6: *go into your room,* and xiv. 23: *he went away by himself up into the mountain to pray.* It is hypocritical to offer private prayer in public. . . . It was, however, lawful to offer private prayers in the sanctuary and in the temple at Jerusalem, as in the examples of Hannah, David and others. (6:673–74)

Thus, Milton has not dispensed with space and style altogether, only melted definitions of and expectations for where his audience has been conditioned to pray, with the hope of instilling in them a varied approach for where and how to meet the holy. It is for them to discern. Milton employs the same strategy when he considers the right time to pray. Just as any place is suitable for praying, so is any time. Yet this omnitemporal principle does not preclude suggestion of appropriate periods in the day synchronized with nature's rhythm: "Similarly there is no time which is not suitable for prayer. . . . But particularly suitable are the evening, the morning and midday" (6:674).

Sometimes a directive about external worship involves a prohibition, as, for example, covering one's head during prayer. Yet here, too, the principle carries no taboo. Once Milton has cited the scriptural text and considered the historical and social contexts then and now, he gives the reason for the change in the respective contemporary customs without stealing anything from the constant theological principle at the core of either age: reverence for the community of believers. While Milton's discussion of "the question of dress," as exemplified by the covering of one's head during prayer, may not seem to warrant lengthy quoting, the effort Milton takes to emphasize the living, progressive church under the guidance of the Spirit at the local level justifies recounting the catalog of customs which reach from Paul's day to Milton's and which illustrate, for Milton, the ultimate criterion for purity of worship—"that the spirit, not the letter of the law [be] observed":

> Paul says, on this subject, I Cor. xi. 4: *any man praying or prophesying with his head covered brings shame upon his head: but any woman who does not keep her head covered when she prays or prophesies brings shame upon her head.* . . . Why was this? Because at that time it was a sign of subjection for either a man or a woman to have the head covered. As a result men prayed and prophesied with their heads uncovered. But nowadays it is a sign of subjection for a man to be bare-headed, and a sign of authority for him to have his head covered. The result is that in most churches, particularly those of Europe, it is the custom to praise God bare-headed in order to show reverence, since that is the way we show it in everyday life, but to prophesy with the head covered, as a sign of authority. It is also customary to listen to prophecy with the head covered, as befitting mature and free-born sons. Thus the spirit, not the letter of the law is observed, which is as it should always be. By the same token, it will be seen to follow that in countries like Livonia or Russia, where the intense cold, or in countries like Asia or Africa, where the custom of the country makes it either inconvenient or improper to uncover the head, it is correct to pray with the head covered. Ludovicus Cappellus, among others, has demonstrated this in a learned note on this passage. (6:673)

So long as the spirit is preeminently observed, all else is negotiable, adaptable, fluid and can be based on what is reasonable, customary, or convenient for that locale where the spirit breathes. Thus, Milton, recognizing fasting as an external aid to prayer, notes that "in ancient times fasting was accompanied by various methods of mortifying the flesh, which were dictated by the customs and the disposition of those nations among whom they were used" (6:679).

Curses and vows are other forms of external worship which Milton takes up and which he conveys in a way similar to those examined above. He begins with a clearly stated, simple catechesis: "We are even commanded to curse, in public prayer, the enemies of God and the church, fellow Christians who have proved false, and anyone who commits major sins against God or even against ourselves.

The same thing is permissible in private prayer" (6:675). Embedded in this concrete teaching on exactly how to pray is a promise that "the prayers of those who pray obediently and with faith will be heard." But this assurance is no sooner given than it is taken away: "It often happens, however, that not all the things for which the faithful pray are granted, whether they asked for them for themselves or for other people" (6:676). To exemplify what he means, Milton refers again to cursing and, in doing so, undoes what was initially perceived as a simple, straightforward command to curse enemies as part of one's prayer: "Among the errors connected with petitions and prayers come rash curses, by which we invoke God or the devil to destroy any particular person or thing" (6:676).

Vow making likewise appears to be spiritually a very desirable thing to do since by a vow "we testify our eagerness and firm resolution to worship God, or perhaps even assure God of the gratitude we shall feel if our request is granted." This "promise solemnly made to God . . . must concern some lawful thing, and sometimes it is even reinforced by the swearing of an oath" (6:680). With principle delivered, qualifier, caution, or condition cannot be far behind. And so, Milton's warning, "But we must be careful not to make a vow which prevents either ourselves or others from using things which God intended us to use," has its own restriction: "We must beware of this except in cases where, by not taking such a vow, we may cause someone else to be tempted" (6:680). Furthermore, even if a vow has passed its definitional criterion of being "lawful," it is not necessarily acceptable. Even the law cannot simplify to the extent of absolving from the task of deciding whether or not a legitimate vow is honorable. Milton provides further comment to aid the prospective vow-maker in assessing the virtue of the task:

> A wrongful vow, however, is not to be fulfilled. . . . Matt. xv. 5: *you say, If a man says to his father or mother, "Anything of mine which might have benefitted you, is a gift for God," then he is innocent. Yet he certainly does not honor his father or mother.* For this man had vowed to God what he ought to have supplied for the upkeep of his parents. Therefore either his vow must go unfulfilled or his parents be neglected. Christ insists that the parents must be cared for and the wrongful vow broken. (6:682)

While the directives to curse and to vow are provided, the "ifs, ands, or buts," here as above, make more of an impression than do the actual declarations and definitions of the various external forms themselves.

In discussing external worship, Milton provides principles of various kinds: some are promotive (cursing, fasting, vowing, covering or uncovering the head); some are dismissive (repeating the Lord's Prayer verbatim, the necessity of raising voices in prayer, making lawful but wrongful vows); some are unitive (praying can be done at any time and in any place). Regardless of the type, though, while the enunciated principle argues the respective external form a certain place in the entire Miltonic scheme of worship, the principle's (sometimes many) qualifications deprive the external of the power of preemptive prescription. Milton's theology has no room for hard and fast rules about verbatim prayers, bareheaded believers, or hours for prayer because Scripture itself (cited often enough to document a practice and to signal a cohesiveness between God's Word and Milton's) is void of such prescriptions. It is as if rigid regulating would prevent the Spirit from blowing where it listeth—a horror to either writer. The individuals who comprise any church are the only ones to decide what externals are just and fitting on the basis of Scripture-and-the-Spirit's operating in the circumstances of the ongoing church. To sum up Milton's methodology, Milton restrains the use of any given principle that, if completely released, would paradoxically restrict the spirit and rigidify the worship and worshiper. We can now look at the execution and effect of Milton's method on the reader, a prospective true worshiper.

As Milton delivers each of these external forms of worship with sometime extended exposition and always scriptural sanction, there is more going on than the eye usually meets in a theological treatise. In his treatment of the Lord's Prayer, use of the voice, solitary prayer, communal prayer, positioning of the body, appropriate dress when praying, the place for prayer, the time, the place of cursing, and the use of vows, Milton gives us ecclesial artifacts that are, in a term given importance by Stanley Fish, "self-consuming." The very externals individually and emphatically raised before our "mental sight" are conveyed and portrayed there, only to be dissolved before our very considering of them so that what worship is left to the reader will be only internal and invisible. Not only are the artifacts self-consuming, therefore, but the experience of church and of worship likewise is. It is this spiritual action that is so essential to Milton's idea of Reform and that is the very experience one can overlook by understanding worship as external and, consequently, as the property of only the visible church. Hill points out that while "the preachers of free grace—Saltmarsh, Erbery, Dell and others—aimed to liberate men and women from the formalism, from the legal calculations of covenant theologians, and from the despair to which predestinarian theology reduced many who doubted their salvation," they and the Ranters—and Milton—had a common enemy: the twin halves of tyranny—oppression and repression. They consequently had a genuine empathy, however different the means to symbolize and articulate the "breakdown of confidence in established forms of religion."[2] In spite of disillusionment with some misbehaving antinomians as well as with self-serving army officers, Milton would, nonetheless, have stood in the company of Muggleton, Reeve, Winstanley, Walwyn, and many like them who emphasized the invisible church.[3]

This catechesis on worship resembles what Stanley Fish finds to be part of the lesson of *Paradise Lost,* namely, "the superfluousness of the mold of experience—of space and time—to the perception of what is true"; and he concludes that "the epic's form is the vehicle of its own abandonment." For Fish, the true form of the epic is not the division of twelve books but the reader's experience: "The action is interior, taking place inside the reader's mind."[4] Regarding worship, the externals of the catechetical exercise and of the supposed eventual worship are not true externals, but only the apparent framework, which is dismantled piece by piece, ultimately leaving only the believing worshiper before God as the only proper external.

In his recent essay, "Driving from the Letter: Truth and Indeter-

2. Hill, *World Turned Upside Down,* 190, 188; for treatment of the Ranters, see chap. 9, "Seekers and Ranters"; chap. 10, "Ranters and Quakers"; and chap. 15, "Base Impudent Kisses." See also Hill, *Experience of Defeat,* 42–50 and 84–97; McGregor and Reay, eds., *Radical Religion,* for an excellent treatment of a variety of Nonconformist groups whose elisions between one and the next often made it difficult to determine definitive characteristics and members of particular groups; Morton, *World of the Ranters;* and Christopher Hill, Barry Reay, and William Lamont, eds., *The World of the Muggletonians;* and Byron Nelson, "Play, Ritual Inversion, and Folly Among the Ranters in the English Revolution."

3. Joan Bennett distinguishes between "humanist antinomianism" and "voluntarist antinomianism" (from which she finds Ranterism "an aberrational offshoot"). She places Calvinists like Saltmarsh and Dell in the "voluntarist" camp, and [John] Goodwin and Milton in the "humanist," whose thinking "reaches from St. Thomas Aquinas through Richard Hooker into the seventeenth century where . . . the traditional beliefs were radicalized" (*Reviving Liberty: Radical Christian Humanism in Milton's Great Poems,* 98–99). Yet this *philosophical* distinction should not suggest impairment of the *spiritual* and *ecclesial* unity and cohesiveness perceived during the mid-seventeenth century by these and other Radical Protestants.

4. Fish, "Discovery as Form in *Paradise Lost,*" 10, 7.

minacy in Milton's *Areopagitica*," Fish makes a similar point about the inadequacy of the external to contain truth or virtue. Through the "self-cancelling sequence" he finds in this treatise, one is ever driven from the letter—of books, of history, of Scripture, of the treatise itself. This "driving from the letter is a strategy that can have no end," for "whatever place or object or condition holds out the possibility of rest and attainment has at that moment become a letter, the occasion for idolatry."[5] It is this occasion that Milton would have one guard against—whether in reading a poem, pursuing truth, practicing virtue, or, as I have been arguing here, worshiping with externals.

While I certainly agree with Fish's "self-consuming" base, his critical treatment—a sort of *via negativa* stating what truth and worship are not—focuses on the process for prevention of the wrong thing (the letter) rather than on what exactly this beneficial process is preserving and projecting one toward (the spirit)—that is, a celebration of union with God, in the context of a continuous ecclesial bond through worship. With a sharpened focus on truth, rather than on the God of Truth, one runs the risk of idolatrizing the process (of being continuously driven from the letter) itself. Milton's concern for truth notwithstanding, in Fish, at times, the rational overshadows the spiritual, particularly in the area of preventing "the occasion for idolatry" and dealing with "the temptation of idolatry."[6] There is a difference between worshiping *in* truth and worshiping truth—a distinction Milton insists on again and again, notably, in *Paradise Lost* (*PL*, 12.485–533), *Paradise Regained* (*PR*, 4.309–64), *The Reason of Church Government* (1:827, 841, 847), *Areopagitica* (2:555–56), *Christian Doctrine* (6:599–600, 666–78), and the *Commonplace Book* (1:423 n.1). In all of these Milton emphatically privileges the indwelling spirit over all else—even truth and virtue, that can at best signal and foster the spirit, but never replace it.

In sum, Milton argues for worship that is as natural and spotless as was Adam's and Eve's in prelapsarian Eden. In the *Christian Doctrine* the visible church consists in believers bonding with one another and to God. What signifies this group who worship "openly . . . in Christ either individually or in conjunction with others" is

---

5. Fish, "Driving from the Letter: Truth and Indeterminacy in Milton's *Areopagitica*," 244.
6. Ibid., 244, 247.

that they worship, not how they worship. The freedom, fluidity, and adaptability, marked at every turn in the excerpted passages above, do not provide merely catechetical information but catechetical exercise. This is revolutionary liturgical preparation. The reading individual or assembly undergoes an internship in worship, ready to do the real thing because of the spiritual conditioning that has occurred through the process of reading.

The whole purpose of this discussion of worship, both internal and external, is to serve an understanding of Milton's ecclesiology. Worship is not the property of the visible and imperfect church as it is typically conceived to be. Instead, it is the property of the invisible church. And as we have seen from the self-consuming exercise of the different external forms that Milton calls up before the visible church, even external worship is ultimately to serve the mystical and spiritual worshiping congregation. This is the primary church and the basis of Milton's ecclesiology. Only within this spiritual body does any other church (small congregation, family, or individual) have meaning, purpose, and identity.

In Milton's ecclesiology, it follows that if church includes everyone "called from any part of the whole world" to "openly worship God the Father in Christ either individually or in conjunction with others," then that visible church may logically and actually be as particular as a single individual. The Reformation, as expressed in Milton's treatise and in numerous other places cited in this study, promised energy, freedom, assurance, and authority. Historians and critics have observed individualism as the natural outgrowth of what the Reformation proclaimed again and again was available to everyone. In spite of the desire to subordinate the individual to the group for cohesion as the Puritan movement stabilized, A. S. P. Woodhouse notes that "the inherent individualism, with its disruptive force, remains and is written in the history of the sects." Perry Miller concurs that the sects "were in large measure a product of the preaching of individualism." About the logical conclusion to this individualistic spirit unleashed at the outset of the Reformation, that came to characterize especially the sects, and that gained massive strength during the mid-seventeenth century, Boyd Berry remarks that "the individualistic pressure broke down churches into sects, sects into churches of one." Milton himself, Parker points out, would eventually embrace "pure individualism in religious belief." Summarizing the development of Milton's extreme individualism,

Douglas Bush delineates Milton's development: "The violent con-
flicts of Milton's age, the Puritan ideal of the holy community, and
the impetus of Puritan individualism led him—he being what he
was—from Anglicanism to Presbyterianism, from Presbyterianism
to Independency, and from Independency to independence. It has
been said that Milton himself " 'was a sect.' " David Quint likewise
arrives at the conclusion of Milton's individualism and inwardness,
but from a political vantage point, thereby reinforcing my claims
from the ecclesio-liturgical one: "If Milton could foresee little political role for the individual against the authoritarian state and urged a
withdrawal to inward piety, this recourse may not have been a wholly
negative gesture. It maintained an area of personal autonomy from
a state that seemed increasingly to intrude upon local and private
reserves." And Arthur Barker analyzes the dilemma of one like Milton
whose conscience becomes the occasion for opposing internal, individual spiritual authority to external, communal political authority:

> The Presbyterians appealed to the Assembly (in which they com-
> manded a majority) set up by the Parliament to interpret God's
> will. But for those who differed from the opinion of the Assembly,
> the ultimate appeal could only be beyond this human authority to
> the individual consciences of those who possessed Christian lib-
> erty. A logical conclusion of this appeal is the belief, at which
> Milton eventually arrived, that *a true church may consist of one
> Christian.*[7]

For Milton, the internal, invisible church is preeminent over the
visible: "We beleeve the scripture not for the churches saying, but
for its own as the word of God, then ought we to believe what in our
conscience we apprehend the scripture to say, though the visible
church [here, intending the outward structures of government]
with all her doctors gainsay" (7:251).

Milton cites Ephesians 2:19, which metamorphoses *"fellow citizens
of the saints"* and Jesus Christ into a *"whole building . . . a holy temple
to the Lord"* (6:500). But, to arrive at the extreme cellular position, as
observed by these recent literary, historical, and theological scholars, Milton would need further doctrine, additional scriptural au-

7. A. S. P. Woodhouse, *Puritanism and Liberty,* 70; Miller, *New England Mind,* 179;
Berry, *Process of Speech,* 207; William Riley Parker, *Milton: A Biography,* 216; Douglas
Bush, *English Literature in the Earlier Seventeenth Century 1600–1660,* 270; David Quint,
"David's Census: Milton's Politics and *Paradise Regained,"* 143; Barker, *Puritan Di-
lemma,* 38; emphasis added.

thority, and an adaptation of the original "building" image, all of which could be suited to the truth of the moment without denying eternal truth. So, Milton makes a spiritual house once again for the spirit of God by edifying humanity, but this time not corporately and publicly, rather, individually and interiorly: "It is certain, too, that it is not the visible church but the hearts of believers which, since Christ's ascension, have continually constituted the *pillar* and *ground of truth*. They are the real *house and church of the living God*, 1 Tim. iii. 15" (6:589). Poetic figure once again becomes literal spiritual truth, but the emphasis is atomistic rather than cosmic and inclusive. The heart as building supersedes the visible church as building, yet without sullying the doctrine of communion, for it is "the *hearts* of believers" (emphasis added) that "are the real *house and church of the living God.*" It appears not accidental that Milton chooses the plural form to express the ideas, when "the *heart* of each believer" would have worked quite naturally if he were aiming not to emphasize believers' spiritual communion with one another.

What we have seen in Milton is that for all the uniqueness that the Spirit and Scripture authorize, they also seal and authorize a particular union among Christ's elect, those en route from the kingdom of grace to the kingdom of glory. As their head, Christ incorporates all his followers into his Body and, by that, no part of his spiritual visible church is ever divided—even the individual. While membership in the visible congregation does not mean membership in the mystic body, a mystical relationship with Christ is certainly not exclusive of visibly belonging to a church. The two (mystical and visible) are not opposites, but merely, as Ames instructed about the invisible and visible church, different "conditions or modes." Belief in the ongoing spiritual inseparability (and the assurance that belief afforded) is one of the chief characteristics among Nonconformists.

In addition to acknowledging Reformation-spawned and Reformation-fostered individuality—taken in our contemporary sense to mean singular, distinct, or unique—we should also understand what the Renaissance understood, which will further authorize the heavy spiritual, mystical, interior emphasis that Milton's concepts of church and worship require. The *Yale Milton* explains, " 'Individual' means 'indivisible' or 'undivided' " (2:609); and Hughes notes, "*Individual* has its Latin meaning of 'inseparable' or 'undividable'."[8] The para-

8. *CPMP,* 289 n. 486.

doxical experience one has in juxtaposing these two meanings provides not only the truest picture of Milton as one who participated
in several movements of Reform while standing aside, but also it
gives what I believe is a Miltonic sense of being mystically, spiritually congregated because incorporated, while worshiping—perhaps alone, though not necessarily. Milton's doctrine on the church
and worship would certainly allow for visibly gathering, though not
requiring it, just as it would for certain externals, though not oblig-
ing them either.

Milton's directory of worship is therefore to serve the larger formal assembly, the small gathering, the domestic church, or the individual—all charged to worship. Being spatially gathered or not, worshiping alone or not, would have no effect on their identity as visible church in which God dwells. In other words, while "the called"
might pray singly for any number of reasons (convenience, conscience, persecution), they never really pray separately, for they are,
in one sense, always gathered. They are literally "individual."
Zwingli calls this body "the communion of saints," a term that he
rightly claims people misunderstand "as the blessedness of those
who out of this time have come to God," but in this perpetual gathered posture, which Milton also presumes and promotes, are "all
godly Christians who will essentially be gathered by God only after
this age; but as long as it is here on earth, it lives in hope alone and
does not ever come together visibly; however in the light of the
divine spirit and faith it is always together, even here; only, not
visibly" (ZW, 45).

What was important to Milton was that their worship was authorized by God's Word, that it was not limited to set place, times,
forms, etc., and that they were not necessarily visibly united with
the rest of the "spotless" church, but were, in truth, united spiritually.

What of particular, visible gathered assemblies that find it necessary to become no longer visible? Perry Miller explains, "When a
Church is dissolved and scattered through persecution, the members
are automatically absolved from the duties of confederacy."[9] Indeed.
But *never* absolved of the status of church—of remembering, celebrating, and deriving strength from continuous intimate, spiritual union
with God, for, as Zwingli stated, "In the light of the divine Spirit and
faith it is always together, even here; only, not visibly."

9. Miller, *New England Mind*, 446.

In the 1520s, the German angel prophesied "a truly evangelical order," which would "not be held in a public place for all sorts of people," and agreed to direct public services "for the time being" (respecting the diversity of local congregations) "until Christians who earnestly love the Word find each other and join together." By the 1650s, the English angel revealed that these Christians had in fact found each other and were indeed ready for this "truly evangelical order." In apocalyptic response, he divined those "rites and methods which [God] himself has prescribed"—the only solution for True Reform—and recorded this revelation in chapters 3 and 4 of the second book of his *Christian Doctrine*. But despite the many externals discussed therein, Milton directed worshipers with a single underlying method: Scripture-authorized transitionality, adaptability, openness, diversity, and recognition of the freedom and autonomy of every local church, however small, especially domestic gatherings and even individual worshipers. Milton gave these Christians exercise in worship that at once purged it of prescriptive, superstitious ritualizing while promoting the free, evangelical order of worship preferred by God—one which Luther surely dreamed of but which only Milton delivered. Milton professed and attempted to promulgate a style of worship that would agree with a multifaceted concept of church which was normative in England during the Revolutionary period.

For Milton and many saintly others, the tenuous, free, flexible, and spiritual came to mean mainly invisible, "individual" (in both senses), and internal. What God had begun in Luther, Calvin, and Zwingli (or Wyclif, as Milton preferred to see things), continued through Perkins and Ames, and inflamed through Dell, Saltmarsh, Everard, Walwyn, Winstanley, and Milton, had been brought to curious completion. Observing how, through the eyes of Milton's writing, is the purpose of succeeding chapters.

II

The Invisible Church

"That Mystic Body"

PREFACE TO PART II

eparating and congregating are twin halves of the ecclesial
condition; therefore, this and the next chapter deal respectively with "being called out of or called away from" and
"being called to." We might refer to these respectively as
the "separatist spirit" and the "the ecclesial spirit"—essential companion aspects of the ongoing reforming ecclesial process.

The separating nature of election is the scripturally founded call
to come away from whatever or whoever endangers believers' predestined sacred spiritual union with God. This antiseptic separatist
spirit is emphasized to preserve the cleanliness and health of the
spiritual life of the church—whether that church be a congregation,
a few believers, a family, or even an individual. The language of the
period attributed this insidious, deadly infecting to Antichrist, the
one whom Milton names as "the great enemy of the church," but
who ironically and paradoxically is "to arise from the church itself"
(6:604).

Christopher Hill traces the development of the people's belief about
the Antichrist during the progression of the seventeenth century
and explains this Adversary's identity variously as Pope, state, bishops, King, and eventually even whatever oppressive or self-serving
pernicious tendencies within their own hearts threatened their spiritual purity and union with God.

By 1640 we have moved from the Pope as Antichrist—a view held
by most Elizabethan and Jacobean *bishops*—to the bishops themselves as Antichrist; for sectaries the whole hierarchy of the Church
of England down to parish ministers was antichristian. [And] by
1640 Charles I had destroyed men's confidence in the godly prince
as effectively as Laud had destroyed their confidence in bishops.
Many conforming Puritans were driven to accept what had hith-
erto been the separatist position, that bishops were incurably anti-

christian. The alliance would not last; but it was powerful in the
crucial years between 1640 and 1643.[1]

The point of this extended discussion on separation from the Antichrist for Milton is to demonstrate that septic conditions in the mid-
seventeenth century were rife in a new way: universal external enemy, perceived variously in the Roman church, the English church
hierarchy, and the King, had become universal internal enemy. This
sort of religious thinking contributed to the accent Milton's doctrine
places on the mystical relationship between Christ and the various
levels of church (world, assembly, household, individual) and paved
the way for the identity of the primary and preeminent concept of
church to be individual, invisible, and interior before it could hope
to break forth and be anything visible and overtly communal. The
next chapter, therefore, focuses on the saints' necessary separation
as the prelude to the desired spiritual union and ecclesial fellowship
to be taken up in the remaining chapters of Part II.

1. Hill, *Antichrist*, 77.

5

To "Stand Separated"

A Rite of Communion for the "Unanimous Multitude of Good Protestants"

ilton holds a concept of church that requires the church to be ever in reform—a scripturally mandated concept that Reformers in the sixteenth and seventeenth centuries reawaken but that, according to Milton, reaches back to an earlier period in England. In *Of Reformation* Milton criticizes England's delinquency in the business of Reform. When her contribution is compared to that of the currently presumed "original" Reforming nations, Milton ponders

> how it should come to passe that England (having had this *grace* and *honor* from God to bee the first that should set up a Standard for the recovery of *lost Truth*, and blow the first *Evangelick Trumpet* . . .) should now be last . . . in the enjoyment of that *Peace*, whereof she taught the way to others; although indeed our *Wicklefs* preaching, at which all the succeeding *Reformers* more effectually lighted their *Tapers*, was to his Countrey men but a short blaze soone dampt and stifl'd by the *Pope*, and *Prelates* for sixe or seven Kings Reignes. (1:525–26)[1]

Christopher Hill remarks that Wyclif "anticipated Luther and Calvin," for "in Milton's perspective the Reformation was only an inci-

---

1. From Edward S. LeComte, *A Milton Dictionary,* on John Wyclif: "That Englishman honored of God to be the first preacher of a general reformation to all Europe, T 222. . . . 'The succeeding reformers more effectually lighted their tapers,' R 5; 'opening our drowsy eyelids leisurely by that glimmering light' An 14 (353)."

dent, part of a rising curve which extended from Wyclif to the English Revolution."[2] Understandably, Milton is able to view England's part in the entire process of ongoing reform only with chagrin: "Me thinkes the *Precedencie* which God gave this *Island*, to be the first *Restorer* of *buried Truth*, should have been followed with more happy successe; and sooner attained Perfection; in which as yet we are amongst the last" (1:526).

While Milton focuses on England, however, his implicit scope involves an international fusion with Reforming predecessors and contemporaries made possible and sustained only by dint of a spiritual communion, standing outside of which should give England pause. Embarrassed by the absence of unity and communion with others, he concludes: "Certainly it would be worth the while therefore and the paines, to enquire more particularly, what, and how many the cheife causes have been that have still hindred our *Uniforme Consent* to the rest of the *Churches* abroad, (at this time especially) when the *Kingdome* is in a good propensity thereto; and all Men in Prayers, in Hopes, or in Disputes, either for or against it" (1:527).

It is important, then, to see Milton's idea on the relationship of the church to the individual believer as occurring within a single relay race toward the goal of true religion. That same team of Protestant Reformers—consisting of Luther, Calvin, and Zwingli in the earlier part of the sixteenth century, then Perkins and Ames at the turn of the century—began sprinting in the mid-seventeenth century with those English Radicals like William Dell, Stephen Marshall, John Saltmarsh, John Reeve, Lodowick Muggleton, Gerrard Winstanley, and John Milton, all carrying the torch to victory. These last were prophet-preachers addressing their world through actual parliamentary sermon, spiritual autobiography, enthusiast movement, religio-political movement, or religio-political tract.

Geoffrey Nuttall raises questions that the saints must have considered in the mid-seventeenth century:

---

2. Hill, *English Revolution*, 85–86. Hill explains: "For [Milton] the true reformers were the Waldenses and in England Wyclif and his Lollard successors, the humble Marian martyrs and the persecuted sectaries" (85). Small wonder, Milton's sympathy with "our first reformers," the Waldenses, whose massacre at Piedmont he commemorated in Sonnet 18, calling them "saints" (1) "who kept thy truth so pure of old" (3). In reading my manuscript, John King pointed out that this view of Wyclif is that of John Bale, Robert Crowley, and John Foxe in the sixteenth century. See also, *CPW* 1:379 n.9.

Had the Reformation been carried far enough? or had it (for whatever reasons) been sinfully halted halfway? . . . At least when the minister was unsympathetic to reformation, not to say "scandalous" in life (as many were), might it be better to stay away from church sometimes, or even altogether, and to worship instead with others eager to share in fruitful times of prayer and bible study? When, furthermore, the majority in the parish, by their spiritual unconcernedness . . . were content with things as they were and supported the minister in his activity, was not some sort of separation the only way open, if holy desires and aspirations were not to be quenched and the Spirit of God within grieved?[3]

Clearly, as Milton asserted in his first treatise, *Of Reformation*, "Exact *Reformation* is not perfited at the first push" (1:536). It is something that must continue to its completion.

Kurt Aland's discussion of the Baptist and Spiritualist element in Germany and Switzerland during the sixteenth century provides insight into the timeless Radical sensibility as well as into the contemporary seventeenth-century dilemma. As if answering Nuttall's panoply of questions in order to agree with Milton's version of Reform methodology, Aland writes:

The movement's roots extend back beyond the Reformation into the Late Middle Ages with its atmosphere of spiritualism, apocalypticism, and social revolution. Common to all of its branches was its radical commitment to its convictions, and its opinion that *the Reformation had stalled halfway to its goal;* it had grown tired too soon and had become a bourgeosie movement. Thus *the "left wing" became the conscience of the Reformation.* This movement which intended to gather the "communion of saints" must always be seen as a check, even though others will never be able to follow fully the demands it makes and the solutions it proposes.[4]

The real question, of course, was how much reform was enough? For the Reformist of mid-seventeenth-century England, the issue was whether or not reforming would suffice or whether there needed to be an overhauling of the elements of church and worship. George H. Williams's useful distinction between *reformatio* and *restitutio*, to distinguish between what all Reformers agreed on and what Radical Reformers (for example, Anabaptists, Spiritualists, and Rationalists) worked for, can serve our greater appreciation of the inten-

---

3. Nuttall, *Visible Saints*, 44–45.
4. Aland, *Four Reformers*, 129–30; emphasis added.

sity shared among Milton and many fellow Reformers.[5] In tracing Milton's increasing emphasis on the reliance upon the interaction of Scripture, Spirit, and inner light of the individual conscience as the ultimate and absolute authority, we find his break with mere reform and adoption of something entirely new for England. Yet, what looked like monumental change to the moderate, relatively satisfied Reformist was, to the gospel purist, nothing more than a return to forms desired and required by God as recorded in Scripture.

John T. Shawcross finds this Radical kind of reform in Milton's politics as Milton addresses his backsliding audience in *The Tenure of Kings and Magistrates*:

> Wherever we look in man's multitude of struggles . . . there are those speakers for the "cause" who harm the cause by drawing back to compromise, who by taking the best from the possible courses only propound a chaotic mess through fear of the new and change. . . . The answer for Milton is to break with the past, cut the roots, and begin anew with the wisdom that the past has afforded. Radical? Yes.

Arthur Barker likewise notes this correspondingly Radical rupture with the past in Milton's religious outlook in *Areopagitica*, wherein Milton's defense of the sects "marks his break with the orthodox puritanism represented by the Assembly." But Barker qualifies this assertion, claiming that although Milton's "sympathy with the left wing of Puritanism was real," much "as his support of the Smectymnuans resulted from common opposition to episcopacy, so his defense of the sects arose from common opposition to Presbyterianism, not from an identity of fundamental principles. . . . In the end the *Areopagitica* is less a defense of the sects than of learning and learned men."[6] This statement seems too strong. Milton was committed to the ideals of tolerance and freedom *for all* but Papists increasingly throughout his prose, long after the Presbyterians were out of the stronghold. Also, already in 1641, in *The Reason of Church Government* (1:841–45), Milton had proclaimed as essential a universal reverence for the dignity and sanctity of *all* believers—the foundation from which he developed in the *Christian Doctrine* (and justi-

5. Williams, *The Radical Reformation*, xxvi. Additionally, see chap. 32, "Law and Gospel: Sectarian Ecumenicity"; and chap. 33, "The Radical Reformation: A New Perspective."

6. Shawcross, "Higher Wisdom," in Lieb and Shawcross, eds., *Achievements of the Left Hand*, 147; Barker, *Puritan Dilemma*, 80.

fied in *The Likeliest Means*) the corollary teaching of the right for anyone endowed by God and taught with Scripture to preach, prophesy, and minister.

Had Barker the historical advantage of Hill's, Lamont's, Reay's, McGregor's, and Morton's scholarship of recent years, he may have dispensed with the qualifier, realizing a greater intimacy between Milton and the sects beyond the exigent "common opposition."[7] Without question there was spiritual communion among them all, and it was Milton's trust in this ultimate truth that formed the basis for his sympathy and support. Refusing to admit a division between sectarians and nonsectarians, corresponding to a division between the learned and the unlearned, Mary Ann Radzinowicz hypothesizes their collaboration:

> Sectarian conflict, Milton wrote, may well have arisen from learned, worthy, zealous and religious men, as appears by their lines written and their many enemies and learned followers. . . . Where men use diligence and sincerity of heart, by reading, by learning, by study, by prayer for illumination by the Holy Spirit, they've done what any man can do: God will assuredly pardon them.[8]

Contrary to Barker's thinking, I would maintain that it was indeed "from an identity of fundamental principles" that Milton (and others like him) defended the sects. University training did have an important function within the church. Its value and purpose were, for the Radical Christian intellectual, to serve God in accord with Scripture, frequently by fighting for one's ecclesiastically equal neighbors.

There are—and must be, of course, for Milton—scriptural Radical models for such a socio-politically and ecclesiastically disengaging position. As Joseph Wittreich points out, Christ and St. Paul provide Milton with precedent for the revolutionary, separated posture adopted in the tracts: "They rebuked custom, flew in the face of tradition, associating both with error and thereby took their place at the head of the tradition of dissent, religious and political, which Milton embraces most directly in *The Judgement of Martin Bucer*."[9]

7. See the historians and literary scholars on Milton's relation to the Radical Puritan tradition, discussed in the introduction to this volume.

8. Radzinowicz, *Toward* Samson Agonistes, 164. Hill, in Hill, Reay, and Lamont, eds., *World of the Muggletonians*, agrees: "Many aspects of this traditional popular theology were accepted by John Milton and other radical intellectuals" (20). See chap. 9, " 'Regenerated by God,' " in this volume.

9. Wittreich, " 'The Crown of Eloquence': The *Figure* of the Orator in Milton's

If, according to Aland, "the 'left wing' became the conscience of the Reformation," then one might say that what unites all Nonconformists is a dissatisfied conscience that the church is not existing as it could and should be according to the roots of the gospel. The fitting response to such twinges is ongoing reform. Luther and Zwingli after a time had finished with dissatisfaction, while in Germany, Karlstadt (for liturgical reasons) and the Peasants led by Thomas Müntzer (for socio-political reasons) and in Switzerland the Anabaptists (for solely religious reasons) clearly had not. So, both Luther and Zwingli, "so divergent in other aspects of their thought, shared a common hostility to the radical movement" (ironically the fruit of their initial labors) even to the point of persecution.[10]

One of the beliefs shared by Radicals was the possibility of the infection of the church through its involvement with secular power. According to true gospel purifying, there had to be separation of the church from the state, of spiritual power from secular. When there was not, particularly amidst the millennial flurry during both the sixteenth and seventeenth centuries, there was communion through obsessive conscience-pricking. Williams writes of this bonding in the context of the imminent coming of Christ: "Almost all the radicals insisted on the utter separation of the church from the state and found in the willingness of the Magisterial Reformers to use the coercive power of princes, kings, and town councilors an aberration from apostolic Christianity no less grievous than papal pretensions." The likelihood of this invasion of one's inner spiritual body by worldly power is the cause of the gradually developed position of separation at work in Milton.[11]

One example of the need for continued reform is the area of church government at the time Milton is writing *The Reason of Church Government* (1641). There needs to be separation of secular governance from spiritual governance both since "the Church coveting to ride upon the Lionly form of jurisdiction makes a transformation of her

Prose Works," in C. A. Patrides and Raymond B. Waddington, eds., *Age of Milton: Backgrounds to Seventeenth-Century Literature*, 10.

10. Richard Bainton, ed. and trans., *Luther's Meditations on the Gospels*, points out that Luther disagrees with Karlstadt whom he labels a "Spiritualist" because Karlstadt "regarded the physical and sensory as inappropriate for the communication of the divine which comes only through the Spirit" and, therefore, "rejected images and church music and denied any physical presence in the Lord's Supper" (14). Edward Peters, *Selected Works*, by Ulrich Zwingli, xxv.

11. Williams, *Radical Reformation*, 860.

self into an Asse, and becomes despicable, that is to those whom God hath enlightened with true knowledge," and also since people then show "the extremity of their bondage and blindnes" "in the reliques of superstition" doing "obeissance to the Lordly visage of a Lion," which is really "an asse" (1:834). The bathos is only heightened in one's realizing the implicit transformation into God's restored image predestined for shepherds and sheep, but forsaken by both for other, more attractive and more tangible metamorphoses: asses for the one and idolatrizers for the other. Along with his diagnosis Milton imperatively prescribes remedy and warning against a setback: "Let England here well rub her eyes, lest by leaving jurisdiction and Church censure to the same persons, now that God hath bin so long medcining her eyesight, she does not with her overpolitick fetches marre all, and bring her self back again to worship this Asse bestriding a Lion" (1:834).[12]

While Milton surely does not excuse the masses, his description of their impaired vision by way of the disease, ill health, blindness figure seems to adjust, if not alleviate in some measure, their culpability for idolatry which does not result from immediate and deliberate preference, but from spiritual blindness prompted by disedifying misgovernance on the part of self-serving church leaders. Furthermore, there is no guarantee against a relapse, however clear-sighted England should become, for her thorough and ultimate health must involve both remedial as well as preventive measures concurrently till the Last Day. Still, even though complete permanent health (that is, Reformation and purity of worship) may not be immediate, because of the "Divine Physician" there is assurance about the outcome, as Jeremiah Burroughs acclaims in *Sions Joy:* "God hath begun a work that he will never leave 'til he hath brought it to perfection. Antichrist shall never prevail again as he hath done." While the Coming that Milton awaited may have been described without the usual immediacy and petulance of the stricter millenarians, nonetheless, as John F. Huntley maintains, "to sympathize with Milton's fervency one must grant his interpretation of reformed reformation and his millenarian faith that his day would behold the 'materialization of the Kingdom of Glory.'" But the issue was how. "Milton is clear about his general priorities for securing the imminent end: a

12. "Milton believes that the cure is still far from being completed" (*CPW* 1:834 n.28).

change of essence precedes a significant change in outward acci-
dents." The Reformation itself with its outside-to-inside approach
needed reforming, for as it stood it would be unable to shape church
and worship to the gospel ideal. "Reformed reformation" required
a shift in emphasis to the inside, an area of focus evident in most
extreme Nonconformists.[13]

In discussing *The Tenure of Kings and Magistrates* (1649–1650), Shawcross argues that because "the interwoven strands of religion and
politics made at least a kind of theocracy viable," Milton "fell into
the trap he himself had already pointed out: conclusion based on
custom and the existing order of things. We do not find a bold pro-
posal that totally separated church and state. Only later did he urge
the kind of separation that many today . . . seem to take for granted
as being necessary." Austin Woolrych likewise observes Milton's
progressive separationism five years hence, when Milton is providing advice along with acclaim for Cromwell in his *Second Defense*
(1654). Milton celebrates the arrival of the Protectorate and Cromwell
who, since he is the most fit, has a right to rule. It was the execution
of that right, however, which prompted Milton's advice, for "Milton
believed as Cromwell did not, that the State should renounce all
authority over matters of religion and should cease to maintain an
established clergy by tithes or any other form of compulsory contri-
bution." Noting the refinement of Milton's position, Austin Woolrych explains that as Milton "focused his mind more and more on
formulating beliefs in *De Doctrina Christiana*, the aim to remove religion entirely from civil power preoccupied him more and more."[14]

Arthur Barker probes whether or not Milton ever accomplished
this separation and maintained it. On the one hand, he argues that
Radicals like Roger Williams are ever out to separate church and
state, religious and civil liberty, the spiritual realm and the secular,
and that Milton is to take his place with those extremists. On the
other hand, even during Milton's silence from 1654 to 1659, at which
time he is closer to Williams than to the nonseparationist Smectymnuans, Barker claims that Milton is ultimately to be distinguished
from Radicals because while Milton approaches that division of realms,

13. Hill, *Antichrist*, 83; Huntley, "Images of Poet & Poetry in Milton's *The Reason of
Church Government*," in Lieb and Shawcross, eds., *Achievements of the Left Hand*, 95.
14. Shawcross, "Higher Wisdom," in Lieb and Shawcross, eds., *Achievements of
the Left Hand*, 152; Woolrych, "Political Theory and Political Practice," in Patrides and
Waddington, eds., *Age of Milton*, 66.

in the end, he is unable to make it. In spite of Barker's tendency to argue in favor of Milton's separationism, unlike Shawcross and Woolrych, Barker argues that this thinking in Milton was only temporary. As Barker sees things, Milton, ultimately impelled to rely on the state, again fuses secular power and interest with spiritual.[15]

In *The Treatise of Civil Power* (1659) Milton does insist that "the settlement of religion belongs only to each particular church by perswasive and spiritual means within it self and that the defence only of the church belongs to the magistrate," but requiring restraint to stave off harm is hardly integration (7:271). In other words, reliance on worldly power to restrict the sprawling effects of the world's perniciousness is certainly not the reconcilement of opposing forces that Barker finds. One need only turn to chapter 32, "Of Church Discipline" in the *Christian Doctrine* for Milton's final word on the subject. In this penultimate chapter to book one, Milton upholds the separation of powers. Asserting and reasserting their different functions, Milton examines the separated spheres wherein each of the two types of power operates:

> The difference between civil and ecclesiastical power is as follows: 1. Every man is subject to the civil authority, that is to say, in civil matters. . . . But only members of the church are subject to ecclesiastical power, and that only in religious matters. Moreover they are liable to ecclesiastical punishment only, that is, punishment within the church. . . . 2. The civil power extends only to the body and the external faculties of man whereas the ecclesiastical power, and it alone, has control over the faculties of the mind. . . . In fact the apostle urges us not to allow men to have any jurisdiction over us in religious matters. . . . Where the civil power is concerned, even those who repent are punished, but the ecclesiastical power grants forgiveness to all who are penitent. . . .
>
> Thus it is a sign of faithlessness, and is also highly derogatory to the power of the church, to imagine that churches need to be ruled by force of arms and by magistrates. (6:613)

Milton's belief that the magistrates' function was mainly one of restraining the reprobates in order to protect the free operation of the saintly community resembles Winstanley's thinking that the government is not intended to get people to behave well, but merely to prevent harm. In 1649 a group of fifty or so, following William Everard and Gerrard Winstanley, assembled on St. George's Hill to

---

15. Barker, *Puritan Dilemma*, 223, 281; see also 89–93, 226.

build their community by first digging the Commons (hence, the name Diggers), having subscribed to the tenet that the earth was a common treasury for all humanity.[16] Because of the collapse of the Digger movement, "largely through the apparatus of the coercive state—troops, lawyers, the rights of private landowners, and the consequent employment of both legal action and physical force," Winstanley became "entirely realistic in seeing that a new kind of government and a radically different system of law were prerequisites for the new society" he desired.[17] But in Winstanley's case, and even more so in Milton's, *using* civil authority is a very different thing from having church authority compromise itself by merging with or serving the state. Assistance from the secular realm is surely not the theocracy that once might have seemed feasible but never came to pass. In such a government the church would have controlled secular power.

While the separation of church and state was a tenet that became clearer to Milton and that demanded more of him, it was a tenet that is evident early on in his political writing. If one allows Milton to speak for himself, one finds this principle very clearly set out already in *The Reason of Church Government* as Milton deals surprisingly not with the macrocosm of the body politic, but with the microcosm of the individual person. While discussing the purpose of "punishment, or censure" as a "saving med'cin as ordain'd of God both for the publick and privat good of man" (1:835), Milton explains the division of the function and focus of "the Church and the Magistrat" in terms of the two kinds of curing necessary for man. Since a person consists "of two parts the inward and the outward. . . . The Magistrat hath only to deale with the outward part, I mean not of the body alone, but of the mind in all her outward acts, which in Scripture is call'd the outward man" (1:835).[18] His mode is restrictive of evil behavior for the protection of the freedom of the virtuous: the "power of the Magistrat which contents it self with the restraint of evil doing in the external man" (1:836). God, on the contrary, is nei-

---

16. Robert W. Kenny, *The Law of Freedom in a Platform or, True Magistracy Restored,* by Gerrard Winstanley, esp. 12–17.

17. G. E. Aylmer, "The Religion of Gerrard Winstanley," in McGregor and Reay, eds., *Radical Religion,* 111.

18. See Luther's "Concerning Christian Liberty," in *Luther's Primary Works,* for the Pauline distinction between the "spiritual, inward, new man" and "the fleshly, outward, old man" based on 2 Cor. 4:16, 256, 259, 272–73. See chap. 9, " 'Regenerated by God,' " in this volume.

ther "judge after the sentence of the Law, nor as it were a school-maister of perishable rites," but

> a most indulgent father governing his church as a family of sons in their discreet age; and therefore in the sweetest and mildest man-ner of paternal discipline he hath committed this other office of preserving in healthful constitution the innerman, which may be termed the spirit of the soul, to his spiritual deputy the minister of each Congregation; who being best acquainted with his own flock, hath best reasons to know all the secretest diseases likely to be there. And look by how much the internal man is more excellent and noble then the external, by so much is his cure more exactly, more throughly, and more particularly to be perform'd. For which cause the holy Ghost by the Apostles joyn'd to the minister, as assistant in this great office sometimes a certain number of grave and faithful brethren, (for neither doth the phisitian doe all in restoring his patient, he prescribes, another prepares the med'cin, some tend, some watch, some visit) much more may a minister partly not see all, partly erre as a man: besides that nothing can be more for the mutuall honour and love of the people to their Pastor, and his to them, then when in select numbers and courses they are seen partaking, and doing reverence to the holy duties of disci-pline by their serviceable, and solemn presence, and receiving honour again from their imployment, not now any more to be separated in the Church by vails and partitions as laicks and un-clean, but admitted to wait upon the tabernacle as the rightfull Clergy of Christ, a chosen generation, a royal Priesthood to offer up spiritual sacrifice in that meet place to which God and the Congregation shall call and assigne them. (1:837–38)

Milton here gives serious attention to the separation of the church from the state based on the two clearly distinguishable dimensions of the microcosm: the internal man and the external man. With the rather extended disease-infirm-physician trope, Milton proclaims the primacy of the "innerman," the spiritual order, and church life. There is such solidarity in the communion of members, as Milton describes their brother- and sister-keeping, that the gathering and barring become almost tangible. Additionally, there is integration here, but the momentum of the passage gathers not to an integra-tion of the spiritual and worldly power in a theocracy, but to an integration between the holy and the people "in a rightfull Clergy of Christ." The secular is thoroughly excluded from the spiritual here as it is in Milton's later prose, though the people are "no more to be separated" from the holy. My purpose here, however, is certainly not to suggest that Milton did not grow in his understanding of the relationship between the spiritual and the secular orders, only to point out that overemphasizing Milton's development can be done at the expense of failing to observe important consistencies in him.

All of this discussion on the separation between the church and the state may seem like much ado about very little and may even seem, particularly as presented so logically and calmly in Milton's *Christian Doctrine,* to be quite Conformist—until one vividly remembers the other side, as conveyed, for example, in Archbishop William Laud's *Constitutions and Canons for the Church of England, 1640:* "The care of God's Church is so committed to kings in the scripture, that they are commended when the Church keeps the right way, and taxed when it runs amiss, and therefore her government belongs in chief unto kings; for otherwise one man would be commended for another's care, and but taxed for another's negligence, which is not God's way."[19] As we have seen above in *The Reason of Church Government,* written within a year or so of Laud's *Constitutions and Canons,* amidst so much else representing the antithetical, Nonconformist or Radical position is the equally shared responsibility among all members of the church both for its government and for its members' correction. Milton claims, in Laudian terms, that to have "one man . . . commended for another's care, and but taxed for another's negligence" is precisely "God's way."

Milton is in perfect keeping with most other Radicals, characterized by George Williams above, who believed that "to use the coercive power of princes, kings, and town councilors" was "an aberration from apostolic Christianity no less grievous than papal pretensions." In his *Treatise of Civil Power,* Milton writes that civil magistrates are worse than Papists in attempting to control spiritual things, for then they make themselves "lord or pope of the church, as far as his civil jurisdiction stretches: and all ministers of God therein, his ministers" (7:253). At least the pope and Papists stay within the realm over which they claim jurisdiction (7:248, 253–56), whereas the magistrate "assumes to rule by civil power things to be rul'd only by spiritual" (7:253).

John Reeve, Levellers like Richard Overton and John Lilburne, and the Digger (or True Leveller) Gerrard Winstanley are English Radicals who, like Milton, maintain this need for separation between

---

19. Laud, *The Works of the Most Reverend Father in God, William Laud, D.D.,* vol. 5, pt. 2, 614.

church and state, matters spiritual and matters secular, for there to be spiritual purity. Reeve, proselytizing and writing in the mid–1650s, represents a lower-class, unliterary, enthusiastic brand of Radicalism. In *A Remonstrance from the Eternal God to the Parliament and Commonwealth of England*, Reeve warns that the duty of magistrates is "to be skilful in the laws of the land" and "to execute justice between man and man." He continues by using personally received injustice from civil authorities to illustrate their inadequacy in dealing with spiritual matters. Having been imprisoned for alleged blasphemy, Reeve, as a martyr, recounts their impropriety amidst his self-exoneration:

> 9. But they have no authority to judge us, that are messengers and prophets sent from God, who are kept by the power of God so innocent from the breach of any civil laws of men. . . .
> 10. Moreover, we declare from the Lord, that no civil magistrate ought to call any man to account for his faith concerning God, or the sacred Scriptures, because there is not a magistrate in the world at this time that doth clearly understand what the true God is, or the truths of holy writ.[20]

Levellers, like Richard Overton, John Lilburne, and William Walwyn, were, according to Brian Manning, "the left wing of the parliamentarian party which won the English civil war." But rather than political, their primary goal was religious, as Manning explains: "Central to the Leveller programme was the demand for religious liberty—for each individual to be free to hold what opinions in religion his reason told him to be true and to worship God in the way his conscience told him to be right, without interference from the state-church. This involved carving out for the individual an area of autonomy beyond the reach of any human power."[21] And so, these three representatives of a rational, religio-political, military approach to the issue carved out such "an area of autonomy." In *The Reason of Church Government* Milton names this space "the innerman" and "the internal man" (1:837), and in *Of Civil Power* he uses "the inward man" (7:257). Overton uses the terms *outward man*, which civil rulers were delegated by God to govern, and *inward man*, whose governance God reserved to himself. Having carved out his impenetrable

20. Reeve, *A Remonstrance from the Eternal God*, 14.
21. Manning, "The Levellers and Religion," in McGregor and Reay, eds., *Radical Religion*, 65, 78.

holy of holies, Overton consequently argues: "Matters of conscience or opinion about Religion or Worship doth not fall under the power of the Magisteriall sword." Lilburne makes the same distinction but dresses the idea in the language of kingdoms. He said that Christ had a kingdom in this world that consisted of believers who obeyed only his laws on issues relating to his kingdom. Walwyn echoed the distinction of realms, but simply translated them into different terms: there were "things naturall" and "things supernaturall," the former under the jurisdiction of the civil government and the latter under the jurisdiction of God only.[22] In the supernatural sphere, because the individual received truth about things of this realm directly from God, he needed obey no one else. Rallying much support from the commoners under the political banner of equality for all and power with all, these and other Levellers put religion to serious military and political business.

Gerrard Winstanley exemplifies yet another type of Radical: a self-educated, but unsophisticated, spiritual leader and community organizer whose writings reveal a man who is as mystical as he is down-to-earth. He, too, focuses on the distinction between the outer world and the inner world, but with a curious twist. Looking a step further behind the problem of tyranny and oppression caused by the intrusion of the civil government into the spiritual, Winstanley considers the externalizing done within the sphere of religion itself. By externalizing God and Heaven, for example, religion—the presumed inner, spiritual order—abets the oppressive political, outer world that is always inimical to things of the spirit. Winstanley sounds almost bizarre in associating an external Christ and the language of heaven after this life has ended with outward political power that represses and enslaves. Wondering "why may not we have our heaven here (that is, a comfortable livelihood in the earth) and heaven hereafter too," and denouncing "God . . . in heavens above the skies" as imaginary, Winstanley proclaims the unequivocal falsity of outwardness and truth of inwardness: "Your Saviour must be a power within you, to deliver you from that bondage within; the outward Christ or the outward God are but men Saviours."[23]

There certainly were educational, spiritual, and political differences between Milton and others of his company. Milton, with his

22. Ibid., 78.
23. See Hill, *World Turned Upside Down*, 139–50, 141.

classical, humanist education, his reverence for reason, and his employment by the Puritan establishment as Secretary of Foreign Tongues, stands out almost in defiance of the branding of "extremist" or "Radical." And yet, what those others share with each other, Milton shares with them: an impassioned commitment to safeguard (call it what one will, "inward man," supernatural sphere, Christ within, or Heaven here) that most sacred space carved out for interaction between God and the individual. This holy ground, they agreed, could only be reverenced and protected from the enemy's invasion through the separation of the church from the state. This holy ground, as their primary and most radical (that is, basic) church, became the spiritual reality that intimately bound all Nonconformists whose corporate conscience, in addition to their individual consciences, was greatly dissatisfied with a truncated Reformation.

Keeping church and state (each good when unengaged) separate was only one dimension of reforming the church, the more obvious one, perhaps, but the less important of the two. Besides this external, organizational overtone, the term *separation* includes the internal, spiritual, intra-ecclesial overtone (as, for example, referring to that apartness or distance that must always characterize the relational location of godly from ungodly). The more subtle aspect, then, of keeping what belonged to Caesar with Caesar and what belonged to God with God occurred *within* the supposedly Reformed church itself: guarding against the remaining "purified" leaders' becoming infected with desire for the things and ways of Caesar and making the visible church once again a conduit for the infiltration of them. Separation, in other words, meant more than keeping church and state disentangled, as well as pure ecclesiastical institution from impure. In the event that the unholy (in persons and practices) could not successfully be routed, the church—that is, the *ecclesial*—in its multiple meanings, would have to remove itself from that continuous occasion of sin. Church members, to protect their church space (that inner place of individual *and* universal contact with the divine) and to protect their right to form a church gathering, would need to separate themselves from the source of uncleanness, as commanded by God, in order to preserve their holy communion with each other and predestinate oneness with him. Separation is, therefore, a condition even to be prayed for, according to the Prayer after the Sermon, from the Middleburg Liturgy of the English Puritans (1586): "It hath pleased thee to call vs to the knowledge of thy holy Gospel, drawing vs out of the miserable bondage of the devil, whose slaves we were, and delivering vs from most cursed idolatrie and wicked superstition, wherin we were plunged, to bring vs into the mer- uailous light of thy truth." Union with others and with God was the goal no one could dispute. How this condition was to be fostered and achieved, however, was very arguable, especially during the Revolutionary period.[24]

A word on the understanding of separationism used in this sec- tion is in order. Horton Davies takes the term *separation* to refer to particular Separatist denominations, such as the Barrowists, Brown- ists, Anabaptists, and the Family of Love, in general to distinguish these groups from the Independents. With Scripture as a base, the term in England as well as on the Continent has even been used to refer to the call for the national church to separate itself from the rest of the nations.[25] I am using the term *to separate,* or *separation,* in a broad sense to describe that scriptural spirit which early Reformers draw upon, but hardly exhaust, and am limiting its use neither to particular sect nor to national communion, though both of these share in the "separatist spirit." Milton himself allows for this broader notion as can be seen in his understanding of sanctification: "The term sanctification is sometimes used in a wider sense to cover any election or separation, either of a whole nation or some particular form of worship or of an individual to some particular office" (6:464). Thus, on the bases of Scripture, the seventeenth-century under- standing of God's calling out from the nations, and Milton's own sense of the term *separateness* in this study should not be taken to refer to particular sects distinguishable because of the hindsight of history more than because of anything else. The concept in Milton's age was less specialized—not denominational but, rather, generally denotative and biblically descriptive—referring simply to keeping isolated from what was unscriptural, untrue, and, consequently, unclean.

In chapter 5 of *The Reason of Church Government,* Milton reminds his readers that the reason for having episcopacy was to quell divi-

---

24. Bard Thompson, ed., *Liturgies of the Western Church,* 330.

25. Davies, *Worship of English Puritans,* 78–82. For England's view of herself as God's Chosen, replicating the type Israel, see Marvin Arthur Breslow, *A Mirror of England,* 140–42, 156; Hill, "The Protestant Nation," in *The Collected Essays of Chris- topher Hill,* 29–30; Barbara Lewalski, *Protestant Poetics and the Seventeenth-Century Religious Lyric,* 129; and Arthur Sewell, *A Study in Milton's Christian Doctrine,* 77.

sion and bring peace—very opposite results of the Prelates' current objectives. If the Prelates are really interested in preserving the garment unrent, as they claim, they should lay down now the office they took up for another age. As is, the Prelacy of the English church, instead of protecting against schism, is, in truth, causing division that results from their "stubbornness and greed" (1:787–88). Protestants, apart from them, in having called a synod evince the true protestant unity: "Noise it till ye be hoarse; that, a rabble of Sects will come in; it will be answer'd ye, no rabble sir Priest, but a unanimous multitude of good protestants will then joyn to the Church, which now because of you stand separated" (1:787–88). In response to the Prelates' presumption of church members' sinful separation, Milton acknowledges this separation as the pivotal point on which he cleverly turns the blame for such condition on the Prelates themselves, at once pointing up the union among the "good protestants" and convicting the bishops themselves of sinful separation from the true gospel of Christ. Having illuminated the object of saintly faithfulness, Milton logically next defends the saintly separation of that "unanimous multitude"—a separation that has been legitimatized, as it always will be, by God himself: "Come out from among them and be ye separate, saith the Lord, and touch not the unclean *thing*: and I will receive you" (2 Cor. 6:17); Hebrews recounts: "By faith Abraham, when he was called to go out into a place which he should after receive for an inheritance, obeyed; and he went out, not knowing whither he went" (11:8); and Revelation, in its caveat against worshiping "the beast," promises that if any "worship the beast and his image, and receive *his* mark," he "shall drink of the wine of the wrath of God" (14:9–11).[26] Since worship, as we have seen in the preceding chapter, is such an integral part of the church, then one must remove oneself from the diseased church whose worship, likewise infected, pays homage to the beast. Separation from wickedness in both church and its worship is, therefore, not sectarianizing but a true rite of communion. This action is mandated by Scripture itself, which contains the principle of separation within its own form of true and recommended worship, in the Psalms: "I have hated the congregation of evil doers: and will not sit with the wicked. Gather not my soul with sinners, nor my life with bloody men. In whose

26. See Nuttall, *Visible Saints*, 47–48 and 52–54 (other pertinent texts include Jer. 15:19, Ezek. 22, Rom. 12, and James 1:27); and see Barker, *Puritan Dilemma*, 38–39.

hand *is* mischief, and their right hand is full of bribes. My foot stand-
eth in an even place: in the congregations will I bless the Lord" (Ps.
26:5–12).

Mid-seventeenth-century England was not the first to know first-
hand that scriptural principle of extricating in order to remain clean.
The priestly establishment, arguing for the sake of church unity,
once criticized Calvin for breaking up the unity. And Calvin, we
should remember, handled his opponents in 1544 at the Imperial
Diet of Spires as Milton does his—with the convention of the initial
innocent blush immediately followed with some very experienced
rhetoric to drive home the quintessence of church doctrine: "The
last and principal charge which they bring against us is, that we
have made a schism in the Church. And here they boldly maintain
against us, that in no case is it lawful to break from the unity of the
Church. Now . . . let them take this brief reply—that we neither
dissent from the Church nor are aliens from her communion" (*NRC*,
211). He appropriately entitles this document *The Necessity of Reforming the Church* since the very substance of *Reform* implies a breaking
away from or out of one form and a bonding to, or a continuation of
bonding to, some other form—in this case, a continuation of bonding to Christ and the True Church.

Calvin cites precedent and authority for his action and motive:
the prophets, with whom Reformers share the same critical, separatist spirit and lineage, since the prophets,

> when they by the command of God, inveighed freely against idol-
> atry, superstition, and the profanation of the temple, and its sa-
> cred rites, against the carelessness and lethargy of priests, and
> against the general avarice, cruelty, and licentiousness, . . . were
> constantly met with the objection which our opponents have ever
> in their mouths—that by dissenting from the common opinion,
> they violated the unity of the Church.

Almost daring his opponents to take on the scriptural giants with
whom Calvin claims that all true Reformers have pitched camp, Calvin concludes with the greatest aplomb: "If the unity of the Church
is violated by him, who instructed solely by Divine truth, opposes
himself to ordinary authority, the prophet must be schismatic; because, not at all deterred by such menaces from warring with the
impiety of priests, he steadily persevered." Calvin, keenly observing his opponents' projection of wrongdoing onto the godly, turns
the tables on them (as Milton does on his), arraigning them for spir-

itual, true separation from that to which they are supposed to be joined: "It is not enough, therefore, simply to throw out the name of Church, but judgment must be used to ascertain which is the true Church, and what is the nature of its unity. And the thing necessary to be attended to, first of all, is, to beware of separating the Church from Christ its Head. When I say Christ, I include the doctrine of his gospel, which he sealed with his blood" (*NRC*, 212–13). Calvin's and Milton's prophetic response is identical: those that *appear* to have removed themselves from Christ's Church have remained, while those who presume to have stood still have drawn far away.

Calvin discusses unity as one of the marks of the Church in the *Institutes*, as noted in my second chapter, but it is in *The Necessity of Reforming the Church* that he elaborates on this most important mark:

> We are as ready to confess as they [the priests and the established church authorities] are that those who abandon the Church, the common mother of the faithful, the "pillar and ground of the truth," revolt from Christ also; but we mean a Church which, from incorruptible seed, begets children for immortality, and, when begotten, nourishes them with spiritual food (that seed and food being the Word of God), and which, by its ministry, preserves the entire truth which God deposited in its bosom. This mark is in no degree doubtful, in no degree fallacious, and it is the mark which God himself impressed upon his Church, that she might be discerned thereby. Do we seem unjust in demanding to see this mark? Wherever it exists not, no face of a church is seen. (*NRC*, 214)

Calvin's question, of course, on the basis of God's Word, disallows a negative answer and discloses the condition of churchlessness when any church is void of that mark "which God himself impressed upon" it. Once the possibility for unchurching is opened, however, at what point must it end? Calvin could hardly have realized that so much churchlessness would have become so visible to the Reformist's prophetic-poetic eye that truth would seem best to be preserved and unity best to be found in mostly secretly or only spiritually related bosoms that seemed so few.

Since unity is that mark which aims to preserve "the entire truth which God deposited" in the Church's bosom, and since it is that mark "which God himself impressed upon his Church," it comes as no surprise that Milton and all Nonconformists always and loudly proclaimed this certain unity.

Calvin has established a tradition, then, which simply refers all allegations of schism to God who prescribes such severance and to the True Church that requires it. To Thomas Edwards's charge that the congregational way of separating from the national church was schism, Katherine Chidley defends that way as the godly way: "God hath commanded all his people to separate themselves from all Idolatry . . . and false worshipping . . . and false worshippers . . . and therefore it is no Schisme (except you will make God the Author of Schisme)." William Chillingworth agrees, but instead of accusing those members who shout "Schism!" of making God responsible for it, he incriminates the decriers' (perceived) church:

> Neither is it always of necessity schismaticall to separate from the externall Communion of a Church. . . . For if this Church supposed to want nothing necessary, require me to profane against conscience, that I believe some error, though never so small and innocent which I do not believe, and will not allow me her communion but upon this condition; In this case the Church for requiring this condition is Schismaticall, and not I for separating from the Church.[27]

And John Owen, one of the foremost Congregational leaders of the seventeenth century, in *Eschol: . . . Or Rules of Direction for the walking of saints in fellowship, according to the order of the Gospel,* names as the fifth of fifteen rules for saints, "Separation and Sequestration from the world and men of the world with all ways of false worship," referring to 2 Cor. 6:14–17 and Rev. 18:4. Like Calvin and Milton, Owen does not take separation lightly, for "causeless separation from established Churches walking according to the order of the Gospel, (though perhaps failing in the practice of some things of small concernment) is no small sin; but separation from sinful practices and disorderly walkings, and false unwarranted ways of worship in any, is to fulfil the precept of not partaking in other men's sins." Owen emphasizes the seriousness of the moral and spiritual imperative: "He that will not separate from the World and false-worship is a separate from Christ."[28] For Owen, Milton, and others seriously committed to the true gospel and to Reform in line with it, the interrelated issues of separation and unity were not mere political, philosophical, or even ecclesiastical theory. The union sought was not with an idea, after all, but with a person, God, through a person, his Son. The spiritual

27. Nuttall, *Visible Saints,* 62.
28. Ibid., 54.

tenor of the age and, certainly, of Milton's theology and ecclesiology is meaningless without this personhood.

If we take Owen's well-reasoned conclusion ("He that will not separate from the World and false-worship is a separate from Christ") as representative of the thinking of the times (and there is every reason to do so), then we might wonder to whom any such person does join himself. Christopher Hill believes: "It is difficult for us to recapture the importance of the Antichrist in the apocalyptic atmosphere of the late forties and early fifties" when Antichrist "seemed intensely real and a very important person." If Christ is the focus from whom the unvirtuous separate themselves and to whom the virtuous join themselves, then Antichrist is the antifocus with whom the wicked affiliate and from whom the just flee. Christ and Antichrist are the cosmic and spiritual antipodes whose realities permeated the everyday world of the seventeenth century. To appreciate the enormity of the spiritual tension which that age believed it experienced from these two Persons, one must consider the influence of the Antichrist experienced in city and country, court and church by the entire range of human society—people including king and subject, bishop and baker, priest and mechanick preacher, philosopher and artisan, parliamentarian and poet. As Hill points out, nation, church, assembly, and individual are not only *permitted* to separate, but even (if they knew their Scripture and their Calvin) have a "religious duty to hate enemies of God or church." That enemy, in a word, is Antichrist, and hatred for him and all his works originates in and is authenticated by God's own command.[29]

Antichrist. What did the term mean? When would he arrive? How should he be pictured to alert people to his danger? What were the signs indicating his arrival? What are his devices? And what did Milton believe about him? These *are* important questions for a study of Milton's idea of church since the overarching business of the entire process of ongoing Reformation was first finding, then separating from, and finally conquering Antichrist. Not to withdraw from institutions and individuals that belong to him was to incorporate into Antichrist.

Calvin and the Genevan translation of the Bible (in its marginal notes for 2 Thess. 2:3–9) identify "the Man of Sin" as Antichrist and further identify this "adversary" as "the mystery of iniquity" with

29. Hill, *Antichrist*, 106, 2; and *English Revolution*, 238.

the Papacy. The term *Antichrist*, or *the Beast*, refers initially, then, to the Pope as a person and to the Papacy as an institution, "subsum[ing] within itself all the evil, coercive, repressive aspects of the secular Empire."[30]

Protestants parceled out Antichrist's parts and properties to various actual men of sin living in their day in order to image these men's sinful incorporation into him. The bishops were often referred to as the limbs of Antichrist; the clergy as his excrement; church courts as his "nerves and joints." The signs of the presence of the Antichrist (as given by Thomas Taylor in the 1620s in *Christ's Victorie over the Dragon*), which were very significant for Milton and all Nonconformists, included excessive emphasis on vestments, persecution of good men condemned for heresy, and the occupation of seats of judicature by ambitious and worldly bishops.[31]

Since the Laudian period is immediately relevant to the church of Milton and his contemporaries, it is worth pausing to determine the state of the disunion within a presumably united Reformed church on the doctrine of the Antichrist. By the time of Laud's ascendancy there were four attitudes, according to Hill, which correspond to four groupings of Protestants. The official doctrine of the Church of England was that the Pope was the Antichrist. The moderate Puritans believed too much of Antichrist remained in the English church yet by way of political power, persecution, and ceremony. Separatists held that the Church of England was so Antichristian that it was impossible to remain in communion with it. And the Arminians, in reaction to the above charges, questioned whether the Pope was Antichristian at all. Thus, the battle against the enemy was far from concerted.[32]

From 1530–1640 critics of the hierarchy were just as much attacking the monarchy and its supportive legal machinery embedded within the system of church government, but, before the Revolution, such assaults could not be made directly against the monarchy and company. People could, however, attack it cryptically as "the Antichrist"—an enemy agreed upon by all. Behind the smoke screen caused by this pointed spiritual reference, with which no monarch could quibble, stood a real political enemy, however vague this cor-

30. Hill, *Antichrist*, 4, 5.
31. Ibid., 60, 48.
32. Ibid., 62.

porate oppressor appeared. "What is new after 1640," Hill explains, "is the breakdown of obstacles to the inhibitions in attacking the government as well as the bishops. Generalized accusations of popery and Arminianism were thrown at bishops and government alike."[33]

It is important to note in this development of the concept of Antichrist in the seventeenth century a clear penchant for a general, rather than a specific, referencing of him, thereby enabling the term to do its spiritual work much more thoroughly than it could by pointing solely to the pope, the episcopacy, or the monarch. If the Antichrist could not be pinned down, he could be throughout England and within the individual. Henry Denne, in *The Man of Sin Discovered* (1646), records, "Some think the Pope of Rome is Antichrist, some the bishops, some the Turk, etc." He prefers to refrain from specific locating, for "to tie the name of Antichrist to a particular man, or to any succession of men is to confine him to too narrow a bound." While acknowledging that "the Pope is a principal member of Antichrist," Denne proselytizes that "the great Antichrist" is "that mystical body of iniquity which opposeth Jesus Christ. . . . Not Rome alone, but the pulpits of England also may be discovered to be filled with the Man of Sin." Joseph Salmon begins (like Denne) by proclaiming Antichrist's unfettered condition and omnipresence, but declares an even nearer, more insidious presence than could occur through national and mystical incorporation into him: "Thou needest not go far to discover" what Antichrist is. "Thou needest not go to Rome, Canterbury or Westminster, but thou mayest find Antichrist in thee. . . . The Spirit of Antichrist is in all of us."[34]

Most important for Milton's ecclesial communion, the idea of Antichrist (like the concepts of church and Christ), becomes universalized, individualized, and internalized as the century progresses.[35] Universal external enemy has become universal internal enemy. Arguing reverence for conscience and disclaiming any sort of coerciveness, Milton, in *Of Civil Power*, contrasts parts of Antichrist's anatomy with those of the True Church in their ability to discipline:

> If apostles had no dominion or constraining power over faith or conscience, much less have ordinary ministers. . . . But some will

33. Ibid., 78.
34. Ibid., 96, 127.
35. Ibid., wherein Hill ascertains a movement "from Antichrist in Rome, through Antichrist in the bishops or the whole state church, to Antichrist in every man" (130).

object, that this overthrows all church-discipline, all censure of
errors, if no man can determin. My answer is, that what they hear
is plane scripture; which forbids not church-sentence or determining, but as it ends in violence upon the conscience unconvinc'd.
Let who so will interpret or determin, so it be according to true
church discipline; which is exercis'd on them only who have willingly joind themselves in that covnant of union, and proceeds
only to a separation from the rest, proceeds never to any corporal
inforcement or forfeture of monie; which in spiritual things are
the two arms of Antichrist, not of the true church; the one being an
inquisition, the other no better then a temporal indulgence of sin
for monie, whether by the church exacted or by the magistrate.
(7:249)

Milton speaks of the Antichrist in his *Christian Doctrine* after proclaiming that the "enemies of the church . . . are all doomed to destruction, Psal. cxxxvii. . . . The great enemy of the church is called
Antichrist. He is to arise from the church itself" (6:604). The last
statement is important, for if one considers Milton's idea of church,
one realizes that Antichrist can sprout at the universal or particular
(which may very well mean individual) levels, for Antichrist makes
the microcosm as well as the macrocosm his scope. Milton recommends scriptural homework:

On this point see II Thess. ii, 3, etc.: *that man of sin, opposing himself
to and exulting himself above everything that is called God, making it
known that he is God . . .* ; I John ii. 18, etc.: *even now there have begun
to be many antichrists: they have gone out from* us *. . .* , and iv. 3: *every
spirit that does not confess that Jesus Christ has come in the flesh, is not
of God; but this is that spirit of antichrist, which you have heard would
come;* and II John vii: *many impostors have come* into the world, who
do not confess that Jesus *Christ has come in the flesh: this is an
impostor and an antichrist;* also almost the whole of Rev., from Chapter xxiii to the end. (6:604)

He then discusses "the cunning devices and methods of persecution which the enemies of the church employ" (6:605)—enemies
after the fashion of "the great enemy."

In *The Reason of Church Government* Milton uses the term *Antichristian* but with staged emotional distance and a consequent only-
the-facts posture, thereby giving greater force to the branding that
the reader himself is called upon to make in the face of Milton's
preselected incontrovertible facts. Milton need not rely on personal
tirade when he has other rhetoric at his disposal. The evidence Mil-

ton marshals of the Prelates' carnality, resulting from their promotion of ceremony and tradition and from the use of violent and secular power, warrants the Antichristian tag:

> And thus Prelaty, both in her fleshly supportments, in her carnall doctrine of ceremony and tradition, in her violent and secular power [goes] quite counter to the prime end of Christs comming in the flesh, that is to revele his truth, his glory and his might in a clean contrary manner then Prelaty seeks to do thwarting and defeating the great mistery of God, I do not conclude that prelaty is Antichristian, for what need I? The things themselves conclude it. (1:850)

Milton's keen eye and clever thinking have enabled him to produce a rhetoric of apparent objectivity and restraint, which aims to get the reader to see Milton's atypical nonconclusion and nondogma as irresistible. Operating on the principle of the dignity of every human being endowed with the operation of God's light through the conscience, Milton is certain that "the absolute voice of truth and all her children" would "pronounce this Prelaty, and these her dark deeds in the midst of this great light wherein we live, to be more Antichristian than Antichrist himselfe" (1:850).

For Milton, church membership based on a maturing ecclesial identity forced separation from the false church and Antichrist, its head. Milton and those in his more apparent spiritual communion knew that one had to protect the ecclesial center with which God had entrusted one in order to safeguard union with God and communion with the True Church.

The problem that Milton, and really all Reformers faced, as Arthur Barker sees it, was an opposition between liberty and reformation: "The liberty demanded by the left destroyed the reformation desired by the right, and the reformation desired by the right denied the liberty demanded by the left." For Barker the two concepts are incompatible; thus, their "conflicting claims could not be reconciled." I would suggest, instead, that although the two concepts seemed irreconcilable and impracticable throughout the Revolutionary period and its aftermath, Milton does not find them to be so. One sees Milton completely poised between the concepts of Reformation and Liberty. This is evident since, on the one hand, Milton is indebted to Reformist predecessors for carrying the taper originally lighted by Wyclif, though nonetheless critical of them for having restricted the implications of gospel liberty and for having truncated the process of discovering truth through the unrestrained cooperation of the spirit and individual conscience. On the other hand, Milton is sympathetic to the plight of the Radicals persecuted for their beliefs, while he is critical of their behavioral or doctrinal libertinism which shuns a certain responsibility that the gospel entails.[36]

Stretched between the two principles of Reformation and Liberty, Milton envisioned the means for genuine spiritual union (in spite of differences he could observe) and a solid common ground. This union and communion demanded the prevention of septic conditions; if that were not possible, the removal of them; and if that were not possible, segregation from them for the good of the mystic body, that True Church. The extent to which some viewed the body as adequately healthy varied. Those like Milton were dissatisfied with the ill health caused by the yet septic conditions and diseased members under Presbyterianism no less than under Prelacy, for "*New Presbyter* is but *Old Priest* writ Large."[37] In the best of all possible worlds, the separated would prefer to be visibly joined as church, yet because of the existing septic conditions, remove themselves. Their consolation derives from the fact that spiritually they are joined to the True Church, however cryptic that union for the time being must remain.

For now, the godly, like Milton and many other extremists, claimed to follow the True Gospel, to belong to the True Church, and, therefore, to be incorporated into Christ. For such determination and commitment, they would have to withstand accusations of "schismatic," "sectarian," "heretic," "Ranter," and worse, and they would have only their communion through separation to rely on externally. The spirit of Wyclif was alive, *brooding*—that is, both guiding and lamenting—over the waters of England's Reform.

36. Barker, *Puritan Dilemma*, 19, 89, 281.
37. *CPMP*, 144–45, "On the New Forcers of Conscience" (l. 20).

6

"Many Schisms and Many Distinctions"

A "Goodly" and "Graceful" Building

piritual unity was at the heart of a very real emerging ecclesial identity that Milton sought, found (in some ways), spoke for, and preached to during the middle years of the seventeenth century. This identity, shared among the radically faithful, was born gradually and only through conflict with Prelates, then Presbyterians, next Independents, and finally the Restored Anglican Church. By examining Milton's progression of responses to this opposition, one can observe the shaping of an ecclesial identity that Milton believed (sometimes correctly, sometimes not) he shared with many others in England and throughout the world. Typical of the various bodies' opposition to what Milton believed to be the True Church was a fear, either genuine or staged, that divergence in scriptural interpretation, theology, congregating, worship, and discipline would cut to shreds the garment of the one Church of England. Safeguarding the unity of the True Church proclaimed by Scripture and incorporated into Christ for perfecting is of enormous concern to any church, and yet, as Milton and many in his communion were to learn, the reflex, "Schism!" could be shouted, not out of care and conviction, but rather out of convenience. They learned that this Prelatical wolf cry could be shouted to justify a suspicion against the individual and conscience and to retain a very limited understanding of truth. In other words, it could be shouted to sustain the concept that the individual and conscience should be means for accepting and passing on truth as something finished rather than as means for arriving at truth often only by arduous diversity and disagreement.

By carefully observing Milton's language in addition to pondering his ideas, one can learn about this spiritual unity, for crucial linguistic transformations evident in Milton's church teaching are very informative about Milton's church itself. We have seen concepts of church and worship undergo change in Part I. The term *separation,* as noted in the previous chapter, and the terms *schism, heresy,* and *license,* in the remaining chapters of Part II experience a shift in meaning as well, but these terms are similar in that they are used pejoratively, leveled as charges by the religious and political establishment. In these cases Milton follows a pattern. Just as he reinterpreted and reassigned both the negative and positive meanings of separation, so will he work the language of schism, heresy, and license. Milton proceeds according to the following design: first, he acknowledges the term as it is traditionally defined and delivered by the malefactor; next, he initially and immediately repudiates the charge based on that definition; according to the spiritual order of things, that is, the way God sees things, Milton then counterapplies the negatively used word to the accusing spiritual enemy (who initiated the attack) for irresponsibility in doctrine, speech, or ministry; finally, after redefining the term, Milton heartily endorses and himself reappropriates the term containing reexplained doctrine to himself and to members of his church.

There was schism, and there was schism. It was simply a matter of whose unity was being torn apart and whose garment rent: the national church or the True Church? the garment of the Antichrist or that of Christ?

In *The Reason of Church Government,* Milton baptizes by immersion his Prelatical opponents into the complexity of schism:

> The Prelates, as they would have it thought, are the only mawls of schisme. Forsooth if they be put downe, a deluge of innumerable sects will follow; we shall be all Brownists, Familists, Anabaptists. For the word Puritan seems to be quasht, and all that heretofore were counted such, are now Brownists. And thus doe they raise an evill report upon the expected reforming grace that God hath bid us hope for. . . . Doe they keep away schisme? if to bring a num and chil stupidity of soul, an unactive blindnesse of minde upon the people by their leaden doctrine, or no doctrine at all, if to

persecute all knowing and zealous Christians by the violence of
their courts, be to keep away schisme, they keep away schisme
indeed. (1:783–85)

Having advanced themselves to importance, the Prelates see their
primary function as guarding against "a deluge of innumerable
sects," but, in actuality, they are only "of the right Pharisaical straine"
(1:786), that is to say, "stressing outward conformity to the ceremonies of ritual without the spirit of piety."[1] The only real schism,
or 'cutting away', as we shall see, will be the discovery of and removal of Prelatical corruption. As for those whom the Prelates have
self-righteously branded,

> those schismaticks I doubt me wil be found the most of them such
> as whose only schisme was to have spoke the truth against your
> high abominations and cruelties in the Church; this is the schisme
> ye hate most, the removal of your criminous Hierarchy. A politick
> government of yours, and of a pleasant conceit, set up to remove
> those as a pretended schisme, that would remove you as a palpa-
> ble heresie in government. (1:786)

The Prelates, having cleverly projected the problem in the realm
onto those who speak truth according to the gospel of Christ, aim to
rivet the nation's attention on these dangerous "schismaticks," while
claiming to protect the English church from sects. Milton gives their
caricature: "If we go downe, say you, as if Adrians wall were broke,
a flood of sects will rush in" (1:786–87). To the Prelates' wolf cry,
"Sects!", Milton deflates their usual custodial self-importance with
the simple piercing query, "What sects?", which, with its flavor of
surprise and innocence, had become a conventional Puritan response
since the time Calvin used it against his adversaries.[2] Milton proceeds by pushing the accusing hierarchy for accuracy and speci-
ficity about the alleged schismatics: "What are their opinions? Give
us the Inventory." The rhetorical ploy aims to make Prelates speechless, impotent before God's (and Milton's) truth:[3] "It will appeare
both by your former prosecutions and your present instances, that
they are only such to speake of as are offended with your lawlesse

1. *CPW* 1:786 n.49.
2. See chap. 5, "To 'Stand Separated,'" in this volume.
3. Someone like Thomas Edwards is anything but speechless. In *Gangraena* he
catalogs Nonconformist groups with ample polemical descriptions.

government, your ceremonies, your Liturgy, and extract of the Masse book translated" (1:787). In other words, these so-called schismatics have rebelled against the *absence* of Reform. Any speaking about danger, in Milton's view, should be done in reference to abuses within the established church and should be addressed to that church.

Out of great confidence and supported by the unity he shares with those committed to Reform, Milton lays down the challenge with flair that is almost Ranteresque: "Noise it till ye be hoarse; that a rabble of Sects will come in, it will be answer'd ye, no rabble sir Priest, but a unanimous multitude of good Protestants will then joyne to the Church, which now because of you stand separated. This will be the dreadful consequence of your removall" (1:787–88). Yet Milton is well aware that he has not made an end of his enemies, for he expects the Prelates "when the quiver of your arguments, which is ever thin, and weakly" is empty, to "betake ye to your other quiver of slander, wherein lyes your best archery." But Milton remains optimistic, encouraged by the fact that Christ, "call'd Samaritan and Belzebub," preceded the True Living Church as victim of slander: "We must not think it strange if his best Disciples in the reformation, as at first by those of your tribe they were call'd Lollards and Hussites, so now by you be term'd Puritans, and Brownists" (1:788). The pattern for renewal of the True Church includes slander as a prelude.

Milton emphasizes the unity of good English Protestants by obliterating alleged sectarian or schismatic distinctions, thereby revealing the Prelates' labeling to be the result of their fantasies:

> But my hope is that the people of England will not suffer themselves to be juggl'd thus out of their faith and religion by a mist of names cast before their eyes, but will search wisely by the Scriptures, and look quite through this fraudulent aspersion of a disgracefull name into the things themselves: knowing that the Primative Christians in their times were accounted such as are now call'd Familists and Adamites, or worse. (1:788)

Seeing all these divisions is imagination at its worst, without any godly regard for Reason and Scripture, the two guides whereby one can see the spiritual reality of unity that does, in fact, exist.[4]

4. The unity in mind here, like that envisioned and hoped for in *Of Reformation* and *Areopagitica*, is English, although Milton places this immediate goal within its larger universal context. In the 1640s Milton had not yet arrived at the radically inward and individual position that launches him so outward that the spiritual unity

Reading and rereading Milton can give one the impression that his not infrequent acerbity with Prelatical opponents and his unrelenting hammering on several points, not only within a single treatise, but several, is overdone, until one considers his formidable and obsessive enemy. This party line might best be represented by that prelate of Prelates, Archbishop William Laud. In the section entitled "Against Sectaries" in the *Constitutions and Canons for the Church of England, 1640,* one can glimpse the nearly mono-maniacal righteousness that propelled all the Laudian rigidity and rigor that wrought havoc among Dissenters:

> Whereas there is a provision now made by a canon for the suppressing of popery and the growth thereof, by subjecting all popish recusants to the greatest severity of ecclesiastical censures in that behalf; this present synod well knowing, that there are other sects which endeavor the subversion both of the doctrine and discipline of the Church of England, no less than papists do, although by another way; for the preventing thereof, doth hereby decree and ordain, that all those proceedings and penalties which are mentioned in the aforesaid canon against popish recusants . . . shall stand in full force and vigour against all Anabaptists, Brownists, Separatists, Familists, or other sect or sects, person or persons whatsoever, who do or shall either obstinately refuse, or ordinarily, not having a lawful impediment . . . neglect to repair to their parish churches or chapels where they inhabit, for the hearing of divine service established, and of receiving the holy Communion according to law.
>
> And further, because there are sprung up among us a sort of factious people, despisers and depravers of the book of Common Prayer, who do not according to the law resort to their parish church or chapel to join in the public prayers, service, and worship of God with the congregation, contenting themselves with the hearing of sermons only, thinking thereby to avoid the penalties due to such as wholly absent themselves from the church. We therefore, for the restraint of all such wilful contemners or neglecters of the service of God, do ordain that the church or chapelwardens, and questmen, or sidemen of every parish, shall be careful to enquire out all such disaffected persons, and shall present the names of all such delinquents at all visitations of bishops, and other ordinaries; and that the same proceedings and penalties mentioned in the canon aforesaid respectively, shall be used against them as against other recusants.[5]

---

he emphasizes becomes clearly more generic (*The Tenure of Kings and Magistrates* and *A Treatise of Civil Power*) and international (*Christian Doctrine*), but he is well on his way.

5. Laud, *Works,* vol. 5, pt. 2, 622.

It is clear that Milton was being neither overly sensitive nor histrionic in dealing with the Prelatical self-serving position and genuinely divisive name-calling. He was merely responding. In Laud's attitudes and policies one can see the typical Prelate's observation of and emphasis on the divisions within the church, the use of "full force and vigour" in requiring religious expression, and the prohibition against worship chosen voluntarily and consisting only of the Word as counting for the required Sunday religious observance. All of these violations horrified Milton as they would any true Reformer bent on Reformation without compromising anything of Liberty, a condition, in addition to Reformation, also promised and ensured by Christ's gospel.

Milton meets his spiritual and ecclesiastical opposition on the turf selected by, and with the tone sounded by, this enemy. It is a methodology that Milton explains and uses in *An Apology Against a Pamphlet call'd A Modest Confutation of the Animadversions upon the Remonstrant against SMECTYMNUUS* (1642) in the serial battle between the Prelates and Presbyterians. First, he attends to the substance of the controversy. He confesses that he has entered the ecclesiastical lists once again (initially in *Animadversions* in 1641), but this time to defend himself as much as the Smectymnuans for whom he originally spoke. Next, he turns to the style that looms larger than the substance. This time, too, perhaps because of the circumstances and personal involvement warranting apologetic particularity, Milton is self-conscious and explicit about the intensity of his demeanor and method. Deeming it "unlike a Christian to be a cold neuter in the cause of the Church," Milton explains his rationale for a zealous approach, having been persuaded "to stand on that side where I saw both the plain autority of Scripture leading, and the reason of justice and equity perswading": "And because I observe that feare and dull disposition, lukewarmeness & sloth are not seldomer wont to cloak themselves under the affected name of moderation, then true and lively zeale is customably dispareg'd with the terme of indiscretion, bitternesse, and choler, I could not to my thinking honor a good cause more from the heart, then by defending it earnestly" (1:868–69). This is merely recapping his original motive for entrance into the conflict by *Animadversions*, but he states that he has begun his *Apology* for them in this way "since the Preface, which was purposely set before them, is not thought apologeticall anough." Consequently, "it will be best to acquaint ye, Readers, before other things, what the meaning was to write them in that manner which I did" (1:871). Milton has "two provocations, his [the Confuter's] latest insulting in his short answer, and their [the Smectymnuans'] finall patience," though "the authors of Smectymnuus . . . were prepar'd both with skill and purpose to returne a suffizing answer, and were able anough to lay the dust and pudder in antiquity, which he and his, out of stratagem, are wont to raise" (1:872). Hence, to Milton "it seem'd an indignity, that whom [the Smectymnuans] his [the Confuter's] whole wisdom could not move from their place, them [the Smectymnuans] his [the Confuter's] impetuous folly should presume to ride over" (1:873). (In other words, realizing that all his wisdom was unable to incite them to furious verbal battle, the Confuter, according to Milton, used his folly to trample over them.) As Milton has considered the Prelatical victims' patience and equanimity, his own emotional pitch, evident in his image of the rough-riding Confuter, has only risen to a level matching the fury of Confuter and company, not exceeding it. Then, while reflecting on allegations of his passionate demeanor and obtrusive levity, Milton reignites that original fervor and relives the spiritual horror that provoked it, despite denial of uncalled-for emoting:

> And if I were more warme then was meet in any passage of that booke, which yet I do not yield, I might use therein the patronage of no worse an author then *Gregory Nyssen*, who mentioning his sharpnesse against *Eunomius* in the defense of his brother *Basil*, holds himselfe irreprovable in that it *was not for himself, but in the cause of his brother; and in such cases*, saith he, *perhaps it is worthier pardon to be angry then to be cooler.* And whereas this Confuter taxes the whole discourse of levity, I shall shew ye, Readers, wheresoever it shall be objected in particular that I have answer'd with as little lightnesse as the Remonstrant hath given example. I have not beene so light as the palme of a Bishop which is the lightest thing in the world when he brings out his book of Ordination: For then contrary to that which is wont in releasing out of prison, any one that will pay his fees is layd hands on. (1:873)

Whether or not Milton has responded only in kind and measure, without excessive warmth and indecorous levity, as *he* saw and felt things, is a question not worth concerning oneself with. What is more to the purpose is his text, in which he has gone to the trouble of citing a patristic authority for having been "more warme then was meet" and in which he has pointed this discussion about his emotional register with biting and/or flippant statement: in one as he changes lightness of rhetoric for lightness of greed, and in the other as he switches the sacramental gesture for a counterpunitive, dismissing one. Neither verbal twist, for all its cleverness, could be called "sleight of hand"; the logical contortions required to get the idea are all too evident and also atypical of Milton, suggesting unusual emotional intensity. The point, in any case, is not to judge whether his emotional pitch is higher than is warranted but to note that Milton has demonstrated the zeal that he has protested he has not overdone. His response is in order because of the Confuter's ravaging attack both on the leaders of Milton's church at the time and on Milton personally, and that response, however "warme" and whenever "light," matches their key according to his sensibility. Milton is once again merely responding, particularly and personally, and hence, for one like the Confuter, too passionately.

The main business of *An Apology,* like that of all of Milton's tracts, is the exposure of falsehood and the proclamation of truth. One of the rhetorical ways to expose falsehood and fight its influence was by portraying it through preaching and writing as the agent for having turned things upside down and inside out from the way they are supposed to be, according to the Spirit's ongoing revelation. As he concludes his *Apology,* Milton demonstrates how the Prelates, for whom the Confuter speaks, have everything backwards, from their argument for the use of riches, to their sacramentality, to an incorrect identification with person and purpose in the Exodus event, to the purpose and style of ministry, to the spiritual nutrition of their sees, and finally to the tradition of their faith.

While "Christ refused great riches, and large honours at the Devils hand," the perverse reasoning of the Prelate attributes that renunciation to the gifts having *"been tender'd by him from whom it was a sin to receave them"* and further to the fact that *"he [Christ] could make no use of such a high estate,"* with the implication that Prelates, of course, can. Milton, challenging logic based on their self-interest with his own logic based on his interpretation of Christ's intention, wonders, "Why then should the servant take upon him to use those things which his master had unfitted himself to use, that hee might teach his ministers to follow his steps in the same ministery." His opponent's confutation, *"But they were offer'd him to a bad end,"* reveals blindness to their own "bad end[s]" besides showing their usual twisted rationalization. Milton concludes, "So they prove to the Prelats; who after their preferment most usually change the teaching labour of the word, into the unteaching ease of Lordship over consciences, and purses" (1:949). This idea of Prelatical sacramental perversion is one of the high points of the treatise: instead of a transubstantiation of "the teaching labour of the word" into the teaching of freedom of consciences and liberality of purses for the care of the poor, the Prelates have perverted the transforming power of the Word. Milton forcefully asserts and shows their twistedness by appropriating a perversion of their usual eucharistic symbolism, which they think applies only to bread and wine, to Prelatical perversion of the source and ground of all Sacrament, the Word.

To justify "capacious greedinesse" (1:948), the Confuter draws a parallel between *the promise of Canaan* with which *"God entic't the Israelites"* and the Prelatical riches and honours used as contemporary ministerial incentives. Through selfish reasoning, Milton's enemy has missed the whole point of the Exodus experience, which is, according to Milton, the possibility of interiorized Egyptian enslavement, and, in so doing, the enemy has misinterpreted Scripture again. To adjust this sort of bad reading revealed through misapplication of it, Milton instructs, "Did not the Prelats bring as slavish mindes with them, as the Jewes brought out of Egypt?" (1:949). They have failed to realize the development of salvation history and its implications for those living in another dispensation: "Besides that it was then the time, when as the best of them, as Saint *Paul* saith, *was shut up unto the faith under the Law* their School-maister, who was forc't to intice them as children with childish enticements. But the Gospell is our manhood, and the minister should bee the manhood of the Gospell, not to looke after, much lesse so basely to plead for earthly rewards" (1:949–50). Prelates look backward rather than forward, glossing their lives in terms of the Old Testament (and that poorly done) rather than in terms of the New, fostering "childish enticements" rather than adult responsibility, which implies self-sacrificing. Furthermore, they shoot themselves in the foot by ensconcing themselves and their argument in the comforts of a bygone dispensation when they have regularly accused Puritans and sectaries of Hebraism.

Identification with scriptural personages like Solomon and Moses, whom the Prelates claim God incited with the means of earthly rewards, further exemplifies their opposition to the truth of Scripture:

Ah Confuter of thy selfe, this example hath undone thee, *Salomon* askt an understanding heart, which the Prelats have little care to ask. He askt no riches which is their chiefe care: therefore was the prayer of *Salomon* pleasing to God; hee gave him wisdome at his request, and riches without asking: as now hee gives the Prelats riches at their seeking, and no wisdome because of their perverse asking. . . . To what reward . . . had the faith of *Moses* an eye to? He that had forsaken all the greatnesse of *Egypt*, and chose a troublesome journey in his old age through the Wildernesse, and yet arriv'd not at his journies end: His faithfull eyes were fixt upon that incorruptible reward, promis'd to *Abraham* and his seed in the *Messiah*, hee sought a heav'nly reward which could make him happy, and never hurt him. . . . But the Prelats are eager of such rewards as cannot make them happy, but can only make them worse. (1:950)

Because the Prelates have inverted the goal of prayer and of life, they use the ministry for self-advancement and self-gratification and see that sort of making-good as being in perfect accord with the truth of the gospel that they follow: "But the Prelats of meane birth, and oft times of lowest, making shew as if they were call'd to the spirituall and humble ministery of the Gospell, yet murmur, and thinke it a hard service, unlesse contrary to the tenour of their profession, they may eat the bread and weare the honours of Princes" (1:950).

In arguing *"Are not the Clergy members of Christ, why should not each member thrive alike?"* the Confuter and his Prelatical company warrant the severity of Milton's scornful labeling, "Carnall textman!", for they have turned priority of values inside out; they have read God's Word by and for the flesh rather than the spirit, seeking "childish enticement" instead of the expected, more responsible emptiness that Christ's true gospel entails:

As if worldly thriving were one of the priviledges wee have by being in Christ, and were not a providence oft times extended more liberally to the Infidell then to the Christian. Therefore must the Ministers of Christ not be over rich or great in the world, because their calling is spirituall, not secular; because they have a speciall warfare, which is not to be intangl'd with many impediments: because their Maister Christ gave them this precept, and set them this example, told them this was the mystery of his comming, by meane things and persons to subdue mighty ones: and lastly because a middle estate is most proper to the office of teaching. Whereas higher dignity teaches farre lesse, and blindes the teacher. (1:951)

By Milton's standards, their performance is abysmal: they "possesse huge Benefices for lazie performances, great promotions, only for the execution of a cruell disgospelling jurisdiction" and "let hundreds of parishes famish in one *Diocesse*, while they . . . are mute, and yet injoy that wealth that would furnish all those dark places with able supply." Perhaps most serious of all, considering the chief goal of the Reformation, is their culpability for having deprived their flock of the spiritual nourishment that must come from the preached Word. Instead, they "chase away all the faithfull Shepheards of the flocke, and bring in a dearth of spirituall food, robbing thereby the Church of her dearest treasure, and sending heards of souls starvling to Hell." Yet spiritual malnutrition also has secular causes and consequences for which the Prelates are responsible. They have managed to gorge themselves, while starving their people spiritually *and* carnally: "They feast and riot upon the labours of hireling Curats, consuming and purloyning even that which by their foundation is allow'd, and left to the poore, and to reparations of the Church" (1:952).

In all of the foregoing Prelatical accusations, the opposite direction of the Prelates' words and actions rends the cover for their rottenness and reveals their commitment to subvert the inheritance of faith, rather than promote it. Milton, with gospel, goals, and vision of a world turned right side up and spirit side out, calls to his readers for "the usurpation of Prelats laid levell, who are in words the Fathers, but in their deeds the oppugners of the faith" (1:952). Reading the signs of the times with the light of the gospel, Milton reveals the Prelates for what they truly are:

> Thus yee have heard, Readers, how many shifts and wiles the Prelats have invented to save their ill got booty. And if it be true, as in Scripture it is foretold, that pride and covetousnesse are the sure markes of those false Prophets which are to come, then boldly conclude these to bee as great seducers, as any of the latter times. For betweene this and the judgment day, doe not looke for any arch deceavers who in spight of reformation will use more craft, or lesse shame to defend their love of the world, and their ambition, then these Prelats have done. (1:952–53)

To the Prelates and the Conformist world, of course, civil war was turning things upside down. However, Milton's clear, reiterated concern for the poor signals an affiliation with them in spirit and in truth that is rooted in Christ, his Church, and that right-side-up world that only true believers can see. Writing only three years later, in 1645, Henry Denne uses the image of inverting, subtextually at work in Milton at every turn, to express very pointedly for himself what is clearly the constant theme of Milton's anti-Prelatical prose, namely, the exposure and removal of falsehood along with the proclamation and establishment of truth. According to the world as it then was in the 1640s, Henry Denne, John Milton, and those with Milton's ecclesial identity would have been guilty of the same crime. "I may peradventure to many," writes Denne, "seem guilty of that crime which was laid against the Apostle, to turn the world upside down and to set that in the bottom which others make the top of the building, and to set that upon the roof which others lay for a foundation."[6]

Reformation, as all Protestants in the seventeenth century agreed, meant the return to Truth. But Truth, as we have seen in previous chapters, meant different things to different Reformers. For the pre-Revolutionary establishment, as represented by the Prelates, truth required opening its repository and setting it out for acceptance; but for Milton, truth required process and progress, racing to a finish line, as Paul had confessed to and exhorted the Philippians: "But *this* one thing *I do*, forgetting those things which are behind, and reaching forth unto those things which are before, I press toward the mark for the prize of the high calling of God in Christ Jesus" (3:7–14). Eventually the various Puritan groups began to disagree among themselves on the placement of the finish line and on the pace needed for reaching their respective conflicting alternate goals. The Prelates, without mark or race, and out of shape, renounced that "reaching forth unto those things which are before" and, as a result, desperately feared the competition. The fact that Truth was something not merely to be assented to, but rather something to be worked for (sometimes with Pauline suffering) before it was arrived at was tied, in the words of Walzer, to "the gradual replacement of a cyclical view of history that underlay the idea [of reformation] with a progressive view that provided a theoretical foundation for the idea of improvement." Stephen Marshall was one of the five Smectymnuans who "in 1642 explicitly rejected the cyclical idea."[7] For Milton and his apparently rather large team in 1642 and much later, *improvement* of both religion and liberty was the

6. Epigraph to chap. 1, in Hill, *World Turned Upside Down*, 13. For an explanation of the use of the term *upside-down world*, see 384–86.

7. Walzer, *Revolution of Saints*, 12, 178. "The idea of the ship of state," Walzer notes, "was closely related to the puritan view of life as a voyage" (179).

substance of the marathon, requiring enormous energy, patience, perseverance, and, perhaps more than anything else, time and scope for the massive competition, for "faith and knowledge thrives by exercise" (2:543).

In a scant two years, by 1644, signs of drastic change were apparent. The Presbyterian Parliament and Westminster Assembly neared their finish line or, worse, had in midrace moved closer the one that they and many had agreed upon. Those who had augured the most promise now proved to be the greatest problem as many of the formerly branded in the Prelatical heyday became the branders. Having inherited that Prelatical dread of "reaching forth unto those things which are before" (in a Pauline-Miltonic word, *knowledge*), Presbyterians, according to Milton, not only withdrew from the competition, but quashed it: "And what doe they tell us vainly of new opinions, when this very opinion of theirs, that none must be heard, but whom they like, is the worst and newest opinion of all others; and is the chief cause why sects and schisms doe so much abound, and true knowledge is kept at a distance from us; besides yet a greater danger which is in it" (2:566). Like their Prelatical predecessors, the Presbyterians feared the upshot of granting time and scope to discover truth, because throughout the process, people might have discovered diversity and come to accept it, love it, and revere it as the only way to determine ultimate Truth. It was far easier to prevent harmful diversity by preventing dispute altogether—an obstacle course Milton was quick to notice:

> When God shakes a Kingdome with strong and healthfull commotions to a generall reforming, 'tis not untrue that many sectaries and false teachers are then busiest in seducing; but yet more true it is, that God then raises to his own work men of rare abilities, and more then common industry not only to look back and revise what hath bin taught heretofore, but to gain furder and goe on, some new enlightn'd steps in the discovery of truth. For such is the order of Gods enlightning his Church. (1:566)

But only the actual race would reveal the losers (who conditioned themselves incorrectly on ease, guile, and greed to have been false prophets) and the winners (who trained themselves on the nutrition, exercise, and selflessness of Christ's gospel to have been true). One discovers Truth and meets God only by being willing "to gain furder and go on," for as Milton knew well, the one who demands the exposure of falsehood and who promises the establishment of

Truth calls from the future. Undaunted, Milton and the Radical church welcomed the challenge of the marathon, therefore, unable to "praise a fugitive and cloister'd vertue, unexercis'd & unbreath'd, that never sallies out and sees her adversary, but slinks out of the race, where that immortall garland is to be run for, not without dust and heat" (2:515). The true wayfaring Christian is always truly warfaring as well, a point emphasized by Milton's own textual revision to "warfaring."[8] There is more than orthographic similarity between Milton's r's and y's and more than diction indecision. There is semantic and scriptural conflation, later historically prompting preference notwithstanding.

Thus, the worries of those branded as "sectarian" or "schismatic" were not over, by any means, with the executions of Strafford in 1641 and Laud in 1645 and with the overall demise of the episcopacy throughout that decade. Those more recently labeled found themselves in a veritable living theater of the absurd as they protested their religious unity before a new establishment, likewise professing Protestant unity, which persecuted them. Milton, familiar with allegations of disunifying and with the mentality behind them (through his ordeal with the Prelates), was able and ready to come to the rescue of new victims at the hands of "Priest(s) writ Large." By 1644 he reresponds in *Areopagitica* to the claim of factions, which in reality he believed was causing them. Although Milton may already have been anticipating serious disagreement with the rather new Presbyterian regime, his previous publicized sympathy with those reputed as "schismatics"—a kind of act of self-sacrifice—formally disposed him to be at odds with the new seat of power or with any that used force and persecution to insure doctrine and discipline.

In this 1644 Address to the fictionally convened English Parliament, Milton pleads his case for trusting in the process of disputation to deliver Truth victorious: "Though all the windes of doctrin were let loose to play upon the earth, so Truth be in the field, we do injuriously by licencing and prohibiting to misdoubt her strength. Let her and Falshood grapple; who ever knew Truth put to the wors, in a free and open encounter. Her confuting is the best and surest suppressing" (2:561). It is common knowledge "that Truth is strong next to the Almighty; she needs no policies, nor stratagems, nor licensings to make her victorious" since "those are the shifts and

8. *CPW* 2:515 n. 102.

defences that error uses against her power" (2:562–63). Consequently, Milton asks that Parliament "forgoe this Prelaticall tradition of crowd-ing free consciences and Christian liberties into canons and pre-cepts of men" and, instead, adopt "a little generous prudence, a little forbearance of one another, and som grain of charity" to "win all these diligences to joyn, and unite into one generall and broth-erly search after truth" (2:554). This enactment of charity, which pre-supposes unity, is the only way if England is to consist of "wise and faithfull labourers," recreated into "a knowing people, a Nation of Prophets, of Sages, and of Worthies": "Where there is much desire to learn, there of necessity will be much arguing, much writing, many opinions; for opinion in good men is but knowledge in the making" (2:554). In other words, there will be the gospel's dyna-mism instead of the Prelatical fixity of thought and structures. He concludes this point by regretting the chimera of divisions: "Under these fantastic terrors of sect and schism, we wrong the ernest and zealous thirst after knowledge and understanding which God hath stirr'd up in this City" (2:554).

Here in *Areopagitica*, with echoes of 1 Cor. 12 on the variety of members within a single body in the background, Milton speaks strongly and spiritually for those "men cry'd out against for schis-maticks and sectaries" (2:555). The rhetoric of the upcoming Milton passage, dazzling as ever in its straightforwardness and concrete-ness, uses a scripturally allusive analogy of the living temple as found in First Corinthians and Ephesians.

> For we are labourers together with God: ye are God's husbandry, *ye are* God's building.
> Know ye not that ye are the temple of God, and that the Spirit of God dwelleth in you? . . . for the temple of God is holy, which *temple* ye are." (1 Cor. 3:9, 16–17)

> Now therefore ye are no more strangers and foreigners, but fellow citizens with the saints, and of the household of God; And are built upon the foundation of the apostles and prophets, Jesus Christ himself being the chief corner *stone:* In whom all the build-ing fitly framed together groweth unto an holy temple in the Lord: In whom ye also are builded together for an habitation of God through the Spirit. (Eph. 2:19–22)

The point of connection between the biblical text and Milton's, which I wish to emphasize, is not merely the identity of the poetic figure, but rather the spiritual union that both texts aim for. To Hughes's observation that "Milton puns on the literal meaning of *schism*, cutting or division,"[9] I would add that such punning on the literal level deflates the literal meaning while directing our attention to the non-literal, spiritual meaning and purpose: that all physical schisms are, in so far as they conform within one large superstructure, un-schismatic. In fact, as is apparent in Milton, such schism is the way to become part of the spiritual architecture:

> Yet these are the men cry'd out against for schismaticks and sectaries; as if, while the Temple of the Lord was building, some cutting, some squaring the marble, others hewing the cedars, there should be a sort of irrationall men who could not consider there must be many schisms and many distinctions made in the quarry and in the timber, ere the house of God can be built. And when every stone is laid artfully together, it cannot be united into a continuity, it can but be contiguous in this world; neither can every peece of the building be of one form; nay rather the perfection consists in this, that out of many moderat varieties and brotherly dissimilitudes that are not vastly disproportionall arises the goodly and the graceful symmetry that commends the whole pile and structure. (2:555)[10]

This Nonconformity is not something out of the ordinary and only to be tolerated. Quite the contrary. It is the rule just as much as spiritual conformity or union is. The goal of Reform about to be accomplished in these last days of the age of the Spirit requires and thrives upon this ecclesial *discordia concors*, whose unity loses nothing from the diversity but, instead, gains Truth, which engenders "a knowing people, a Nation of Prophets" at once completing Reform and fulfilling Moses' dream: "Let us therefore be more considerat builders, more wise in spirituall architecture, when great reformation is expected. For now the time seems come, wherein *Moses* the great Prophet may sit in heav'n rejoycing to see that memorable and

9. *CPMP*, 744 n. 242. See Lieb, *Sinews of Ulysses*, 33–35.

10. Stanley Fish, in "Driving from the Letter," deals with this passage but conflates the "thousand pieces" of Truth and the "many distinctions made in the quarry and in the timber" of "the Temple of the Lord," emphasizing a rational rather than a spiritual architecture. In Fish's view, the goal is "the making of us into members of [Truth's] incorporate body" (246–47). Milton, in fact, reverses the emphasis, very definitely and explicitly centering on incorporation of the members—with their "many moderat varieties and brotherly dissimilitudes"—into "the Temple of the Lord," or "house of God" (*CPW* 2:555).

glorious wish of his fulfill'd, when not only our sev'nty Elders, but all the Lords people are become Prophets" (2:555–56).

In Milton's view there are those who "fret, and out of their own weaknes are in agony, lest these divisions and subdivisions will undoe us," and "the adversarie again applauds, and waits the hour" (2:556). But Milton emphasizes that the inability to see the union for the ostensible divisions follows the very misguidance of "the adversarie": "When they have brancht themselves out, saith he [the adversarie], small anough into parties and partitions, then will be our time. Fool! *he sees not the firm root,* out of which we all grow, though into branches: nor will beware untill he see our small divided maniples cutting through at every angle of his ill united and unwieldy brigade" (2:556; emphasis added). Faith, as the belief in things unseen, allows the believer who is ingrafted into Christ to see and to trust the unity that is not apparent.

For the Prelates, schism invited a lurking "adversarie"; for King Charles, it splintered the national church and was, therefore, to be regarded as seditious (a point Milton makes in *Eikonoklastes* in 1649). But as Geoffrey Nuttall points out, for Congregationalists, "The Church of England, as a national church was not, and never had been, truly the Church at all." The logical conclusion to such a position was traumatic for its opponents, for "if the body, which those accused of schism were charged with rending never was, never could have been, the Church, then obviously there could be no schism from it." Jeremiah Burroughs dispels the notion of a national church on the same grounds as Milton, namely, that Christ never intended one:

> That we may call the church in England a National Church because of the many saints in it, who are the body of Christ, I deny not, nor ever did. . . . But that its by the institution of Christ formed into one political Church, as the Nation of Jews was, this is no Independency to deny. Where are any particular men standing Officers to the whole Nation by divine institutions? What National Worship hath Christ instituted?[11]

Having granted that the English church may be described as national because of its people, but not its polity, Burroughs, in soliciting answers to questions (on "Officers" and "National Worship") that have

---

11. Nuttall, *Visible Saints,* 62, 63, 64.

none, effectively attempts to work his rhetorical ploy, bringing opponents to a silence of guilt.

In *Eikonoklastes,* when Milton decries Charles's confessed aim to
uphold a Church of England, he provides the governing principle
for distinguishing schism from church:

> It is a rule and principle worthy to be known by Christians, that no
> Scripture, no nor so much as any ancient Creed, bindes our Faith,
> or our obedience to any Church whatsoever, denominated by a
> particular name; farr less, if it be distinguisht by a several Govern-
> ment from that which is indeed Catholic. No man was ever bidd be
> subject to the Church of *Corinth, Rome,* or *Asia,* but to the Church
> without addition, as it held faithfull to the rules of Scripture. . . .
> That Church that from the name of a distinct place takes autority to
> set up a distinct Faith or Government, is a Scism and Faction, not a
> Church. It were an injurie to condemn the Papist of absurdity and
> contradiction, for adhering to his Catholic Romish Religion, if we,
> for the pleasure of a King and his politic considerations, shall
> adhere to a Catholic English. (3:571–72)

Milton turns the argument that the state makes about schism on
itself just as he had turned the Prelates' claim about schism against
them. Here it is the national state (or head of state) that, through its
(his) fear of sects, creates them in imagination and persecutes them
in reality.

7

"When They Cry Liberty"

A Rhetoric of License for "Bad Men"

ilton's lifelong quest was to find and bond with "good men" and, in the process of his search, to reform "bad men" (3:190). This two-part mission—whose scope was national at first—was to yield a true church for Milton in which he would find reformed communion. After the anti-Prelatical pamphlets (by 1643), he begins to de-emphasize the national dimension of church unity and to search for some other sort that even an English ecclesia, should it turn harmful, would be unable to threaten or undo. He looks for a "fit audience . . . though few" that would act as leaven (PL, 7.31). But, as Joseph Wittreich rightly points out, Milton's distinction "between levels of audience . . . is made in terms of morality, not class."[1]

If Milton missed or lost his audience (as some critics maintain),[2] that audience was a visible, political, narrowly focused one that was stunting Milton's concept of church. As this audience faded, another,

---

The treatment of "license," reprinted with changes by permission of Roy C. Flannagan, editor, appeared first in my article, "*License* Reconsidered: Ecclesial Nuances," in *Milton Quarterly*.

1. For a superb treatment of the shift in Milton's audience, see Wittreich, " 'Crown of Eloquence,' " in Patrides and Waddington, eds., *Age of Milton*, 16. This analysis lays the groundwork for my ecclesiological argument that Milton's expanded *audience*, in fact becomes expanded *congregation*.

2. See Bush, *English Literature*, 373; Florence Sandler, "Icon and Iconoclast," 167–68, and Shawcross, "Higher Wisdom," 145–48, in Lieb and Shawcross, eds., *Achievements of the Left Hand*; and Woolrych, "Political Theory and Political Practice," in Patrides and Waddington, eds., *Age of Milton*, 66–67.

spiritual audience (already existing for Wyclif and sixteenth-century Radicals who followed in his footsteps) was coming into focus for Milton. This new audience became spiritually more and more visible to Milton's eye, "med'cin'd" by God through a variety of political and ecclesiastical hardships. In 1649, in *The Tenure of Kings and Magistrates*, Milton glimpses that spiritual communion, still at a distance, demonstrated by the universal interiorizing principle that he will increasingly rely upon to enable him to determine the ecclesial intimacy inherent in any true church: "Nor is it distance of place that makes enmitie, but enmity that makes distance. He therefor that keeps peace with me, neer or remote, of whatsoever Nation, is to mee as farr as all civil and human offices an Englishman and a neighbor" (3:215). What is "English" has gone beyond the physical, external, national bounds, just as what is "alien" has. In redefining what it means to be "English" and in widening the audience he desires to address, Milton has stepped into the spiritual realm. This teaching on the church is later expressed in the *Christian Doctrine* where he proclaims that he is not limited by "spatial considerations" but participates in the invisible church and, so, enjoys "mystic" communion with the other members who comprise "the body of Christ" and "WHO ARE CALLED FROM ANY PART OF THE WHOLE WORLD," for "THE PEOPLE of the universal church are all nations" (6:500, 568, 573). Because of his ecclesiology, *audience*, for Milton, becomes *congregation* (invisible primarily, though visible as well in certain quarters already and everywhere ideally and eventually). Also because of his ecclesiology, Milton, instead of mere orator, becomes shepherd in pursuit of his flock that is, for him, not yet entirely found and certainly not yet gathered.

Without ignoring the English "members of Christ's body," Milton found it necessary to enlarge his sympathies and the communion of Protestant Reformers. Milton's quest for unity shifted to Radical Puritans at home then grew to include Radical Puritans throughout the world. While this expansion began as early as 1643 and 1644 with the divorce pamphlets and *Areopagitica*,[3] it became doctrinally explicit and more vocalized in the *Christian Doctrine* between 1658 and 1660. The English saints, in Milton's view, did not, could not, and would not fit the Prelatical, Presbyterial, and eventually even Congregational structures that had all grown too small for the zeal of those who

---

3. Wittreich, " 'Crown of Eloquence,' " in Patrides and Waddington, eds., *Age of Milton*, 14–19.

had not seen enough Reform. But this was all part of a larger shift in focus: away from the national and external and toward the internal but without forsaking attention to the pure believers still at home: "Who knows not that there is a mutual bond of amity and brotherhood between man and man over all the World, neither is it the English Sea that can sever us from that duty and relation: a straiter bond yet there is between fellow-subjects, neighbors, and friends" (3:214).

The gradual spiritual, inward thrust that is evident in Milton's later work, however much owing to domestic dissatisfaction, occurred alongside Milton's attention to that broader, spatially unconfined international group of saints who were ingrafted into Christ's Mystical Body as the Church. This is ecumenicity that bonds believers in a way that Prelatical, Presbyterial, and even looser Independent organizing could never accomplish and foster. George Williams describes the beginning of this Radical Protestant development a century earlier:

> Ecumenicity in the sixteenth-century Radicals was a combination of the sense of the inwardness of the Kingdom of God, the experience of the universality of the work of the Holy Spirit, the impatience of the territorialization of the Reformation, and the overwhelming conviction as to the actuality of the New Covenant. The experience of the new creation in the Spirit gave all the Radicals a feeling of comradeship in Christ and in longing to share their Christian fellowship in solidarity with saints and would-be saints of all times and in all climes.

If any renewed and renewing vision helps to explain Milton's post-Restoration days and later poetry as optimistic or hopeful, it is this enlarged sense of communion where church and worship, despite all sorts of political and ecclesiastical traumas (even persecution), perdure. Williams elaborates: "Just as there was a 'unitive Protestantism' of the Magisterial Reformation that cut across the territorial boundaries, so likewise there was an underlying catholicity in the Radical Reformation, even though divisive sectarianism and conventicular fission seem to have bulked very large."

What was true of radicalism then had changed very little in England during the next century. Perry Miller points to the signs of this bonding there and then:

> Sects of enthusiasts multiplied [during the 1640s] beyond number; whatever their differences or their eccentricities, these "gan-

graena" were united in their hostility to universities, college gradu-
ates in the pulpit, and the monopoly of religious instruction by the
formally educated. . . . The Presbyterians and Independents were
even then engaged in a furious combat over the form of church
polity, but they both strove to remain loyal to orthodox Calvinism
and to the orthodox conception of the necessary alliance between
religion and learning.[4]

Milton is often about tearing down old definitions and building
up new ones, especially with ecclesiological terms basic to Protestant church doctrine in England during the 1640s. Thus, for him,
separation will mean spiritual communion (*Reason of Church Government* 1:787–88); schism will refer to a morally informed, alert, and
zealous Christian (1:783–85) or to the necessary variety of living stones
cut for the living temple, enhancing its proportion, design, and cohesiveness (*Areopagitica* 2:555); and heresy, as we shall see, will mean
any scripturally based opinion one holds as the church progresses
to Truth (*Of Civil Power* 7:250). With the rebuilding and reuse of these
and other church terms, the term *license* too deserves serious recon-
sidering in an ecclesiological context. What does Milton have in
mind? Does it characterize those we often and most easily presume:
the uneducated, bacchanalian, raucous rabble? And is the looseness
referred to mainly sociological? By examining Milton's pertinent
prose and by remembering one of his chief concerns, namely, a completely reformed church, we can historically, thus accurately, understand who Milton believed were crying "liberty" when they meant
"license," and how an audience that was "morally" fit had to behave.

Milton shared such ecumenicity with extremist groups, particularly those who through charity were socially more responsible, and
who through internal discipline were not libertine. Included among
these Radicals were Seekers, Reevonians, Muggletonians, and Diggers who unselfishly followed Winstanley's vision. Union with those
at home, in spite of differences, was a concrete, local expression of
the larger Radical reform with which they were mystically interfused as church.

Sects may have regarded their differences with great significance
(just as mainline Puritanism regarded its distinguishing orthodoxy),
but, as William Haller notes, and as I think Milton believed, "In
everything that seems significant to us, the Puritan sects were far

---

4. Williams, *Radical Reformation*, 815; Miller, *New England Mind*, 74.

more alike than they were different."[5] It is, of course, important to be aware of the differences, but for an accurate reading of the period retrospectively it is just as important not to ignore the very tool that helps to explain the period and its people: an emphasis *not* on what distinguishes these religious dissenters, but on what unites them. In contrast to Puritan orthodoxy, as represented by the Presbyterian government, the leftist Puritans (even the Independents to some degree, however much their motivation differed) abounded in tolerance and pluralism that was rooted in a deep mystical union. Their cry, as Brookes's was and Milton's became, was "Liberty!"

Milton was certainly aware that liberty could be mistranslated as license; hence, his chastising in Sonnet 12 (164?) of those who mean license "when they cry liberty" (l. 11). A surface reading of this sonnet might seem to suggest Milton's unequivocal disaffection with misbehaving Radicals that espoused varying degrees of (antinomian) sensuality. The unarguable disgust, however, is aimed elsewhere: at attackers of his prose who have become part of the self-serving and narrow-minded new establishment. This and the previous sonnet refer to William Prynne's attack on *Tetrachordon* and *Colasterion*[6]— "barberous noise" (3) that Milton must endure because he has cast his

> Pearl to Hogs,
> That bawl for freedom in their senseless mood,
> And still revolt when truth would set them free.
> (8–10)

To Milton's Radical mind, license refers to the pattern of ecclesiastical self-will, doctrinal stubbornness, self-protecting hypocrisy, and unchecked use of force to accomplish the preceding ends; that is, it refers to all that stands opposed to liberty. This point is clear from Milton's use of the word *license* in his prose, where it refers to irresponsibility through looseness of speech and irresponsibility through self-serving tyrannical government. Milton is not referring to those

---

5. Haller, *The Rise of Puritanism,* 180.
6. Sonnet 12, in *CPMP,* 143 n. 1. Barker, *Puritan Dilemma,* generalizes about the period of the divorce pamphlets and Milton's doctrinal dissent: "It is impossible to fix the time at which this reinterpretation [possibility of salvation extended to all] began to develop in his mind; but it is clear that it was in his defense of the will in divorce that he first came into collision with the uncompromising Puritan attitude towards human nature" (310).

Radicals whose social manners are looser than he himself and other respectable citizens would have liked.

In *The Reason of Church Government*, for example, Milton, announcing his inability to suppress truth that he is impelled to proclaim, points out the Prelates' inability to do little but repress truth and scathe its prophets in order to protect their scandalously usurped sources of "pleasure and commodity" (1:803–4).[7] Liberty, for Milton, means exercising the freedom to teach truth and serve others honestly. Falsehood and selfishness (from having oppressed others) distinguish license from liberty; release, alone, does not. Prelates exercise license; Milton exercises liberty: "For me I have determin'd to lay up as the best treasure, and solace of a good old age, if God voutsafe it me, the honest liberty of free speech from my youth, where I shall think it available in so dear a concernment as the Churches good" (804). The contrasting treasures only underscore the selfishness of the presumed servants as opposed to the selflessness of the real prophet-servant. And as Milton points out in *An Apology* (1642), the Confuter also illustrates looseness, for he "hath licenc't himself to utter contemptuously of those reverend men [the Smectymnuans]," provoking Milton "to doe that over againe which some expect I should excuse as too freely done," that is, speak out loudly in their defense (1:872).

The irresponsibility of self-serving tyranny, as exemplified by the King, is at the heart of *The Tenure of Kings and Magistrates* wherein Milton, complimenting England's direction to date (1649), encourages constancy to that single-minded goal of uprooting tyranny. Envisioning Parliament and the military held up to posterity as examples of virtue, wisdom, and magnanimity for calling their king to account, he describes this "better fortitude" that earns fame not by pursuing fame abroad through military victory, but by daring at home

to execute highest Justice on them that shall by force of Armes endeavor the oppressing and bereaving of religion and thir liberty

7. John N. King, *English Reformation Literature: The Tudor Origins of the Protestant Tradition*, points to the Royal Injunctions' (1547) licensing all to read and interpret Scripture and to Parliament's repeal of all treason and heresy statutes since the time of Edward I as signs that Edward Seymour—Protector-uncle during the reign of Edward VI—"execute[d] the intentions of the radical Protestant faction" (85). With discussion encouraged and censorship lifted, "English printers produced books at the highest rate ever known" before Elizabeth's reign (88). For discussion of this "libertarian policy," see 76–94.

at home: that no unbridled Potentate or Tyrant, but to his sorrow, for the future may presume such high and irresponsible license over mankind, to havock and turn upside-down whole Kingdoms of men as though they were no more in respect of his perverse will than a Nation of Pismires. (3:238)

Here, license means unchecked and unaccountable use of power by a ruler who has so forgotten that the power of ruling comes from God to the people, with whom he has covenanted to lead and to protect their rights, that he handles mutual covenanters as if they were ants. Clearly, what does cause "havock and turn upside-down whole Kingdoms of men" is not raucous, ranting antinomians, but irresponsible, self-licensing tyrants.

Yet this tyrannizing spirit is not restricted to kings or Prelates. It can occur within anyone who reveres the wrong things. After discussing the double tyranny of custom and blind affections in *The Tenure*, Milton differentiates between good and bad men: "For indeed none can love freedom heartilie, but good men; the rest love not freedom, but license; which never hath more scope or more indulgence then under Tyrants" (3:190). Milton shows here the bond that "tyrants" and "bad men" share, and he points up the deceit of evil at court as these "bad men" disguise their base compliances with the name of "Loyalty and Obedience" (3:191). But what is frightening to Milton and what prompts this treatise is that deceit of this sort is not a device of the past. Preachers who had incited the people for seven years against their king now denounced regicide.[8] Milton was aware that since the burdens of Prelatical governance, "dumb" preaching, and the ban against Puritan ministers had been largely lifted, the source of all that misery and spiritual error seemed far less monstrous and guilty. But, Milton refuses to allow reneging Presbyterians to get away with the political and spiritual tyranny—tyranny they themselves once denounced, upon the arrival of worldly convenience (manifested by a Presbyterian Parliament, Westminster Assembly, and a financially successful middle class). Thus, he targets their "license" as a signal of an absence of spiritual substance:

Although sometimes for shame, and when it comes to thir owne grievances, of purse especially, they would seem good Patriots, and side with the better cause, yet when others for the deliverance of thir Countrie, endu'd with fortitude and Heroick vertue . . .

8. Parker, *Biography*, 347–48.

would goe on to remove, not only the calamities and thraldoms of a People, but the roots and causes whence they spring, streight these men [the Presbyterians], and sure helpers at need, as if they hated only the miseries but not the mischiefs, after they have juggl'd and palter'd with the world, bandied and born armes against thir King, devested him, disannointed him, nay curs'd him all over in thir Pulpits and thir Pamphlets, to the ingaging of sincere and real men, beyond what is possible or honest to retreat from, not only turne revolters from those principles, which only could at first move them, but lay the staine of disloyaltie, and worse, on those proceedings, which are the necessary consequences of thir own former actions. (3:191)

The obvious enemy of liberty for revolting Presbyterians had been Royalism—an enemy that they presumed could be easily spotted and combatted only in others. But the matter was not that simple, for the real enemy was and always is Tyranny, which can be closeted even in the self-aggrandizing Puritan Presbyterian. Shawcross explains:

Although the Royalists exhibit these vain loves of custom and self, Milton is talking to those who have alleged a deep-seated antipathy to the Tyrant, those who have seemingly opposed him. The Tyrant—that is, anyone who exerts his will over another without restraint, without relief, and without consultation with the governed—owes his position to custom and to self-centered hope. Men deceive themselves by words—mere words—like *Loyalty* and *Obedience*, but their end is gain for themselves in a *known* world. Men fear tyrants because of their hopes for themselves.[9]

While Milton does aim to attack morality and manners with the term *license*, his target is not the tavern-frequenting, street-dancing segment of English society, but that "courtly" coterie—old or new. Presbyterian Puritans, with whom Milton had originally allied himself, cried "license" not only at Royalists, but also against sectaries to the left of themselves. As things had developed, however, Milton's spiritual sensibility allowed him to minimize his former concern over the alliance between monarchy and popular festivity. By comparison to the "license" of ease and self-service that pitched camp within Presbyterianism, festivity was hardly a genuine spiritual enemy in Milton's eyes and could, therefore, at least be overlooked

9. Shawcross, "Higher Wisdom," in Lieb and Shawcross, eds., *Achievements of the Left Hand*, 144.

if not excused. Any government, church or political, that depends on preserving itself and securing its pleasures by wordiness to obscure its oppressiveness, by slander, by superstition, or by custom— in short, by tyrannical license—is the deadly enemy for Milton and those members in communion with him. Thus, tyrants of any sort who promoted this kind of governing became the focus of Milton's verbal venom, not sometimes shocking Radicals, however embarrassing their proclaimed Gospel-authorized release may have been.

Milton himself was branded as "licentious" for his views on divorce by that new Presbyterian coterie, who presumably espoused liberty on the basis of their recent religio-political platform that advanced them to power. According to William Riley Parker, this fact gives even greater significance to Milton's use of the term *license*:

> The entire first edition of *The Doctrine and Discipline of Divorce*, a printing of perhaps twelve hundred or more copies, was exhausted within five or six months. Since nothing of this sort had happened to the earlier pamphlets . . . , Milton must have been surprised. He was far from pleased, however, when he learned what people were saying. Although "divers learned and judicious men testified their daily approbation of the book," by most of his readers he was "esteemed the deviser of a new and pernicious paradox," "a novelty of licence" and of "libertinism." His central thesis was one easily distorted, and to the casual reader, even to his recent confederates the Presbyterians, he seemed to be advocating "divorce at pleasure." To heresy-hunters of all sorts he became fair game. His views were labelled "licentious, new, and dangerous"; His book was called "lewd"; its anonymous author was lavishly traduced. . . . The "odious inferences" of the vulgar public he had half expected, but he was totally unprepared for the attitude taken by some of the clergy.

Parker notes, in addition, that Milton "was treated as the spokesman for a heretical sect, the Divorcers, in the second edition of Ephraim Pagitt's *Heresiography, or a Description of the Heretics and Sectaries of These Latter Times*" (1645). "Divorcers" were those "that would be quit of their wives for slight occasions" and would "let loose to inordinate lust" the bonds of marriage.[10] To Milton, however, "let[ting] loose to inordinate lust" through the pleasure of noxious verbal wallowing without point or purpose was the sort of antinomian heresy that needed to be expurgated.

10. Parker, *Biography*, 244, 287.

Pagitt's and the typical Presbyterian name-calling over the doctrinal question of divorce paved the way for Milton's affinity with many other Radicals who, in his view, were just as foolishly and irresponsibly labeled one thing (in this case "lewd" or "licentious") when they often were pursuing something else, namely, liberty. They were in the same religio-political boat of being persecuted, or at least denounced, for their spiritual, ecclesiastical, and/or social beliefs by others who were fornicating with ignorance, custom, uniformity, prestige, and worldly goods. The diversity of views among those branded by the Presbyterians as "loose" did not matter. What did was the common enemy that enabled them to unite and focus their energies. Moreover, as they gradually pondered Reform through the indwelling Spirit, their plight enabled them to know and rely on a spiritual communion when ecclesiastical and political ones failed.

Milton calls things as he spiritually sees them: he is about "truth [that] would set them free"; and though his Presbyterian opponents "cry liberty," it is "License they mean." The tyrannical, self-serving, and self-preserving "bad men" always get things backwards; it is the duty of "good men" to set them right. The rhetorical twist with license works to great purpose since it allows Milton to use the precise term as delivered by the malefactor. He takes the traditional meaning of a term like license, as used by the religious and sociopolitical establishment, and transforms it into something so radically new that he can use it against the accusing spiritual enemy (who initiated the attack) for looseness of speech, governance, ministry, or the use of goods. The corollary is the implicit application of the wholesome value (in this case, "liberty"), formerly assumed as the aim of Milton's adversary, to be reassociated where it belongs: with the preaching prophet of the true and right order.

In sum, license refers to the pattern of ecclesiastical self-will, doctrinal stubbornness, compromising hypocrisy, and unchecked use of force to support positions of power. For the Radical Milton, who is bent on turning given things inside out, license actually refers to all that stands opposed to internal and mystical ecclesial liberty. Milton takes this term that, according to things *presumably* right side out, describes those libertine Radicals whose social manners are looser than respectable, orthodox Puritan society would like. Once he has emptied the word of its standard associations and has redefined it as irresponsibility through looseness of speech and irresponsibility through self-serving, tyrannical government, then this new definition implicates the political and religious establishment without excusing the undisciplined antinomian sensuality of certain Ranterist assemblies. When the renovated definition operates, the formerly supposed *un*licentious are guilty. And jarred by the sound of "licentious"—a tag formerly typifying the most despicable and ill-mannered of society, the new guilty are invited to be horrified at their own license—looseness able to do much greater harm than what they regarded as the license of the rabble's social improprieties. The irony is that, spiritually speaking, some of the ill-mannered may exemplify the converse of license taken in the usual sense. Because they refrain from tyrannizing over others' consciences as well as from impeding the free movement of the Spirit, these, ostensibly guilty of license, may in fact be graced with the beginnings of true spiritual liberty and, consequently, may be genuine initiates into real religious Reform and political liberty.

The verbal renovation evident for terms like *separation, schism, heresy,* and *license* is significant for Milton's church, because the transformative pattern, in turning things right side up as God would have them, reveals the spiritual world in which Milton finds his essential church membership and meaning. This verbal pattern is also important because once Milton has this ecclesial center, he formulates teaching for those, still in the flesh, who, "though they be many, yet need not interrupt the *unity of Spirit*"—and who, like Milton himself, see Christ, "the firm root out of which we all grow" (2:556).

This emphasis on political and religious unity among Nonconformists was not a momentary response for a few Reformers on the fringe of the Revolution. Bonding by appreciating diversity, by reverencing the individual conscience, and, for some serious about the spiritual life, by celebrating all of this within a perceived true spiritual communion summarily accomplished the overthrow of Presbyterian tyranny, advancing the runners in the race of Reform to a new stage. Independent and extreme Nonconformists joined together to stave off Presbyterian polity.

Perry Miller terms the situation for Independents as "sadly muddled because the Independent divines, who in speculative matters were at one with their enemies the Presbyterians, were yet forced to argue for toleration of the sects in order to gain allies against the Presbyterians during the battle over church polity." But this need to commune amidst difference and disagreement was nothing new to England in the promotion of Protestantism. As Christopher Hill points out, since England was relatively isolated as a Protestant power on the defense against world Catholicism, "at least one section of Elizabethan and Jacobean governments wished to maintain close links with continental protestants, embarrassingly radical though some of them were."[11]

While one might be unable to distill the real motive among the Independents, that is, whether they were prompted to unify primarily for religious or political reasons, or both, the fact is that their ultimate political and religious positions produced, legitimated, and fostered reverence for pluralism—a position that enables Woodhouse to name Independents as "the party of toleration." Robert S. Paul explains the process that "forced Independent churchmen to move from a position that had been at least sympathetic to uniformity, to an enthusiastic support of religious toleration":

> The Independents always found themselves out-voted in the Assembly, sometimes outmanoevered in Parliament, but never outfought on the field of battle . . . because . . . they attracted those who stood to lose most by the imposition of religious uniformity of any sort. The Radicals in the army may not have agreed about the form of the Church, and the Army debates were to show that they would not agree about the shape of society, but they had been forced to make common cause first in opposition to Archbishop Laud and his priests, and then by discovering that "New Presbyter is but old Priest writ large."[12]

From the ecclesio-religious angle, "as a result of this *marriage de convenance* the Independents moved naturally first to the hope of accommodation, next to the plea for toleration, then to the principle of Liberty of Conscience, and hence eventually to a more inclusive

11. Miller, *New England Mind*, 75; Hill, *Antichrist*, 63.
12. Hill, "John Reeve and the Origins of Muggletonianism," in Hill, Reay, and Lamont, eds., *World of the Muggletonians*, comments: "The distinction we draw today between 'religion' and 'politics' does not apply in the seventeenth century. Religion was concerned with life on earth. . . . So religion was politics" (82). Walzer in *Revolution of Saints* argues that Radical politics was impossible without religion (261–63); Woodhouse, *Puritanism and Liberty*, 17; Paul, *The Assembly of the Lord: Politics and Religion in the Westminster Assembly and the "Grand Debate,"* 122, 59; see also 122–23. Morton in *World of the Ranters* notes: "The sects gained confidence from the outstanding role their members played in the Army, the Presbyterians became increasingly alarmed, and anxious to establish their systems while they still had power to do so" (145).

doctrine of Church." According to Paul, Independents "began to discover unsuspected breadth within their own ecclesiology. . . . By cooperating politically with other sects, and by fighting side by side with them in the same regiments, the Independents learned to respect other Christians' faith and biblical integrity" and to recognize that "other churches might also be true churches and hence to concede that there might be several ways of interpreting the scripture which all professed to revere."[13]

Thus, whether one, following Christopher Hill, labels Milton "a radical" in close touch with "the third culture" or whether one, following Andrew Milner, considers him "an Independent" in socio-economic opposition to Levellers, one must recognize the church communion Milton surely discovered and participated in, resulting from some sort of ecclesial bond between Independents and leftist non-Independents. "These first moves toward an ecclesiology that had room for plural forms of Church" are evident in Milton's constant and increasing commitment toward toleration. Intolerance metamorphoses one into a wolf that rends the garment of Christ's Church. William Walwyn remarked that Thomas Edwards's intolerance was dangerous because it divided Presbyterians from Independents in a way that could only benefit the Royalists: "Whosoever doth, or shall endeavor to perswade the godly and honest Presbyters to abandon, discourage or molest the faithful, helpfulls valiant and assured friends of other judgements (whom Mr. Edwards would have to be out worse then dogs) they are at best, but wolves, or wolves' friends and seek the destruction of all honest people, of what judgements soever."[14]

From the time of Colonel Pride's purge of the Presbyterian element in Parliament in 1648 and thereafter, there was a range of Independents whom it is confusing, if even possible, to categorize. And to attempt to delineate them would serve no purpose here. It is safe to say, however, that there were Independents to the right and others to the left: those to the right wedded other Independent groups and Radical groups mainly for socio-political convenience; those to the left united with other things in mind: for spiritual fellowship and out of sincere reverence for the individual and conscience. If we

13. Paul, *Assembly of the Lord*, 59, 50–51.
14. See the introduction in this volume for more on Hill's Milton vs. Milner's; Paul, *Assembly of the Lord*, 51; Morton, *World of the Ranters*, 35.

are to view Milton as an Independent at all during this period, in which Independency was a viable party opposing Presbyterianism, we can regard Milton as being of the second type. But once in power, as the Commonwealth (1648–1653) and the Protectorate (1654–1660) developed, Independency, too, eventually became intransigent, oppressive, and, hence, despicable as a possible alternate church base for Milton.

8

"Heresie"

"Against the Light" of God's "Secretary"

ary Ann Radzinowicz has pointed out that "Milton never changed his opinion on crucial issues of tolerance and disestablishment." And Joseph Wittreich talks of that "larger unity" (suggested by Milton) that his tracts be gathered under, namely, "liberty—religious, domestic, and civil."[1] The importance of the connection between respect for the individual conscience on the one hand and liberty of the individual and society on the other cannot be overemphasized in bonding together many different kinds of Nonconformists in the battle against the new form of tyranny. It is this emphasis on the individual's conscience and liberty that forms the basis for the increasing atmosphere of interiority and individualization in which Milton's Radical notions of church and worship develop and, in which, as the 1640s turn to the 1650s, he finds spiritual communion almost solely with those to the left even of Independency.[2] Unity with others could only result from a respect for the individ-

---

1. Radzinowicz, *Toward* Samson Agonistes, 146; Wittreich, " 'Crown of Eloquence,' " in Patrides and Waddington, eds., *Age of Milton*, 28.
2. Regina M. Schwartz, "Citation, Authority, and *De Doctrina Christiana*," shows how Milton's absolute authorization of Scripture authorizes himself (and other legitimizing legitimized) absolutely, making Scripture and Spirit contingent upon the individual conscience. The political result of such contingency is that the church and state could be dismantled while each individual's freedom of conscience could be protected (230, 233, 238).

ual's conscience—the fundamental rule for the new ecclesial order, making the internal, invisible church preeminent: "We beleeve the scripture not for the churches saying, but for its own as the word of God, then ought we to beleeve what in our conscience we apprehend the scripture to say, though the visible Church with all her doctors gainsay" (7:251).

What was this conscience that united and divided Protestants, all of whom rallied to the call of Reform? In *The Reason of Church Government* Milton calls conscience God's "Secretary" (1:822), that is, one "entrusted with the secrets or commands of God." Milton's age understood conscience "as a God-given sense which knew the right intuitively; hence it is privy to God's commands and secrets."[3] In his first tract, *Of Reformation,* Milton signals this important aspect of conscience as the ultimate guide on earth while railing against abuse resulting from the bishops' interpretation of "Indifferency" to suit their ends: "What more binding then Conscience? what more free then *indifferency*? cruel then must that *indifferency* needs be, that shall violate the strict necessity of Conscience, merciles, and inhumane that free choyse, and liberty that shall break asunder the bonds of Religion" (1:585). With ironic, taunting surprise Milton seizes on presumably innocuous indifferency to stress the absurdity if it interferes as a nonessential with conscience, which is an essential, for only through "the strict necessity of Conscience" do "the bonds of Religion" exist. In attempting to execute their will, rather than God's, under the guise of indifferency, the Prelates have only tried to give truth the slip. Very early on, then, we find the importance of "free choyse, and liberty" to Milton's theology in his repudiation of the Prelates' "merciles, and inhumane" version of the same.

The church has been given power symbolized by the keys, but evidence of this power, Milton makes clear in *The Reason of Church Government,* comes not from external and internal coercion, but rather from allowing the Spirit to prompt and guide:

> For when the Church without temporal support is able to doe her great works upon the unforc't obedience of men, it argues a divinity about her. But when she thinks to credit and better her spiritual efficacy, and to win her self respect and dread by strutting in the fals visard of wordly autority, tis evident that God is not there; but

3. *CPW* 1:822 n. 159.

rather her apostolick vertu is departed from her, and hath left her key-cold. (1:832–33)

Milton's treatises are replete with cognitive statements about divinity, but not affective ones. Here, in discussing the consistency of approach that should characterize both the Church and the God whom it knows and worships, Milton proclaims gentleness and trust as God's sort of power. God, through his instrument Milton, recommends this unusual disarming manner and method. Also in this tract we find Milton's patience with the multitude—a quality at this early stage that anticipates the pluralism and toleration of Independents and that foreshadows a clear and growing sympathy with Radical sects and Separatists: "If the multitude be rude, the lips of the Preacher must give knowledge, and not ceremonies" (1:828). Shawcross observes, "Milton foresaw the need to educate the masses to understand and accept the truth of the few."[4]

In *Areopagitica* several years later, Milton argues for toleration not for individuals so much as for the larger issue, that "[Truth] and Falshood grapple" (2:561). Truth "needs no policies, nor stratagems, nor licencings"; Milton pleads only that his listeners "give her but room" (2:563). This general principle introduces Milton's position on conscience in this tract: "How many other things might be tolerated in peace and left to conscience, had we but charity, and were it not the chief strong hold of our hypocrisie to be ever judging one another"; "this doubtles is more wholsome, more prudent, and more Christian that many be tolerated, rather then all compell'd" (2:563, 565).

Milton gives his most extensive consideration of conscience and its response to the interaction of the two guides, Scripture and the Spirit, in *A Treatise of Civil Power* (1659), even though his professed audience is magistrates and his announced argument is the unlawfulness of judgment and coercive force by the magistrate in matters of religion (7:254–63). God compels, instead, through "the inward perswasive motions of his spirit and by his ministers: not by the

---

4. Shawcross, "Higher Wisdom," in Lieb and Shawcross, eds., *Achievements of the Left Hand*, 155. Milton decries "planting our faith one while in the old Convocation house, and another while in the Chappell at Westminster; when all the faith and religion that shall be there canoniz'd, is not sufficient without plain convincement, and the charity of patient instruction to supple the least bruise of conscience, to edifie the meanest Christian, who desires to walk in the Spirit, and not in the letter of human trust, for all the number of voices that can be there made" (*CPW* 2:567).

outward compulsions of a magistrate or his officers" (7:262). In fact, as Busher in 1614 points out, "Bishops forcing consciences play the antichrist." In spite of Barker's claim that Milton was concerned in this treatise "not so much with the responsibilities of individual Christians but with the duties of magistrates," the treatise is informed by Milton's spiritual purpose (which has become much more focused, definitive, and vocalized through successive Reformational disenchantments by the time of this treatise's composition). This spiritual orientation, made explicit in the *Christian Doctrine* that was written at the same time, not only allows inclusion of the individual conscience but demands that it receive primary and prominent attention. Through Milton's explicit and implicit attention to the "inward man" and to conscience, this treatise indicates Milton's mature development as he nears his final word in the *Christian Doctrine*.[5]

Sewell, in contrast to Barker, argues another line: while his earlier works are confined to the natural plane, "it is in 1659, when [Milton] came to write *A Treatise of Civil Power* that the supernatural aspect of Gospel Liberty begins to determine the logic of his view." Noting Milton's growth, Sewell explains that although Milton does not yet say that the Mosaic law was abrogated in its entirety, "for the first time Milton begins to speak vigorously of that sweeping away of the 'weak and beggarly rudiments' of the Law, which until the gospel had served instead of man's free conscience." Sewell detects a calm and confident tone evident in the *Christian Doctrine* but lacking in the earlier prose: "The old asperity in argumentation has gone; gone, too, is the old assertive confidence in the citation of scripture." There is no less inward certainty, only now "a quieter confidence."[6]

Milton gives his stricture against the use of outward authority, which appears to be the main business of this seemingly pragmatic treatise: "That for beleef or practise in religion according to this conscientious perswasion no man ought to be punished or molested by any outward force on earth whatsoever" (7:246). But he makes this point by application of his major premise: Scripture-enlightened conscience is the spiritual foundation for this practical laissez-faire method. Milton first provides a definition: "Whence I here mean by conscience or religion, that full perswasion whereby we are assur'd that our beleef and practise, as far as we are able to

5. See Parker, *Biography,* 519; Hill, *Antichrist,* 59; Barker, *Puritan Dilemma,* 248.
6. Sewell, *Milton's* Christian Doctrine, xi, 53, 70, 71.

apprehend and probably make appeer, is according to the will of God & his Holy Spirit within us, which we ought to follow much rather then any law of man, as not only his word every where bids us, but the very dictate of reason tells us" (7:246). Then he explains "why it is unlawfull for the civil magistrate to use force in matters of religion" (7:257): he lacks competence and right.

He lacks competence because what is required of the individual by God through the Scriptures is illuminated by the Spirit within and for that individual only:

> First it cannot be deni'd, being the main foundation of our protes-
> tant religion, that we of these ages, having no other divine rule or
> autoritie from without us warrantable to oneanother as a common
> ground but the holy scripture, and no other within us but the
> illumination of the Holy Spirit so interpreting that scripture as
> warrantable only to our selves and to such whose consciences we
> can so perswade, can have no other ground in matters of religion
> but only from the scriptures. And these being not possible to be
> understood without this divine illumination, which no man can
> know at all times to be in himself, much less to be at any time for
> certain in any other, it follows cleerly, that no man or body of men
> in these times can be the infallible judges or determiners in mat-
> ters of religion to any other mens consciences but thir own. (7:246)[7]

Furthermore, "if apostles had no dominion or constraining power over faith or conscience, much less have ordinary ministers" (7:249). And if the church, through its apostles and ordinary ministers, can-not discern conscience, how much less can civil magistrates who feign success at such a task before proceeding to judge, force, and condemn.

Besides the ability "to judge . . . , though we should grant him able, which is prov'd he is not, . . . as a civil magistrate he hath no right." Conscience belongs under the jurisdiction of another:

> Christ hath a government of his own, sufficient of it self to all his
> ends and purposes in governing his church; but much different
> from that of the civil magistrate; and the difference in this verie

7. Edward Seymour, Protector of King Edward VI, likewise "assumes that truth should be determined by the individual conscience on the basis of scriptural author-ity" (King, *English Reformation Literature,* 84). Socinians maintained "the notions that every man must be ruled by his conscience and that no man is so free from error that he may dictate what others must believe." Such a position meant that "no power existed in human form that could absolutely declare what is truth" (Haller, *Rise of Puritanism,* 197).

thing principally consists, that it governs not by outward force, and that for two reasons. First because it deals only with the inward man and his actions, which are all spiritual and to outward force not lyable: secondly to shew us the divine excellence of his spiritual kingdom, able without worldly force to subdue all the powers and kingdoms of this world, which are upheld by outward force only. (7:257)

Having brought the document to its spiritual climax, Milton elaborates on this spiritual realm housed by the "inward man":

That the inward man is nothing els but the inward part of man, his understanding and his will, and that his actions thence proceeding, yet not simply thence but from the work of divine grace upon them, are the whole matter of religion under the gospel, will appeer planely by considering what that religion is: whence we shall perceive yet more planely that it cannot be forc'd. What euangelic religion is, is told in two words, faith and charitie; or beleef and practise. . . . Both these flow either the one from the understanding, the other from the will, or both jointly from both, once indeed naturally free, but now only as they are regenerat and wrought on by divine grace. . . . Nay our whole practical dutie in religion is containd in charitie, or the love of God and our neighbour, no way to be forc'd, yet the fulfilling of the whole law. . . . If then both our beleef and practise, which comprehend our whole religion, flow from faculties of the inward man, free and unconstrainable of themselves by nature, and our practise not only from faculties endu'd with freedom, but from love and charitie besides, incapable of force . . . how can such religion as this admit of force from man, or force by any way appli'd to such religion, especially under the free offer of grace in the gospel, but it must forthwith frustrate and make of no effect both the religion and the gospel? (7:257–58)

If people eschew giving the individual conscience its rightful preeminence, it is owing to a phobia of its produce, heresy. Milton anticipates this objection by practicing what he has elsewhere preached, the need for educational response: "Some who write of heresie after their own heads, would make it far worse then schism; whenas on the contrarie, schism signifies division, and in the worst sense; heresie, choise only of one opinion before another, which may be without discord" (7:250).[8] Therefore, Presbyterians and Indepen-

8. Recalling this definition of heresy from *A Treatise of Civil Power*, written without question by Milton and at the time of his work on *Christian Doctrine* and *Paradise Lost*, might calm orthodoxy anxiety in readers like Hunter (see also introduction in this volume).

dents can be considered heretics in the literal sense, Milton remarks, as if to force them to reexamine finger pointing before indulging or after having already enjoyed themselves. He schools these ignorant ones in the truth of apostolic tradition: "In apostolic times therfore ere the scripture was written, heresie was a doctrin maintaind against the doctrin by them deliverd: which in these times can be no otherwise defin'd then a doctrin maintained against the light, which we now only have of the scripture." As this finger pointing can only return to them, the branders once again become the branded self-righteous who stand to be condemned according to God's Righteousness unless they see the light:

> Seeing therfore that no man, no synod, no session of men, though calld the church, can judge definitively the sense of scripture to another mans conscience, which is well to be known to be a general maxim of the Protestant religion, it follows planely, that he who holds in religion that beleef or those opinions which to his conscience and utmost understanding appeer with most evidence or probabilitie in the scripture, though to others he seem erroneous, can no more be justly censur'd for a heretic then his censurers; who do but the same thing themselves while they censure him for doing so. (7:250–51)

The root of the problem is authority. Forcing presupposes judging; and judging presupposes the rule of Scripture. The issue is who in the end is to decide what that rule means: visible church, minister, Scripture scholar, or individual believer? Milton's clarity on this point reveals that primacy of interpretation rests with the individual believer: "We ought to beleeve what in our conscience we apprehend the scripture to say, though the visible church with all her doctors gainsay" (7:251). Thus, Milton shows his kinship with that increasing individualism which marked the sects through the midcentury, despite the attempt by the Cromwellian regime during the late 1650s to mute their voice.

One can barely judge one's own conscience much less another's since one cannot know "this divine illumination . . . at all times to be in himself." To support the inscrutability and awesomeness of conscience, Milton retrieves the traditional Calvinist trapping of spiritual nervousness that characterized orthodox theology, sermons, and spirituality of days well before the "settlement" wrought by the Revolution. Milton, however, has reversed its typical direction, using it against orthodoxy and leadership, in a word, against the new establishment that has typically tried to make edgy the problem believers who spurned conversion or discipline. Now the individual was able to be just as sure or unsure of divine illumination. Geoffrey Nuttall describes this shift:

> In the seventeenth century a man's reliance upon his own conscience and his demand for liberty to obey its dictates despite the contrary requirements of authority, were thus neither new nor a Protestant monopoly; but during the hundred years following the death of Mary Tudor, the *common man had risen steadily in power and independence,* until at last lords spiritual and temporal, no less than Pope and King were all fallen before him.[9]

One such common man, standing in this line in the 1650s, is John Reeve, self-proclaimed as one of the two last witnesses prophesied in Revelation (chap. 11), who represents for commoners the currency and prominence of the individual conscience. In *A Remonstrance from the Eternal God to the Parliament and Commonwealth of England,* Reeve makes his plea to Parliament that the people of England be able to "enjoy not only civil liberties, but the liberties of their consciences also towards God": "You and the people, for *liberty of conscience,* did join together as one man and have conquered all ecclesiastical *tyrants* and *monsters* of men. . . . We beseech you let your brethren, the free-born people, enjoy the liberty of their conscience which they have bought at so dear a rate." But on this point and by this time there is no difference in the point that Milton and Reeve are making. Their purpose is spiritual; their focus single-minded: freedom to enjoy conference and commerce with God through the instrument God has created for such use, namely, conscience, without interference. Radzinowicz observes that the last tracts, including *A Treatise of Civil Power* and *The Likeliest Means . . . to Remove Hirelings,* are "bluntly anti-elitist Radical documents. . . . People don't need a learned ministry since free study is a sufficient path to truth." Wilding concurs, citing the doctrine of the inner light, "the belief that God's word is available directly to every man, illuminating his life, his way": "With the inner light, there is no need for bishops, rituals, churches, church hierarchies. . . . Each man can receive the word of God directly, and act as his inner light,

9. Nuttall, *Visible Saints,* 102.

his illuminated conscience, directs him; authorities hence become redundant and restrictive."[10]

The slight, almost constant spiritual edginess (of not knowing at any given moment that one might have slipped or, at any future moment, could slip from divine illumination) leveled all believers to a position of stillness and silence when they might be tempted to judge another. Resistance to that temptation could be interpreted as that first sign of confidence to which true believers were entitled and which would increase so long as pride of spiritual success and its companion self-righteous judgment remained in exile. To speak out against another believer or group of believers was presumptuous:

> But if any man shall pretend, that the scripture judges his conscience for other men, he makes himself greater not only then the church, but also then the scripture, then the consciences of other men; a presumption too high for any mortal; since every true Christian able to give a reason of his faith, hath the word of God before him, the promisd Holy Spirit, and the minde of Christ within him, 1 Cor. 2. 16; a much better and safer guide of conscience, which as far as concerns himself he may more certainly know then any outward rule impos'd upon him by others whom he inwardly neither knows nor can know; at least knows nothing of them more sure then this one thing, that they cannot be his judges in religion. 1 Cor. 2. 15 *the spiritual man judgeth all things, but he himself is judgd of no man.* (7:247)

If there is mortal sin within the theology of the extremely Nonconformist church, it is this self-advancement to the heights from which one presumes to know more than the church, the scriptures, and even God himself, whose message is uniquely and privately revealed only to his "Secretary," Conscience (1:822).

Refraining from judgment implies trust, another aspect of liberty and toleration that Milton shares with the Radical Puritan tradition. We see this trust in Winstanley's acceptance of Ranters, that catchall term for those Radicals at the furthest edge of Nonconformity that surely tested any true believer's trust in conscience. The selfishness shown by their crude reactions to middle-class society, as T. Wilson Hayes notes, "merely universalizes the vileness of private property, reduces the five senses to the bestial level, and denies the socially

10. Reeve, *Remonstrance,* 17, 18; Radzinowicz, *Toward* Samson Agonistes, 163; Wilding, "Regaining the Radical Milton," 127.

acquired characteristics of thinking, observing, reflecting, caring, and nurturing."[11] The adversary was not the Ranters, as Conformist orthodox perception would assume, but rather that spirit (in other words, "Antichrist," [7:247]) which would have lured one to mistrust, judge, and consequently tyrannize over others who dissented in a way that caused practical socio-economic and political problems. Indeed, any system may have its abuses, and any community its abusers whose efforts will go toward sliding convenience and selfishness into acceptance, but the greater principles of freedom and trust and the related condition of nonpersecution far outweigh the alternatives of suspicion and tyranny. We have seen this identical trust and patience above promoted in Milton's *Areopagitica* and *Reason of Church Government*.

Thus, the level of certainty that one can enjoy comes from knowing the self and knowing that others cannot know for the purpose of judging in religion. While Milton is consistent in his assertion of the primacy of Scripture throughout his prose, there is important development in his understanding and use of that authority. Barker maintains that the emphasis on Scripture's authority in the argument of the later pamphlets is greater than it was in the earlier, "for to that [emphasis] has been added the positive assertion that it can be interpreted only according to the divine illumination within the believer." The logical and dangerous conclusion to such a tenet is mental, emotional, spiritual, and ecclesial isolationism. A century earlier, Stephen Gardiner, Bishop of Winchester, observed the beginnings of accenting the sufficiency of an individual's interpretation of Scripture and envisioned the result: "Each one man" becomes "a Church alone." Each person fasts alone and prays alone. And so each person is "alone, alone, alone, mine own self all alone." Gardiner continues his caricature: "And such men lay their hands on their breast and say they spake as their conscience serveth them, or tell how they have prayed for grace and cannot believe the contrary; . . . And thus as they would have it they will have it, and be clearly deaf to any other teaching." Their conviction and confidence were claimed to be based not on the self, but on Scripture. But that does not assuage Gardiner: "There was never any heretic but boasted Scripture." As Milton well knew, isolationism could be ruinous to one's mental, spiritual, and ecclesial health, but it could be checked

11. Hayes, *Winstanley, the Digger*, 173.

by the necessary balance that only Scripture and the continuous awareness of spiritual communion provided within the conscience, God's "rationall temple" (1:758).[12] Milton's position on Scripture and the individual presupposes an intimacy between God and the believer not evident in Gardiner's position.

There are numerous references in Milton's *Christian Doctrine* to the prominent place conscience holds in the faith of the believer. Two will suffice here to show the continuity of Milton's position on the primacy of the individual conscience as the supreme authority on earth for determining God's Word and will: "Every believer is entitled to interpret the scriptures; and by that I mean interpret them for himself. He has the spirit, who guides truth, and he has the mind of Christ. Indeed, no one else can usefully interpret them for him, unless that interpretation coincides with the one he makes for himself and his conscience" (6:583–84). Milton here reiterates the point made in numerous places, especially in *A Treatise of Civil Power* and *The Reason of Church Government,* of the impermissibility of external force used by the visible church or magistracy to tamper with the inner life: "No visible church, then, let alone any magistrate has the right to impose its own interpretations upon the consciences of men as matters of legal obligation, thus demanding implicit faith" (6:584). Milton expected true believers to be thoroughly engaged with Scripture's text and, through the experience of grappling with it, of observing it, and of employing it within their everyday lives, to arrive at a faith that was lively, original, free, and active, rather than mindlessly transmitted. With so careful and involved a reading, they were to be stimulated and raised to the spiritual realm, even to intimacy with God himself.

It cannot and should not be determined whether trust, exercised by reverence for the individual conscience, causes the experience and perception of unity for the Radical church, or whether unity, experienced because of an impinging establishment, prompts the need for and eventual experience of trust. Trust and unity, unity and trust are necessary companions for true spiritual solidarity in

---

12. Barker, *Puritan Dilemma,* 225; J. A. Mueller, *Stephen Gardiner and the Tudor Reaction,* 130, 129; Schwartz, "Citation, Authority," finds authority to be distributed among three sources: interpreter, Scripture, and Spirit (233). I would add church communion (the members of any particular congregation); hence, Milton's recommendation for joining such a society of believers, and his great emphasis on discernment by and discipline within this local church communion.

Christ; hence, Milton's constant, though increasingly more vocal and definitive, assertion of their prominence and potency. Allowed to walk freely hand in hand, trust and unity feed and foster a living, healthy Church as the Body of Christ. If what made the extreme Nonconformists extreme were their emphases on Scripture, trust, spiritual unity, and the obedience to conscience, then in their own view they were merely heeding Christ's commands with all the precision and passion that they believed he intended.

In another sense, then, Milton was not extremist at all, though he may have been radical (that is, faithful to "the root"—to the original aim and contract of Puritan Reform, which claims to be faithful to God's Word and will). Gerrard Winstanley reminds his contemporaries of how far back they must reach to find the measuring device for spiritual Reform: "The Reformation that England now is to endeavor is not to remove 'the Norman Yoke' only and to bring us back to be governed by those Laws that were before William the Conqueror came in as if that were the rule or mark we aim at: No that is not it; but the Reformation is according to the Word of God and that is the pure Law of righteousness before the Fall."[13] If the Reformation is regarded in this way, Milton felt that the purity championed and promised by the novel Presbyterian program was never delivered because these recent English Reformers broke their contract in having second thoughts about deposing and killing their king, in reintroducing ceremonialism and making it mandatory, in preventing gathered assemblies and their prophesyings, in attempting to know and force consciences, and in persecuting heresy (in Milton's sense of different religious belief or opinion). Milton all along understood the essence of Puritanism to be respect for the individual illumined by Scripture and Spirit to choose the way to God. His participation in the labors of the Revolution was based on a personal contract, as Milton viewed things, with the Presbyterians to ensure the preservation of this ideal as well as to keep that promise to God which the gospel involves.

We know how important covenant keeping is to Milton, for *The Tenure* and *Eikonoklastes* use this concept as the basis for the argument that power resides with the people who contract with their ruler to protect them and preserve their liberty. From the time that people realized that absolute power could corrupt absolutely,

13. Aylmer, "Gerrard Winstanley," McGregor and Reay, eds., *Radical Religion*, 104.

they were constrain'd . . . to put conditions and take Oaths from all Kings and Magistrats at thir first instalment to doe impartial justice by Law: who, upon those termes and no other, receav'd Allegeance from the people, that is to say, bond or Covenant to obey them in execution of those Lawes which they the people had themselves made, or assented to. And this ofttimes with express warning, that if the King or Magistrate prov'd unfaithfull to his trust, the people would be disingag'd. (3:200)

Thus, when power from free-born men is "derivative, transferr'd, and committed . . . in trust," it involves "a mutual Covenant or stipulation" between King and people" (3:199, 201, 202, 226). *Eikonoklastes* echoes the same idea, the difference in this case being that Milton defends not only deposition, but its logical conclusion in Charles's case, regicide:

Those . . . Oaths of Allegeance and Supremacy we swore, not to his Person, but as it was invested with his Autority; and his autority was by the People first giv'n him conditionally, in Law and under Law, and under Oath also for the Kingdoms good, and not otherwise: The Oaths then were interchang'd and mutual; stood and fell together. . . . There was no reason why the Kingdom should be furder bound by Oaths to him, then he by his Coronation Oath to us, which he hath every way brok'n. (3:592–93)

Agreement for anyone, even a king (how much more so for any other body of men), is never permanently secure, but always conditional: "As for the Covenant, . . . [it] gives unlimitable exemption to the Kings Person, but gives to all as much defence and preservation as to him, and to him as much as to thir own Persons, and no more; that is to say, in order and subordination to those maine ends for which we live and are a Nation of men joynd in society wither Christian or at least human" (3:593–94).

But this discussion concerns the political covenant. Holding fast applies even more to the spiritual covenant of the gospel, which, Milton states in *The Reason of Church Government*, "is the straitest and the dearest cov'nant can be made between God and man, wee being now his adopted sons, and nothing fitter for us to think on, then to be like him, united to him, and as he pleases to expresse it, to have fellowship with him" (1:837).

While discussing in particular the powers given of God by Christ to people, Milton gives his general theory of power and the limited extent to which power—however initially good, derived, and contracted—is to be respected. As Milton points out in *The Tenure*, this theory comes neither from Milton himself, nor from Parliament, but from the very ground and authority of all religion and Reform, Scripture:

> If such onely be mentioned here [1 Pet. 2. 13 & c.; Rom. 13] as powers to be obeyd, and our submission to them onely requir'd, then doubtless those powers that doe the contrary [terrorize the good, not the evil] are no powers ordain'd of God, and by consequence no obligation laid upon us to obey or not to resist them. . . . Both these apostles [Peter and Paul] whenever they give this precept, express it in termes not *concrete* but *abstract*, as Logicians are wont to speake, that is, they mention the ordinance, the power, the autoritie before the persons that execute it; and what that power is, least we should be deceav'd, they describe exactly. So that *if the power be not such, or the person execute not such power, neither the one nor the other is of God, but of the Devil, and by consequence to bee resisted* [emphasis added in this sentence]. (3:209–11)

Anti-Christianity, wherever it exists in government, church, society, or self, is always "to be resisted" and, of course, automatically nullifies any agreement previously conceived in good faith or believed to be so conceived.

In the areas of God's Word, True Religion as conveyed through it, True Church headed by Christ, and covenant keeping with God as well as with the members of Christ's Body, Milton had not budged. In this world, ordered according to the highest regard for the spiritual, Milton was truly conservative (as was the entire communion of those who had often been viewed as extreme, Radical, or worse); conversely, Prelates, Presbyterians, and many Independents were the truly dangerous "radicals," "extremists," or "anti-Christians" for having strayed so far from center to the very fringe of Christianity.

For an index to Milton's unswerving sense of commitment to God based on the primacy of conscience, one can look back to Savonarola whom, for his steadfastness, Milton regards as a heroic model, which he cites in the *Commonplace Book*, under the topic "LAWS" (1:423). Summoned to Rome after having been threatened with excommunication by Alexander VI if he did not cease preaching, Savonarola did not cease and did not go but rather hoped for the order to come that he might cite Scripture: "It is necessary to obey God rather than men." The parable referred to by Milton, which Savonarola uses to illustrate his conviction and determination to his fellow monks, Dominico and Silvestro, comes from *Oracolo della Renovatione della*

Chiesa (Sermon on the Renewing of the Church) delivered on February 17, 1496. The *Yale Milton* summarizes as follows: "The owner of a vineyard is duped by rascals into believing that his good son had turned into an evil doer. When the father sends for the son, he refuses to come, knowing that the vineyard will be despoiled by the villains in his absence. Certainly, Savonarola concluded, 'the son acted most prudently, not against, but according to, the will of the father.'" Savonarola had acted just so in refusing to cease preaching and leave the city, for his departure would have meant bodily and spiritual ruin for the people.[14]

In referring to the parable and in agreeing with Savonarola's stated moral, Milton allows him to speak for himself: "By [it] he shows 'that one should obey the spirit rather than the letter of the law'" (1:423).[15] Both the man and message stand as a kind of picture and poem, serving for Milton as an ecclesial emblem of faithfulness to a Father, who cannot be duped and is not suspicious—a Father who has entrusted his vineyard to preaching prophets. A man of principle and conviction (however the labels, faces, and accusations shift), Milton too would "obey the spirit of the law" and refuse to swerve from his covenant with God and from his commitment to tend his flock (wherever it grazed) through his writings. He too would act "most prudently, not against, but according to the will of the father." Such zeal in the face of any establishment that is not only unzealous, but often downright spiritually apathetic or indolent clearly seems and is extreme. The uncompromising passion about God's Word and will is what the establishment (Prelatical, Presbyterian, or Independent) lacks, and what so-called Radicals like Milton thrive upon. Milton's only other reference to Savonarola occurs in *Animadversions:* "Most true it is what *Savonarola* complaines, that while hee endeavour'd to reform the Church, his greatest enemies were still these lukewarm ones" (1:683).[16]

---

14. See Ruth Mohl, *John Milton and His* Commonplace Book, the section headed "Laws," 223–27, which notes Milton's emphasis on the spirit of the law. *CPW* 1:423 n. 1. See Mohl, *Milton and* Commonplace Book: "Shortly after making this entry, in 1639 or 1640, Milton entered into public controversy in the early anti-Prelatical tracts of 1641 and 1642; it is interesting to note that in *Animadversions* of 1641 he introduces a parable similar to that of Savonarola" (224). The story is of a "good gardener" who "refuses to yield up his garden to the intruder" who wishes (like the Prelates) to take over the garden, though knowing nothing about gardening (224–25).

15. See Mohl, *Milton and* Commonplace Book, 226–27.

16. For this observation see *CPW* 1:423, n. 1. In *Animadversions*, as Mohl in *Milton*

The Savonarola entry, made into the *Commonplace Book* in 1639–1640, is significant because the origin as well as the development of Milton's ecclesiology is able to be distilled from his treatises. Like Wyclif, whom Milton cites numerous times in the prose of this same earlier period, Savonarola is a heroic forefather in the single long-distance race of Reform. Examining the range of Milton's writing, one realizes that Savonarola (like Wyclif) provided Milton with spiritual fellowship and with a spiritual reference point from which he never deviated. At the heart of Milton's spirituality and ecclesial identity, Milton had not changed at all.

Original covenanting aimed to protect the sacred dignity and freedom of every individual whose soul was "his rationall temple" (1:758). A noble ideal, for certain, but there had been neither time nor practice to test out and refine its consequences. Haller suggests that this "active individual religious experience" was evident at the outset of Puritan Reform and that the state itself was indirectly responsible for it. Analyzing what I consider to be the keystone for the entire Radical communion in England, Haller writes:

> [The Puritan reformers] were far from approving in principle the tolerance by which they profited. Their ideal was uniformity based upon the will of a godly civil state. They would have the state set up presbyterianism first and trust the preachers to render the people godly afterwards. As it was, the condition imposed upon them by the policy of the government was that they begin by trying to convert the people and trust in God to bring about presbyterian reform in his own time. The immediate result was that, in the hope of establishing ultimately their cherished scheme of uniformity, they spent two generations preaching a doctrine and a way of life which promoted active individual religious experience and expression, promoted it much faster than means could be found to control or direct it. . . . The ultimate effect, as later the reformers learned to their sorrow, was to encourage in their followers the habit of going each his own way toward heaven and the notion that it was every man's native right to save himself or not in his own way, without interference from anybody.[17]

and Commonplace Book explains, at this point "Milton is taking to task Bishop Hall and other bishops for just such a middle-of-the-road position" (225).

17. Haller, *Rise of Puritanism*, 173. Shawcross analyzes apparent but insubstantial bonding between those claiming to be ready for change and those who really are: "The liberal majority always seem to see the other man's point—largely because it is to their advantage to do so—but draw back in time to make sure that nothing really changes. Indeed, the most subversive of all political groups is that which outwardly

In the end, the new establishment tried to restrain what it had released. And what it had released for free development, namely, Radical Evangelical existence, Milton remained committed to. "New presbyters" had "prov'd unfaithful to [their] trust," and he, though in spiritual covenant and communion with others, "would be disengaged" from the new orthodoxy and establishment. What began as a blessed movement all too soon became bourgeois in England. Milton's treatises, as we have seen, recognize this progressive moral degeneration and convey directly proportional disappointment with one ecclesia as his hopes began to build for another—a church that was mainly spiritual, international, and inward.

The strife continued. The fear of individuality would be endless. By 1652 another burgeoning establishment, Independency, was becoming the opposition to gospel freedom and Reform. Independents, too, would eventually urge the church to institutionalize, centralize, uniformalize. Parker provides the following summary:

> Proposals had been made by certain Independent ministers with a design to perpetuating an Established Church with a state-paid and state-controlled clergy. The idea had been closely connected with the hue and cry over the [heretical] Racovian Catechism, and Milton feared that Parliament, frightened as it was by an apparent excess of toleration might favour such proposals. He urged Cromwell, therefore, to throw the weight of his personal prestige on the side of religious liberty.[18]

Beyond doctrinal formulation was the seemingly perpetual rub of the minister's recompense that, try as he might to overcome the temptation to greed and gratification, all too frequently led to collusion with the civil magistrate with each trying to further his own interests by way of the other—and always at the expense (spiritual as well as material) of the multitude that needed tending. "Presbyterians and Independents alike had become a hireling crew. The situation was so bad that 'now commonly he who desires to be a

---

agrees but essentially—perhaps unconsciously—rejects the basic philosophy of the group of which it somehow has become a part. But the adherents of reformative action are so gratified to have support for their ideas—particularly from those who might otherwise not be thought of as swelling their numbers—that they do not look into the essential ideology of this 'liberal majority' and thus do not recognize that the impending withdrawal of support will go far to subvert the action deemed necessary" (145).

18. Parker, *Biography,* 413.

minister looks not at the work but at the wages.' "[19] But mammon is only the external manifestation of a massive cankerous inner, spiritual malaise that Milton probes in *The Likeliest Means to Remove Hirelings out of the Church Wherein is also discourc'd of Tithes, Church-fees, Church-revenues* (1659). His summary analysis targets the core of the problem and reveals the fact that little seemed new under the sun:

> Neither speak I this in contempt of learning or the ministry, but hating the common cheats of both; hating that they who have preachd out bishops, prelats and canonists, should, in what serves thir own ends, retain thir fals opinions, thir Pharisaical leaven, thir avarice and closely thir ambition, thir pluralities, thir nonresidences, thir odious fees, and use thir legal and Popish arguments for tithes: that Independents should take that name, as they may justly from the true freedom of Christian doctrin and church-discipline subject to no superior judge but God only, and seek to be Dependents on the magistrate for thir maintenance; which two things, independence and state-hire in religion, can never consist long or certainly together. For magistrates at one time or other, not like these at present our patrons of Christian libertie, will pay none but such whom by thir committies of examination, they find conformable to their interest and opinions: and hirelings will soone frame themselves to that interest and those opinions which they see best pleasing to thir paymasters; and to seem right themselves, will force others as to the truth. (7:318–19)[20]

By "forc[ing] others as to the truth," these Independents seek to reinforce their self-righteousness and the need for their system by manufacturing a mimicking majority consisting of theological and ecclesiastical automatons who, like their makers, are without spiritual substance as well as the critical eyes and voices to safeguard it. There were, unfortunately, even "new[er] forcers of conscience" in 1659, thus making New Independent but Old Presbyterian writ almost the same. Barker gives a concise summary of the ecclesiastical and doctrinal results of this transfer of power:

> They were now occupying the defensive position surrendered by the presbyterians, and their recommendations were based only on a more liberal interpretation of the principles expressed in the *Westminster Confession*. They believed that the magistrate must be a nursing father to the church; and consequently proposed the es-

19. Ibid., 531.
20. The link between tithes, university learning, and ministerial elitism is treated extensively in Part 3.

tablishment of congregationalism as the national discipline, with a ministry supported by tithes or some other civil maintenance, and commissioners appointed by parliament to approve or dismiss ministers. And though they denied that churches themselves could exercise material power, they proposed toleration outside the establishment only for such as accepted the fundamentals of Christian religion—the doctrine of the Trinity, the Incarnation, justification by faith, the necessity of forsaking sin, the Resurrection, the Scripture as the only certain revelation of the divine will, and the necessity of worship.[21]

These developments would be difficult enough to observe within a segment of church and society to which one did not belong; but they could only be torturous for Milton who affiliated with Independency and had put his hopes for true religion, the individual conscience, and liberty in it. As Hughes points out, "Milton regretted the concessions which the Moderate Independents . . . at the Savoy, were willing to make to the principle of an established church"— especially problematic for Cromwell's latter Protectorate, in Milton's view, because of a tax-supported salaried clergy.[22]

With the Restoration, mutual fidelity between God and his people was all but impossible unless it were observed underground or inward. If one looks to the external, established church and compares the articles of 1627 with those of 1662 one can monitor the absence of change. One notices the restrictiveness of the pre–Revolutionary Conformist Church in John Cosin's *Articles to be Inquired of by The Churchwardens And Swornmen of Every Parish within the Archdeaconry of the East Riding in York in the Ordinary Visitation of the Archdeacon There*, Anno 1627 (from chapter 2):

> "Concerning the Clergy, the Service, the Sacraments,
> and other Rites of the Church"
>
> 2. Whether is he [parson, vicar, or minister] a graduate of one of the Universities of this Kingdom, or not?
> 3. Is he a preacher licensed either by the bishop, or by one of the Universities of this realm, under their writing and seal? . . .
> 8. When there is any sermon together with the service, doth it come in orderly and in due place, namely, after the reading of the gospel and the profession of the Christian faith in the last service, as is prescribed in the book? . . .

21. Barker, *Puritan Dilemma*, 221–22; see also 172 and 252 for the restrictiveness of the center party of Puritanism in 1659.

22. *CPMP*, 878 n.54. For Milton's disenchantment with Cromwell, see Parker, *Biography*, 468.

12. Doth he add unto the public prayers and service of the Church, any prayers of his own, or other men's framing? Doth he substitute of his own head and appoint any other psalms, hymns, or lessons, in the place of those which are appointed by law? . . .

46. Doth he appoint, hold, and uphold, any fasts, prophecies or exercises? Hath he been present at any conventicles or meetings of silenced and suspended ministers, or others, to use any repeatings or preachings whatsoever, to deprave the doctrine and discipline established, or to use any other form of prayer than what is enjoined in the churchbook?

One notices this same restrictiveness at the time of the Restoration. Only by that time, because of recent Revolutionary turmoil, most easily imputed to the Radicals, suppression and repression became even more essential and monstrous. Cosin's *Articles of Visitation and Inquiry 1662 addressed to the Ministers, Church Wardens, and Sidemen of every parish within the Diocese of Durham* reveal that the same spirit of obsessive control through uniformity, which desperately feared diversity, had merely slept awhile to gain strength. The first article, "Concerning the Parishioners," will suffice to illustrate the sort of ecclesia that returned to power:

1. Is there in your parish any person, who is commonly known or reputed to be an heretic or schismatic? Any papist, presbyterian, familist, anabaptist, independent, quaker, or other sectary, that refuses to come unto the public assemblies, prayers, or services of the Church, or that makes profession of any other religion, than what is established in the Church of England? and, if there be any such, what are their names?[23]

There is a crucial linguistic transformation that occurs, which clues us to Milton's new ecclesia. What we saw occurring with the term *separation* occurs with the terms *schism, license,* and *heresy.* There are three movements: embarrassed rejection of a term, angry counter application of it, and reappropriation of the metamorphosed term where it morally fits. After the initial and immediate repudiation of the alleging and traditionally defined label, there is then the counterapplication based on that overturned world now righted as Luke (Acts 17:6–7), Denne, Milton, and others in their company saw that God had fashioned it. Finally, there is a reassignment of that

23. John Cosin, *Works* 32:6–9, 15 and 34:513–14.

inverted term, whose renovation is symbolized by its overhauled image, to any individual or community whose identity as Church must not only be spiritual, but separate and schismatic. Milton's turning of phrase that we witnessed in *An Apology* (the images of lightness and laying on of hands), on closer examination, then, is neither awkward nor gamesome but the required regimen for any-one who must do the same for concepts of church, worship, holi-ness, clergy, Sacrament, and Scripture. Milton provides the same sort of exercise with accusations of license and heresy, whereby his accusers ultimately become guilty of the very spiritual-ecclesiastical respective crime attributed, at their own instigating, to the more innocent Radical(s).

The identity of church that emerges for Milton and those in his spiritual communion did indeed mean being schismatic, but truly schismatic, that is, ever-cutting because one "spoke the truth against . . . high abominations and cruelties in the Church" and because one aimed at "the removal of criminous Hierarchy" (1:786)—and eventually also of "criminous" Presbyterianism and Independency, both of which soon lost sight of the root of the Reformation. "Schis-matick" for the Radicals *was* an appropriate term, but the cutting that they performed made them not poor tailors, but excellent sur-geons—well-schooled experts not irresponsibly rending a garment but very conscientiously and precisely removing all malignancy. The maturing ecclesial identity of Milton's Radical spiritual broth-erhood was primarily schismatical. But to be so was an attribute of honor to be welcomed and cherished. It dignified while it identified. "Schism," in Milton's new *surgically* metaphoric sense, was the only way of purifying and preserving what belonged to God most of all, his Church. To be skillful at this sort of schism required, of course, knowledge and training, but *this* education was available to *anyone* through Scripture and at home. The risky linear (progressive) ap-proach to Truth comprised this rigorous course of study, which au-gured improvement as it taught what and how to cut, so long as all this learning were exchanged and tested against other colleagues' and then used.

Those participating in the True Church with Paul, Silvus, Jason (Acts 17), and James (James 1:27; 4:4) in the seventeenth century, having turned the world not only upside down but right side out, see only the spirit of Christ. Those like Wyclif, Hus, Savonarola, Winstanley, Saltmarsh, Denne, and Milton will also have "set that in the bottom which others make the top of the building, and set that upon the roof which others lay for a foundation," as Denne had said. But to appear to have done so is nothing else than to be one who, in Milton's words, "*sees . . . the firm root*, out of which we all grow" (2:556; emphasis added).

III

The Visible Church

Reformed and Resignified

PREFACE TO PART III

P revious chapters have described a many-sided Milton: the Reformer with Wyclif, Luther, Calvin, Perkins, and Ames; the antiseptic Separationist with Chidley, Dell, and Colonel Hutchinson; the "Schismatick"—in his transformed sense, that is, surgically cutting away diseased tissue (1:783–86, 2:555)—with Lollards, Hussites, Brownists, Familists, and Adamites; and the Milton who, consequently and summarily, stands as Uniate with "a unanimous multitude of good Protestants" (1:788) in pursuit of radical (as in root) gospel truth. These several portraits complement rather than contradict one another as they come together in Milton—in the man, in his ecclesiastical doctrine, and in the experience of ecclesia as recorded throughout his writings.

In Part II, I discussed the ecclesial identity of a body of believers that had emerged during Milton's lifetime with greater definition, energy, voice, and inner strength than ever before. This segment of the church (and society) was regarded as extremist, leftist, ultra-Nonconformist, and Radical. I have shown the development of the identity of this church mainly in terms of opposition it faced from Conformist or less Nonconformist Reformers. In Part III, I would like to consider the concrete expressions of the Radical church evident in Milton, to observe the ways in which Milton's ecclesial identity took flesh within the Radical communion of believers.

As documented in previous chapters, Morton, Hill, McGregor, Reay, Lamont, Manning, Walzer, and others have recently researched the many Radical groups from a historical perspective. Hughes treated the influence of Milton's revolutionary religious and ecclesiastical posture on his Radical politics. Hill, using Milton's prose and poetry, has attempted to show Milton's place within the Radical, populist segment of society. Wilding, too, uses Milton's writing to discover the real, historical Milton, citing the need not to search for new documents to fill in the gaps, but to sift the already available material with history to find the true, Radical Milton. Berry applies the observations on individualism made by Bush, Barker, Miller, and Parker to his updated reading of Milton. Desai, Pecheux, and Schultz all employ church concepts (received or Miltonic) to serve their reading of Milton's poetry. But, as I pointed out early on, no one has thoroughly examined the doctrine of church that Milton shares with those viewed as extremist or schismatic when Milton was writing to and for them as ecclesia—not only in his *Christian Doctrine*, but also in his earlier, not exclusively doctrinal prose, especially *The Reason of Church Government*. And this omission has sometimes been the negative cause of erroneous conclusions, notably those arrived at by [M. M.] Ross who faults Milton for ignoring the visible church and for draining the Mystical Body of significance by having removed the Eucharist from the center of things to satisfy a growing secular impulse and ethical purpose. I shall argue just the opposite: that Milton emphasizes the Mystical Body *and* attends quite systematically to the visible church. Since Ross's reading exemplifies erring by omission, it can serve as a point of reference for measuring how far one can wander from Milton's actual doctrine; hence the elaboration on Ross.

In spite of noting Milton's acknowledgment of " 'the mutual fellowship of the members of Christ's body among themselves' in the invisible church," Ross regrets that "the church is *utterly* invisible, as is the fellowship it is said to contain. And the faithful enter this invisible fellowship, if at all, by equally invisible means."[1] This is simply wrong. The invisible, spiritual relationship of the church members to Christ as well as to one another is, indeed, primary for Milton, but he in no way sells the visible dimension short.[2] Chapters 29 through 32 of book 1 of the *Christian Doctrine* signal Milton's regard for the visible and external. A closer reading will show there is much to be said for the visible and external, even though "it is not the visible church but the hearts of believers which, since Christ's ascension, have continually constituted the *pillar* and *ground of truth*" and *"the real house and church of the living God,* I Tim. iii. 15" (6:585). In the entire process of conversion to the primacy of the interiorized

1. Ross, *Poetry and Dogma*, 189.
2. See the introduction, esp. 5–6; chap. 2, "Milton's Ecclesiology"; and chap. 3, " 'That Mystic Body' and 'Societ[ies] of Persons,' " in this volume.

Word for an invisible, spiritual church, one begins with the visible and external:

> We believe in the scriptures in a general and overall way first of all, and we do so because of the authority either of the visible church or of the manuscripts. Later we believe in the church, in those very manuscripts, and in particular sections of them, because of the authority and internal consistency of the whole scripture. Finally we believe in the whole of scripture because of that Spirit which inwardly persuades every believer. (6:589–90)

It is by visibility, then, that a member is first conveyed to invisible, spiritual communion, realizing, for the first time, two very important maxims: (1) that "on the evidence of scripture itself, all things are eventually to be referred to the Spirit and the unwritten word," and (2) that "each believer is ruled by the Spirit of God" (6:590). Thus, nothing can be further from Milton's ecclesiological truth than Ross's thinking: that "the old lines of communication between the visible and the invisible are discarded," and that "the Mystical Body is retained as a thoroughly bodiless concept," with "Milton's . . . assertive individualism threaten[ing] the concept itself."[3] Besides recognizing that it is the visible church whose authority, as a rule, is responsible for aiding believer's acclamation of the Scriptures (6:589–90), Milton exhorts "every believer to join himself, if possible, to a correctly instituted church" (6:568), so that the respective visible particular church can be "organized for the purpose of promoting mutual edification and the communion of saints" (6:593). Milton regards the external and visible as important enough to warrant the following directives in "the uniting bond of any particular church," which he calls "CHURCH DISCIPLINE." To the community he advises: "It is a prudent and pious custom to make a solemn renewal of the covenant when establishing any particular church" (6:607). And to the individual he advises corresponding visible observance for entry into an actual, defined church society: "Similarly, when any individual joins a particular church he should, as if he were entering into a covenant, make a solemn promise to God and to his church that he will, insofar as he is able, carry out every office, both towards God and towards that church, which may concern either his own edification or that of his fellows" (6:608).

3. Ross, *Poetry and Dogma*, 189.

In overlooking the emphasis on the suitable place of the "visible," "particular," "external," dimension in at least four of Milton's chapters in book 1 of the *Christian Doctrine,* Ross himself has rather hastily untied the very knot between God and humanity, spirit and flesh, the invisible and the visible, which he claims Milton has undone. Milton's teaching in his successive, thematically well-integrated chapters ("Of the Visible Church," "Of the Holy Scripture," "Of Particular Churches," and "Of Church Discipline") is unarguable proof that the Mystical Body in Milton is anything but "a thoroughly bodiless concept" and that the lines of communication between the invisible and visible church, while certainly refurbished, are anything but "discarded." They are open and very evident.[4]

Unlike Ross, I would suggest that the ways Milton's church doctrine and the Radicals' church doctrine are put into practice solidly agree with each other, primarily because both are centered on the teaching of the Mystical Body, which is reinforced and recalled again and again through the intimate, vital connection between the invisible and visible church. The community of membership as ecclesia is not exhaustively explained by its spiritual invisibility. Visibility plays an important part and not only as a vehicle for introducing one to the Scriptures or for sustaining the organization of a particular group so that it can continue to be edified or disciplined. The visible aspect of church must be more than pragmatically causative. It must be pragmatically consequential as well. For Milton, visibility, as it refers to the concrete expression of spiritual membership in the invisible Body of Christ, is at least as important as being numbered among a particular church. In other words, visibility is to be a viable principle of church doctrine that must be exercised regularly; it must be dynamic rather than static; and it must be expressive of the living flesh of that spiritual community, not only emblematic of its particular solemn covenant (6:607–8). A critical question for the progress of the Reformation in the mid-seventeenth century is the means whereby the Radical spiritual communion (both ecumenical, yet separated) to which Milton belonged made its passionate invisible relationship with its Spouse visible. Milton's ecclesiastical, political, and theological tracts supply a clear and systematic answer to this fundamental question.

4. See bk. 1, chaps. 24, 25, and 29–33; bk. 2, chaps. 3 and 4 (*CPW* 6:498–514, 563–633, 656–83).

The foundation of the specific attributes shared by those within a Radical ecclesia is the reclaimed and proclaimed dignity of the individual. Successful promulgation of this particular doctrine—lost for too long beneath layers of ecclesiastical machinery, elitism, abusiveness, and self-service—would smooth the way for the Reformed, True Church to operate. Visibly, practically speaking, this Church would break through many of the old ecclesial barriers and venture into new and promising land. It would dissolve the distinction between "clerical" and "laick," for example. It would disempower the network of tithes, university, and caste that perpetuated itself and guarded the corner it claimed to have on spiritual knowledge and ecclesiastical governance. It would, instead, initiate a new type of ministry, foster another sort of sacramentality, and find a corresponding fitting church for religious intercourse between God and his people. In addition, it would institute a ceremonialism whose "works" would promote a harmony between the inner, spiritual life and the daily goings-on that would concretely express one's saintly, renovated status by attending to the practical and spiritual needs of others in one's particular religious society. Most of all, this Radical ecclesia would promote, protect, and preserve this "charity" as the source and sign of both the invisible and visible modes of church. In accomplishing these goals, Milton and the rest of the Radical Reformers believed they gave dynamic and expressive, rather than static and solely emblematic, visibility to their spiritual, invisible brotherhood. In this part I shall examine how each of these goals was to be pursued and achieved if their true ecclesia were to keep good Reformist pace to the finish line.

9

"Regenerated by God"

The Dignity of the Individual Believer

everence for the individual believer and his conscience is the practical expression of the foundation of Radical spirituality, namely, the dignity and holiness of each human being—both naturally, since all people "were borne free" (*The Tenure* 3:198), as well as supernaturally through adoption (*Christian Doctrine* 6:495–97), for as chosen, they are God's "anointed" (*Eikonoklastes* 3:586).[1]

Such dignity derives from the originally created condition of "being the image and resemblance of God himself" (3:198), which, after the Fall, needed refurbishing through Christ's redemption. One must recognize the importance of the tenet of universal dignity and holiness if one is to appreciate the actual church tradition that Milton embraced and within which he found more satisfying communion than he found anywhere else. Part II explained that *this* church, spiritually guided and encouraged by the sixteenth-century Reformers, existed before Luther nailed his theses in 1517 in Wittenberg; it existed with Wyclif, Hus, and their followers, originating, happily for Milton, in England.[2] The proper lineage of Milton's application

1. Sacred anointing, cited in the Scriptures by those aiming to defend rulers as being above the law and the people, refers to the annealed condition of all God's chosen people. Milton explains this common gift in *Eikonoklastes*: When "God himself says to Kings, *Touch not mine anointed*," he means "his chos'n people, as is evident in that Psalme [105, 15]" (3:586–87). Anointing is not for vertical discrimination among humans, but for horizontally setting apart the chosen community from the rest of humankind.

2. See chap. 5, "To 'Stand Separated,'" in this volume.

of the gospel's renovative power, making all people free at birth, stems from the time of the Peasants' Revolt in 1381 and has served as a "traditional *lower-class* reading of the Bible."[3] Thus, the origins of opposition to and separation from Prelacy, or Presbyterianism, or Independency, or anything that denies or denigrates the sacred dignity of the redeemed and renovated human person had an older and a native history with which Milton continually felt it necessary to challenge opponents and encourage supporters.

"MAN'S RESTORATION," Milton explains, "is the act by which man freed from sin and death by God the Father through Jesus Christ, is raised to a far more excellent state of grace and glory than that from which he fell" (6:415). The restoration consists of two components: redemption, "THAT ACT BY WHICH CHRIST, SENT IN THE FULLNESS OF TIME, REDEEMED ALL BELIEVERS AT THE PRICE OF HIS OWN BLOOD," and renovation, "by [which man] is BROUGHT TO A STATE OF GRACE AFTER BEING CURSED AND SUBJECTED TO GOD'S ANGER" (6:415, 453). "Renovation takes place either naturally or supernaturally" (6:453)— that is, either by invitation to fallen humanity for salvation and proper worship or by restoration of the "natural faculties of faultless understanding and of free will more completely than before. But what is more, it also makes the inner man like new and infuses by divine means new and supernatural faculties into the minds of those who are made new." This process of supernatural renovation is called "REGENERATION and INGRAFTING IN CHRIST" (6:461).[4]

The idea of the holiness and dignity of every believer, stressed by Milton and other Radicals as *a*, if not *the*, fundamental doctrine of their ecclesia, derives from their belief in the regeneration of the inner man, a tenet expressed by Milton in his *Christian Doctrine:* "REGENERATION means that THE OLD MAN IS DESTROYED AND THAT THE INNER MAN IS REGENERATED BY GOD THROUGH THE WORD AND THE SPIRIT SO THAT HIS WHOLE MIND IS RESTORED TO THE IMAGE OF GOD, AS IF HE WERE A NEW CREATURE. MOREOVER THE WHOLE MAN,

---

3. Hill, *English Revolution*, 100. See also Hill, "Why Bother about the Muggletonians?" in Hill, Reay, and Lamont, eds., *World of Muggletonians:* "Much of [the Muggletonians' theology] derived from commonplaces of the radical heretical milieu, which can be traced from Lollards via Familists and Anabaptists to Baptists, Seekers, Socinians, Ranters, and Quakers. Many aspects of this traditional popular theology were accepted by John Milton and other radical intellectuals" (20).

4. See chap. 3, "'That Mystic Body' and 'Societ[ies] of Persons,'" where I have discussed the effects of Ingrafting in Christ, one of which enables the elect, though not without flaws, to be regarded as perfect because of their incorporation into Christ.

BOTH SOUL AND BODY, IS SANCTIFIED TO GOD'S SERVICE AND TO GOOD WORKS" (6:521).[5] In talking of universal dignity, I have coupled universal holiness with it. The intimacy of the relationship is called for, not so much because it is thematically suitable or theologically plausible, but because Milton intends it within his discussion of terms that may be used interchangeably: "Thus regeneration is sometimes called sanctification, and indeed this is the right name for it, *regeneration* itself being merely a metaphorical term" (6:464).

With this renovated internal condition comes a renovated external one: Liberty, "the first result of adoption," which enabled "the descendants of Abraham, even under the law of servitude" to refuse "to be bound even by ceremonies of religion, whenever charity demanded that they should do otherwise. . . . But liberty, like adoption, has appeared in a much clearer light since the coming of Christ. That is why it is called Christian liberty" (6:496). Devoting an entire lengthy chapter later to this doctrine, Milton elaborates: "CHRISTIAN LIBERTY means that CHRIST OUR LIBERATOR FREES US FROM THE SLAVERY OF SIN AND THUS FROM THE RULE OF THE LAW AND OF MEN, AS IF WE WERE EMANCIPATED SLAVES. HE DOES THIS SO THAT, BEING MADE SONS INSTEAD OF SERVANTS AND GROWN MEN INSTEAD OF BOYS, WE MAY SERVE GOD IN CHARITY THROUGH THE GUIDANCE OF THE SPIRIT OF TRUTH" (6:537). The effects of this holiness or dignity are conveyed through images that suggest the completion of growth, the fulfillment of awaited development, and the arrival of the Spirit.

In this new age, the Spirit will govern the meaning of what has been written as well as the message of what still needs to be spoken. This sort of divine communication, called the Everlasting Gospel, was one of the most prized Radical doctrines since it prevented any human or institution from interfering with the Word spoken purely

5. See pp. 90–95 in this volume. Cf. Luther's "Concerning Christian Liberty," in *Luther's Primary Works:* "Man is composed of a twofold nature, a spiritual and a bodily. As regards the spiritual nature, which they name the soul, he is called the spiritual, inward, new man. . . . We first approach the subject of the inward man, that we may see by what means a man becomes justified, free, and a true Christian; that is a spiritual, new, and inward man" (256). Camille Adkins argues the importance of the idea in Blake and in Milton that "redemption of the tarnished image of the godhead depends upon the individual's recognition of the divine in himself" and explains that, in contrast to Satan, Adam "will acknowledge the image of God in himself (by recognizing his relation to the Christ) and will gain access to the 'paradise within,'" ("Adam's Room: Incarnation of the Divine Image in *Paradise Lost* and *Jerusalem,*" 3).

and exclusively by the Spirit to the individual.[6] This doctrine is evident in Milton as a by-product of Christian liberty: "Once the gospel, the new covenant through faith in Christ, is introduced, then all the old covenant, in other words the entire Mosaic law, is abolished" (6:525–26). The status of such absolute freedom, which Milton declares that believers enjoy, likens Milton more to Winstanley, Reeve, Muggleton, even Clark, Coppe, and Saltmarsh, than to Calvin and Luther on the point of Christian liberty and its ramifications. Milton's Magisterial unorthodoxy appears on two accounts: first, Luther, Calvin, and other mainline Reformers "generally hold that Christ's sacrifice abolished the ceremonial and civil portions of the Mosaic law but left the moral part as useful for self examination"; additionally, "the gift of Christian liberty . . . is limited to the spiritual life of believers, and has no bearing on civil and political matters." The Yale note concludes: "Milton, who arrived at his heterodox doctrine between 1643 and 1645 . . . argues that Christ's sacrifice abrogated the total Mosaic law, moral as well as ceremonial and civil, and bestowed on believers a complete Christian liberty that frees them from the judgments of men and from civil or ecclesiastical coercion in religious matters."[7] This unorthodoxy is fundamental to Milton's Christian humanism as well as to his theory of toleration.

Reaffirming holiness and dignity was necessary to reclaim a posture that would allow all people to refute and mute the loud traditional authority which ever championed their tame subjection. It was necessary to shape their own church without feeling dwarfed by contrast with the well-organized, mammoth institution (Roman or Anglican) they knew. And it was necessary to trust that their worship was not only acceptable, but was the type even preferred by God because its form was unforced and fluid.

The formulation of theological doctrine on the dignity, holiness, and liberty (which all Christians enjoy), while stated systematically in the *Christian Doctrine*, certainly appeared earlier in Milton's writing. This doctrine was stated nearly twenty years before in *The Reason of Church Government* where Milton records the controversy between the Prelates and the people over whose right and responsibility it was to govern the church. This treatise is valuable in illuminating

---

6. See chap. 15, " 'Written Records Pure,' " in this volume.
7. *CPW* 6:521 n. 1.

two practical goals of the doctrine of universal dignity. The first is moral virtue or, in Milton's words, "honourable duty of estimation and respect towards [a man's] own soul and body"; in other words, "this hilltop of sanctity and goodness above which there is no higher ascent but to the love of God which from this self-pious regard cannot be assunder" (1:842). But Milton is a master of psychology. He realizes that one cannot simply hear the religious cant of redemption and re-creation, and then be treated irreligiously (that is, barred from governing, leading worship, touching sacred things) without experiencing one's self as nonhonorable, nonrespectable, unsanctified, and inferior. Milton penetrates the surface and goes to the heart of the problem to provide a rationale that will move believers to respond to "the high calling of God to be holy and pure" (1:823). If the theology were believed and adhered to, a dignified moral life would follow. However, a poor self-concept, like the one promulgated to the laity by the Prelates, can only issue forth a base, unworthy morality:

> We have learnt that the scornfull terme of Laick, the consecrating of Temples, carpets, and tablecloathes, the railing in of a repugnant and contradictive Mount Sinai in the Gospell, as if the touch of a lay Christian who is never the lesse *Gods living temple*, could profane dead judaisms, the exclusion of Christs people from the offices of holy discipline through the pride of a usurping Clergy, causes the rest to have an unworthy and abject opinion of themselves; to approach to holy duty with a slavish fear, and to unholy doings with a familiar boldnesse. For seeing such a wide and terrible distance between religious things and themselves, and that in respect of a woodden table & the perimeter of holy ground about it, a flagon pot, and a linnen corporal, the Priest esteems their lay-ships unhallow'd and unclean, they fear religion with such a fear as loves not, and think the purity of the Gospell too pure for them and that any uncleannesse is more sutable to their unconsecrated estate. (1:843–44; emphasis added)

Aiming to redress that "unworthy and abject opinion of themselves" caused by the Prelates, Milton bridges the gap between laic and cleric, unconsecrated and consecrated so that every Christian values himself or herself as "Gods living temple."

In removing that "wide and terrible distance between religious things and themselves," Milton likewise abolishes that chasm between ordained governors and unordained governed. Here, in *The Reason of Church Government*, Milton arrives at the second practical goal of his theological doctrine on the dignity of all believers: sharing the responsibility of church governance with every person previously regarded as "lay" since "as he is call'd by the high calling of God to be holy and pure, so is he by the same appointment ordain'd, and by the Churches call admitted to such offices of discipline in the Church to which his owne spirituall gifts by the example of Apostolick institution have autoriz'd him" (1:843). The strategy goes like this: if you want people to act like reputable shareholders in a reputable corporation, welcome them in, dissolve dichotomies, and give them responsibility for the incorporating. "Prelacy cannot conform to God's plan," Radzinowicz observes, "because it denies the progressive liberation of all believers by forbidding them a place in the government of the church."[8] Once he has exposed the problem and its cause, Milton articulates the remedy—redignifying: "And if the love of God, as a fire sent from heaven to be ever kept alive *upon the altar of our hearts*, be the first principle of all godly and vertuous actions in men, this pious honouring of our selves is the second, and may be thought as the radical moisture and fountainhead whence every laudable and worthy enterprise issues forth" (1:841; emphasis added). Milton recapitulates: to be virtuous one needs to perceive oneself as sacred place, as church; further, one must assume the role of presiding sacramental officer—a role heretofore usurped by Prelates and priests. "Honouring of our selves" allows the waters of "laudable and worthy enterprise[s]" to spew forth from the sacred "fountainhead" of the newly honored self.

Milton can conclude his point, bolstering the spiritual confidence of all believers, while still cautioning against antinomian abandon for which the freedom of the gospel might be mistaken:

> But he that holds himself in reverence and due esteem, both for the dignity of God's image upon him, and for the price of his redemption . . . accounts himselfe both a fit person to do the noblest and godliest deeds, and much better worth then to deject and defile, with such a debasement and such a pollution as sin is, himselfe so highly ransom'd and enobl'd to a new friendship and filiall relation with God. (1:842)

In his argument Milton, thus far, has opposed ceremonial, liturgical trappings to ceremonial, liturgical essentials: temples, car-

---

8. Radzinowicz, *Toward* Samson Agonistes, 73.

pets, tablecloths, table, and so on to "God's living temple" and "the altar of our hearts." I wish to emphasize here that Milton has not abandoned liturgical language or the supernal realities to which they refer, so long as language and liturgy are dictated by Scripture literally or authorized by Scripture spiritually.[9]

Milton proceeds in this renovated liturgical vein by discussing the human person as more sacred than any altar, an unholy heart as the only potential means for sacrilege, and the priesthood shared by all believers as the single acceptable order of priesthood:

> But when every good Christian throughly acquainted with all those glorious privileges of sanctification and adoption which render him more sacred then any dedicated altar or element, shall be restor'd to his right in the Church, and not excluded from such place of spiritual government as his Christian abilities and his approved good life in the eye and testimony of the Church shall preferre him to, this and nothing sooner will open his eyes to a wise and true valuation of himselfe . . . and will stirre him up to walk worthy the honourable and grave imployment wherewith God and the Church had dignifi'd him: not fearing lest he should meet with some outward holy thing in religion which his lay touch or presence might profane, but lest something unholy from within his own heart should dishonour and profane in himselfe that Priestly unction and Clergy-right whereto Christ hath entitl'd him. Then would the congregation of the Lord soone recover the true likenesse and visage of what she is indeed, a holy generation, a royall Priesthood, a Saintly communion, the household and City of God. And this I hold to be another considerable reason why the functions of Church-government ought to be free and open to any Christian man though never so laick, if his capacity, his faith, and prudent demeanour commend him. And this the Apostles warrant us to do. (1:844)

The issues—what is holy? who are holy? who should govern?—are all of a piece. According to the purest perspective on Reform, only

9. See chap. 4, "'Rites and Methods which [God] Himself Has Prescribed,'" in this volume. Studies that argue Milton's sacramentalism, thereby supporting my argument of his re-sacramentalizing rather than un-sacramentalizing, are those by Fixler, "The Apocalypse Within *Paradise Lost*"; Lieb, *Poetics of the Holy*; Schwartz, *Remembering and Repeating*; Galbraith Crump, *The Mystical Design of* Paradise Lost; and John C. Ulreich, Jr., "Milton on the Eucharist: Some Second Thoughts about Sacramentalism." Ulreich points up sacramentalism in Milton's poetry, and rescues Milton from his frequently received stereotype of absolute and rampant later iconoclasm. Studies that argue an un-sacramentalizing or an anti-sacramentalizing are those by Ross and Kent.

by abolishing the distinctions between what the clerical view has labeled "sacred" and "profane," "clerical" and "lay," "governing" and "governed" can the divorce between moral vision and the enactment of moral virtue disappear and their wedding, predestined by God, transpire.

In his discussion on the visible church in the *Christian Doctrine*, Milton elaborates on the practical ramifications of dissolving the distinction between lay and cleric and of emphasizing the priesthood of all believers—a universal clergy. Believing that the word *clergy* is informed by the Latin *clerus* (heritage),[10] Milton derives the institution, integrity, and sufficiency of a lay ministry: "Any believer can be an ORDINARY MINISTER, whenever necessary, so long as he is provided with certain gifts (which constitute his mission)" (6:570–71). Proclaiming the clerical privilege common to all God's people from the Old Testament, through the New, and continuing in the Everlasting Gospel, Milton traces the line of succession for a common clergy from its origin down to his own day: "Before the law the fathers or eldest sons of families came into this category, as, for example, Abel, Noah, Abraham, etc., and Jethro. . . . Also in this category, under the law, came Aaron and his posterity, the whole tribe of Levi, and lastly the prophets" (6:571).

Even the Law lacked a rigidity as to the qualifications of ministering: "Furthermore, anyone who seemed suitable, although neither priest nor Levite, was able to teach publicly in the synagogue: Christ was given permission to do this; so was Paul, Acts xiii. 15." One naturally expects that "it is even more allowable under the gospel, for any believer endowed with similar gifts to do the same," but such is not the case: "Our modern clergy, if that is the right name for them, who claim the right of preaching as theirs alone, would not have been glad had they seen this grace extended to the laity, as they call them, but would have been more likely to condemn it" (6:571). Milton concludes this ministerial family tree, as recounted in Scrip-

10. For Huguelet's idea of heritage as a commonplace Protestant translation for *clerus*, see *CPW* 6:572 n. 12. Milton echoes Luther's and Calvin's emphasis on the priesthood of all believers, based on the biblical text, " 'But ye are a chosen generation, a royal priesthood, an holy nation, a peculiar people; that ye should show forth the praises of him who hath called you out of darkness into his marvelous light' (1 Pet. 2:9). Since Calvin had declared (*Institutes of the Christian Religion*, 12, xix) the liberty of Christians from the Jewish ceremonial and civil law, this verse had been a rallying cry of all who challenged the rights of any hierarchy which seemed to derive in any way from the Jewish priesthood" (*CPMP*, 681 n. 231).

ture, by correcting the misdefinition of clergy that has perniciously diseased the church for too long: "If the term *clergy*, which ecclesiastics have since appropriated to themselves, means anything here, then it must signify the whole church." Retaining but universalizing the clerical status is the deathblow to the concept of church as hierarchical institution and, consequently, to an age that perceived the church solely in that way. Just as the notion of priesthood has been revamped, so must the notion of prophecy be: "Moreover the term *prophet* is applied not only to a man able to foretell the future but also to anyone endowed with exceptional piety and wisdom for the purpose of teaching." Prophecy, too, has been universalized—a truth evident in the most common of Milton's contemporaries *if* they excel in edification through example and spiritually competent pedagogy: "Thus under the gospel the simple gift of teaching, especially of public teaching, is called *prophecy:* . . . I Cor. xiv. 3: *he who prophesies speaks to men for their edification*" (6:572).

In Milton's statement on a thorough appreciation for "all those glorious privileges of sanctification and adoption" in *The Reason of Church Government* (1:844), which include priesthood and prophecy potentially for all, we approach the sacred center of Milton's doctrine on the church, on its gospel, and on its worship. We learn what to value as holy and liturgical. Milton follows the Psalmist (who knows that God prefers contrite hearts to oblations), prophets like Ezekiel, Hosea, and Amos (who announce, either explicitly or implicitly, God's law written in the heart), and he follows Christ (who shifts attention from sacred mountain to sacred believer).[11] Milton gives his rendition of the same principal value: "glorious privileges of sanctification and adoption . . . render ["every good Christian"] more sacred then any dedicated altar or element" (1:844). Milton's renovated term *sacred* is simultaneously universal and particular; surprisingly common (that is, including all), though still elite—only now, *morally* elite (that is, superior for having acknowledged Christ as exclusively justificatory).

If Milton's methodology is operative, this sacred status surely qualifies all Christians to be involved in church government, for all Christians, having their eyes opened "to a wise and true valuation" of themselves, will have been stirred "to walk worthy the honour-

---

11. See Ps. 51; Ezek. 36:26–27; Hos. 6:6 and 10:1–10; Amos 5:21–27; John 2:19–22, 4:21.

able and grave employment wherewith God and the Church hath dignifi'd" them. The Prelates object to including the laity in church governance because "this will bring profanenesse into the Church." But Milton's reply holds to the prophetic tradition that seeks to turn the world inside out: "None have brought that in more then their own irreligious courses; nor more driven holiness out of living into livelesse things" (1:844).

Just as the Prelates have imagined sects and schism in their zeal to preserve church unity,[12] so too have they imagined profaneness residing within the laity—the main business Milton sets out to disclaim in the second book of this treatise. The Prelates have flown in the face of Scripture's truth, which proclaims the holiness of *all* God's people, just as it does the union in Christ of all those bent on true Protestant Reforming. Additionally, they have ignored the instruments of reason and the Spirit, which assist in grasping Scripture's plain intent. Instead, they have neatly dichotomized into "holy" and "profane," then externalized the dichotomies. Most horrifying and dangerous of all to the Radical brethren, these Prelates have, in their bifurcation, projected a deficiency of holiness and worthiness onto the "laicks" and reserved holiness and worth for themselves and for things traditionally regarded as ceremonial. Milton is enlightening on the perversity of their theological system that has ignored God's will:

> For whereas God who hath cleans'd every beast and creeping worme, would not suffer S. *Peter* to call them common or unclean, the Prelat Bishops in their printed orders hung up in Churches have proclaim'd the best of creatures, mankind, so unpurifi'd and contagious, that for him to lay his hat, or his garment upon the Chancell table they have defin'd it no lesse hainous in expresse words then to profane the Table of the Lord. And thus have they by their Canaanitish doctrine (for that which was to the Jew but jewish is to the Christian no better then Canaanitish) thus have they made common and unclean, thus have they made profane that nature which God hath not only cleans'd, but Christ also hath assum'd. (1:844–45)

In short, they have worked to undo the ennobled station of mankind—to undo Christ's work of sanctification and adoption. Milton's intention here is to set things right by turning all the received ecclesiastical custom and tradition inside out and upside down, thereby

---

12. See chap. 6, " 'Many Schisms and Many Distinctions,' " in this volume.

exposing the Prelatical lie and the evangelical truth: regenerated, redeemed, and renovated ordinary people are dignified, while their clerical, Prelatical counterparts are tyrannical, debased, and duplicitous. Filled with rottenness, the Prelates can only misreference words to things, calling that which is good or true, "evil" or "false," and that which is holy, "profane." They had made their own game and rules to determine and bestow dignity, but true "Nobility," as Milton recorded under the entry so titled in his *Commonplace Book,* comes about in another way, without game; instead with nature and grace: "From the spirit of God it must be derived, not from forefathers or man-made laws, as the high-born Roman martyr in Prudentius is of noble spirit: 'Let it not be that the blood of my parents proves me noble, or the law of the Curia', & c.; and then, 'We first had our being from the mouth of God, our Father; whoever serves Him, he is truly noble'" (1:471–72).

In rescuing the common people, Milton is at one with Radicals like Dell, Walwyn, Winstanley, and Muggleton. The Leveller William Walwyn also opposed exclusive professionalism that gave "university-reared ministers . . . a monopoly in the word of God." He championed "the reasoning and disinterested layman, both in religion and politics, who brought to them adequate gifts with which he believed all men were, at least potentially, endowed by God and nature." In his sermon *The Stumbling Stone* (1653), locating himself in the sort of Reform that predates Luther and Calvin, Dell is definitive about the only way to ensure Reform: "I cannot choose but conclude with John Hus, that all the clergy must be quite taken away ere the church of Christ can have any true reformation." But clergy was much more than a body of men. Clergy was a system that perpetuated and sustained itself by keeping knowledge to themselves and keeping the poor ignorant. Winstanley, in *The Law of Freedom* (1651), explains how this process worked:

> For so long as the people call that a Truth which they call a Truth, and believe what they preach, and are willing to let the Clergy be the Keepers of their eyes and knowledg; . . . Put out their eyes to see by theirs, then all is well, and they tell the people they shall go to Heaven.
>
> But if the eyes of the people begin to open, and they seek to find knowledg in their own hearts, and to question the Ministers Doctrine: . . .
>
> Then do the Ministers prepare War against that man or men, and will make no Covenant of Peace with him, till they consent to

have their right eyes put out, that is, to have their Reason blinded, so as to believe every Doctrine they preach, and never question anything.

Lodowick Muggleton, too, in *A True Interpretation of the Eleventh Chapter of the Revelation of Saint John* (1662), echoes Milton, Winstanley, and Dell in his scriptural commentary: "Believers have been trodden under foot. . . . They have been kept under darkness and blindness, as believing that the learned men and priests of the earth, had power successively to set up gospel ordinances, or visible worship, to please God."[13]

13. Morton, *World of the Ranters,* 195; Hill, *Antichrist,* 98; Winstanley, *The Law of Freedom in a Platform, or True Magistracy Restored,* 70; Muggleton, *A True Interpretation of the Eleventh Chapter of the Revelation of St. John,* 6.

10

"Thir Own Abilities and the Church"

Vocation to the New Ministry

The iconoclastic spirit evident here among the Radicals was directed not only at the clergy themselves, but at the entire network of universities, tithing to support the universities, the sacramental system, the self-proclaimed indispensable priestly caste, and the all-too-compromising, state-acquiescing church. This system churned out a steady supply of clergy who thrived on having distinction, who claimed exclusive knowledge to substantiate their unique dignity, who claimed custody over sacraments and holy things, and who sought the state's sanction and support in accomplishing their goals as well as in muscling any who presumed to edge beyond their "laick" station.

The typical Radical church doctrine (held by those like Winstanley, Reeve, and Milton), which was emphasized in reaction to that nefarious network, maintained that the special priestly caste, out to get power and wealth, had deceived people ever since the original corruption within the early church and had used their knowledge and a mandatory sacramental system as a means for keeping their self-gratifying hold. Winstanley, in *Fire in the Bush* (1653), like Milton, denounces the priesthood for its deception because

> the Scriptures of the Bible were written by the experimental hand of Shepherds, Husbandmen, Fishermen, and such inferior men of the world; and the Universitie learned ones have got these mens writings; and flourish their *plaine language* over with their dark interpretation, and glosses, as if it were too hard for ordinary men

to understand them; and thereby they deceive the simple, and make a prey of the poore.[1]

Those called "extremist" in the seventeenth century, like Walwyn, Dell, Winstanley, and Milton, followed in the steps of their forebears Wyclif and Hus in having as their primary practical target a cultic coterie who proclaimed as essential for salvation vehicles of grace that only they could provide. James Nichols explains that Reformists rejected the "correlative ideas of a special priesthood for sacrifice and of the propitiatory interpretation of the Eucharist, which established themselves late in the third century, . . . as unworthy reversion, or to use modern terms, an illegitimate 'development.'" But genuine, thorough Reformists, aiming as always to get to the *bottom* of abuse and anti-Christianity, looked further—to the spawning areas of this ministerial elitism—and found the universities to be the culprits. They taught this supercilious superiority and superficial sanctity, causing Winstanley to view those ministers trained there as the Man of Sin, or Antichrist.[2] Likewise convinced and concerned about the danger of the university to the church and its ministers, Milton states the same truth as Winstanley, only more positively: "It is not the Universities, then, but God who has given us pastors and teachers: that same God who gave us apostles and prophets" (6:572).[3] And looking even beyond universities, these purist Reformers also found tithes to deserve the blame.

But the matter went even beyond clergy, university, and tithes—to the all-too-intimate relationship between the church and the state— a relationship that (as Milton stresses in *Of Reformation*) seeks, finds, and fosters an infectious materialism:

> We have tri'd already, & miserably felt what *ambition worldly glory & Immoderat wealth* can do, what the boisterous & contradictional hand of a temporall, earthly, and corporeall Spiritualty can availe to the edifying of Christs holy *Church*; were it such a desper-

1. Hill, *Experience of Defeat*, 294; Gerrard Winstanley, *The Works of Gerrard Winstanley*, 474.

2. Nichols, *Corporate Worship in the Reformed Tradition*, 27; Hill, *Antichrist*, 137.

3. Margaret Lewis Bailey, in *Milton and Jakob Boehme: A Study of German Mysticism in Seventeenth-Century England*, notes: "Learning is opposed to the 'inner light' because inspiration can never be a product of reason." With such reasoning, when classical learning competes with divine learning or spiritual wisdom, other kinds of learning must always take a subordinate place. It is according to such a hierarchy of learning that Milton's repudiation of worldly knowledge, especially before an audience like Satan, is right and even reasonable.

ate hazard to put to the venture the universal Votes of *Christs* Congregation, the fellowly and friendly yoke of a teaching and laborious Ministery, the Pastorlike and Apostolick imitation of meeke and unlordly Discipline, the gentle and benevolent mediocritie of Church-maintenance, without the ignoble Hucsterage of pidling *Tithes*? (1:613)[4]

Prophetically explaining and exposing both evil and evil ones, Milton in his theological compendium is very clear on the matter: "To bargain for or exact tithes or gospel-taxes, to exact a subsidy from the flock by force or by the intervention of the magistrates, to invoke the civil law in order to secure church revenue, and to take such matters into the courts—these are actions of wolves, not of ministers of the gospel" (6:598).

But stalking church and society to discover the evil and obliterate the wolves responsible for it does not automatically inseminate goodness and bring about a noble replacement. What will restore a pure ministry? What will ministry consist of? Who will minister? Where will these servants come from? Where and how will they be trained? How will they be paid—and if not paid, how will they survive?

The remedy was to educate and dignify the people. This education did not refer to university training, but to gospel training that would free and redignify believers so that they could preach and minister. By dint of "their spiritual priesthood" all have "equal access to any ministerial function," Milton claims in *The Likeliest Means*, as long as "thir own abilities and the church" summon them, "though they never came neer commencement or universitie" (7:320).[5] He asserts: "It is a fond error, though too much beleevd among us, to think that the universitie makes a minister of the gospel . . . : but that which makes fit a minister, the scripture can best informe us to be only from above" (7:316). Here, near the end of the treatise, Milton speaks about the most desirable place of training for the ministry:

4. See pp. 86–95 and 114–17 in this volume; and see Hill, *English Revolution*, 84. For the dynamics between the clergy-education-tithes-university system and the universal competency to divine and preach, see McGregor, "The Baptists," in McGregor and Reay, eds., *Radical Religion*, 50; also Miller, *New England Mind*, 79, 82. Richard L. Greaves, *Saints and Rebels: Seven Nonconformists in Stuart England,* cites the new system of education, based on Scripture and tailored to the particular abilities of students, which Francis Bamfield aimed to put into operation. Education was not to be monopolized by a few. Bamfield "urged the appointment of lecturers in every county to teach biblical subjects in English" (194–96, 202).

5. See Barker, *Puritan Dilemma*, 229. See also *CPW* 6:571–73 on the need for the endowment of certain gifts to prophesy and preach.

(1) "what learning either human or divine can be necessary to a minister, may as easily and less chargeably be had in any private house"; (2) libraries, not those valued at £600, but those at £60, can contain what a minister needs for reference and direction; (3) "it were much better . . . that they who intended to be ministers, were traind up in the church only, by the scripture and in the original languages therof at schoole; without fetching the compas of other arts and sciences, more then what they can well learn at secondary leisure and at home" (7:317–18). Regarding this third item, one should note that Milton's purpose in *The Likeliest Means* is to attack "the usual pretences of hirelings, colourd over most commonly with the cause of learning and universities: as if with divines learning stood and fell; wherein for the most part thir pittance is so small" (7:318). (These divines, in Milton's view, erroneously literalize the synecdoche that the learned are the source, measure, indeed, the very repositories of learning.) The essence of the education advocated by Milton is place more than curriculum: home and church over university is the point, not multilingual preparation for scriptural exegesis. Learning and the concomitant wherewithal for knowing Scripture do not result *because* of a university system, but *because* of the Spirit and its tutelage that can be provided at home. Furthermore, Milton is not requiring that every minister have this curriculum. If aspirants desire this valuable instruction and have the ability to grasp it, they can learn "the original languages" of Scripture "at schoole"; as for Scripture itself, they are better off to be "traind up in the church only."

Ministers were to come from anywhere and everywhere. Every congregation would call forth one of its own members whom they believed to be knowledgeable, disciplined, and saintly. The belief that ministers were to be elected by plain artisans, whom defenders of prelacy called "the mutinous rabble," was evident early on in Milton's political and religious life. Christopher Hill insists that this belief was "soon . . . to unite him with all true radicals in the English Revolution."[6] For Milton and those of his company, the emphasis was on a church from below, rather than from above:

> Heretofore in the first evangelic time (and it were happy for Christendom if it were so again) ministers of the gospel were by nothing els distinguishd from other Christians but by thir spiritual knowl-

6. Hill, *English Revolution*, 84.

edge and sanctitie of life, for the which the church elected them to
be her teachers and overseers, though not thereby to separate
them from whatever calling she then found them following besides,
as the example of S. *Paul* declares, and the first times of Chris-
tianitie. When once they affected to be called a clergie, and became as it were a peculiar tribe of levites, a partie, a distinct order
in the commonwealth, bred up for divines in babling schooles and
fed at the publick cost, good for nothing els but what was good for
nothing, they soon grew idle: that idlenes with fulnes of bread
begat pride and perpetual contention with their feeders the despis'd
laitie, through all ages ever since: to the perverting of religion,
and the disturbance of all Christendom. (6:320)

The simplification of the entire process of this pure, egalitarian
church's degeneration—conveyed for the most part in ordinary, tangible diction (for example, "partie," "bred up for divines in babling
schooles and fed at the publik cost," "fulnes of bread," and "feeders")—underscores the ideal of the common, mainly since the principle preached is immediately enacted, albeit in the pejorative description of current church conditions. With a truly Reformed church
there was to be no patronage system, which had always insured
that the clergy were *appointed* by the ruling class.[7] Also universities,
which had been the seat of clerical Christian education and which
had been associated with Prelatical government of the church and
with social privilege, were now suspect and would have to defer to
the newer assembly and home seats of power that were based almost solely on the Word itself.[8] Milton, therefore, argues in *Of Education*, "Any yeoman or tradesman competently wise in his mother
dialect only" is as competent and worthy to take his place in church
governance and ministry as a university wit (2:370).[9] Milton's point
here is that "language is but the instrument convaying to us things

7. Hill, "Irreligion," in McGregor and Reay, eds., *Radical Religion*, 196. Social dif-
ferentiation became for the Levellers an index for religious discrepancy, the degree
of material prosperity inversely proportional to the spiritual. They saw the religion
of the rich and powerful to be a "false religion" and the religion of the poor and
powerless to be "the true religion" (Manning, "The Levellers," in McGregor and
Reay, eds., *Radical Religion*, 76).
8. Hill, *Antichrist*, 137–38.
9. See the link Hill, "The Religion of Gerrard Winstanley," in McGregor and Reay,
eds., *Radical Religion*, makes between Winstanley and Milton on God's practical concern for the lowly: "Winstanley was certainly no Fifth Monarchist . . . , but with
Milton and almost all the radicals he shared generally millenarian expectations, fore-
seeing a time when God will reveal himself to 'the despised, the unlearned, the
poor, and nothings of this world' " (193). See also Hill, *English Revolution*, 107–8.

useful to be known."[10] Without "the solid things" (that is, reference to reality and usefulness) in "all the tongues," a multilinguist is actually *less learned* than a unilingual "yeoman or tradesman," who knows both the realistic meaning of words as well as the practical use to which they can be put (2:369–70).

Recalling Milton's statement in *The Likeliest Means*, that prospective ministers should be "traind up in the church only, by the scripture and in the original languages therof at schoole," one is not to presume that Milton was uncertain, much less contradictory, about the type of schooling suitable for a minister. There, his aim is to drain the university and its graduated divines of prestige, preeminence, and necessity in the preparation of ministers; it is *not* to degrade the university. In fact, as I pointed out in chapter 2, university training, even for nonministers, "did have an important function within the church. Its value and purpose were, for the Radical Christian intellectual, to serve God, in accord with Scripture, frequently by fighting for one's ecclesiastically equal neighbors." The university gave one (minister or not) the linguistic capability of disputing by enjoying the same linguistic advantage as one's intellectually, university-trained opponents. Milton's purpose in *Of Education* is different. Here, he is primarily concerned about the value of a human being and wishes to underscore that this value has nothing to do with a university education (an agent to be inferred from one of its chief contemporary metonymies, mastery of languages). Milton achieves his purpose by deflating multilingual ability as a superior and an essential criterion for knowledge and by elevating unilingual ability if it brings one to know "the solid things" in the words. To summarize, *The Likeliest Means* dignifies the home as a seat of scriptural (though not linguistic) learning; *Of Education* dignifies the pragmatically educated learner (unilingual or multilingual) who is adept at linking language to life.

Barker observes that Milton's concept of education becomes Radical, as his later recommendations, seen in *The Likeliest Means* and the *Christian Doctrine*, repudiate the evaluation of learning expressed in the *Areopagitica* and *Of Education*. Like Christian rationalists who, with their contempt for scholasticism, valued education to raise the improvement of natural understanding, Milton, Barker argues, re-

10. *CPW* 2:369 n. 20: "Read as a whole and in its context, this sentence affirms that utility is the primary, but not necessarily the exclusive value, of language study."

flects "the sectarian demand for a wholly practical education and for a ministry dependent not on learning, which 'is but the tradition of men,' but on the inner light."[11] In fact, though, as I have stated earlier in this chapter, much of what comes to completion in *The Likeliest Means* and in the *Christian Doctrine* is much more than just seminally present in the earlier *Reason of Church Government*. If one sees Milton's base as not primarily educational or even political, but spiritual (or ecclesial) and scriptural, then Milton's Radicalism, while increasing, is nonetheless constant in character—focused on church and on every individual's dignity and virtue.

Barker then claims that Milton ultimately returns to faith in education for inculcating principles of virtue in addition to conveying knowledge. Perhaps Milton changed less than Barker presumes. Reason leads to faith, and faith to virtue—no matter how much Milton seemed to Barker to have adopted the sectarian dichotomizing attitude toward learning, where knowledge is concerned with the natural and the practical and where faith, independent of reason, is the result solely of "the inner light." Milton, like some other Radicals, had continuously honored reason that, as common sense, could be used as a check against illogical doctrine and scripturally forbidden worship. Similarly, he had not given up the importance of "the inner light" to his final doctrine on Scripture and the individual believer. If raising the natural understanding became a goal for Milton, this development was not a departure from his commitment to learning as expressed in *Areopagitica* and *Of Education*—a point that Barker does maintain. In that middle period, I would argue, Milton had only expanded the curriculum to include material that would educate the natural understanding of all humankind. Milton's ultimate aim, like that of the minister, is to raise the understanding, piety, and virtue of the entire person—body, mind, and soul (1:845).[12]

Profit made from the gospel was one of the sins that the scrupulous conscience of the Radical church wished to avoid. Milton was thus on guard since he felt that "monetary considerations should weigh least of all with anyone who preaches the gospel." Buying the gospel is wicked enough, but selling it "must be much more wicked" (6:598). As Milton's irritation over hirelings mounts, he chants an antilitany of accusatory exclamations:

11. Barker, *Puritan Dilemma*, 231.
12. Ibid., 276, 281.

If the flock does belong to the minister, how avaricious it is for him to be so eager to make a profit out of his holy office; and if it does not, how unjust his behavior is! How officious, to force his instruction upon those who do not want to be taught by him at all! How extortionate, to exact payment for teaching from a man who rejects you as a teacher, and whom you reject as a pupil if it were not for the money! For *the hireling, to whom the sheep do not belong, runs away because he is a hireling and because he does not care for the sheep,* John x. 12, 13. (6:599)

Needing to subsist, yet forbidden to be a hireling—what's a minister to do? Milton concedes that "some remuneration is allowable" but insists that "it is better to serve God's church for nothing and, following our Lord's example, to minister and to serve without pay" (6:595–96). Ministers may accept gifts "freely and spontaneously given," as did Paul, who nonetheless felt "guilty of robbing" (6:597). Yet they should be "worried and annoyed," as was Paul, if they must accept aid from the churches "by dire necessity." But such reliance on providence through "the willing flock" is preferable to a reliance on "any edicts of civil power" (6:597). Anticipating the pointed question that has gained rhetorical force by his having forestalled it till now, Milton proceeds: "How are we to live then? you may ask," only to embarrass with an exclamatory repetition ("How are you to live!") those foolish enough to have asked such a thing. But Milton is well aware that this rhetorical rebuff will not intimidate or satisfy anyone whose natural reasoning has been too dulled to figure the obvious solution, so he provides scriptural exemplars who have figured it, complete with their resumes. Contemporary ministers are to live

as the prophets and the apostles used to live, by making use of your abilities, by some trade or some respectable profession. Follow the example of the prophets; they were quite accustomed to chop wood and build their own houses, II Kings vi. 2. Follow Christ's example: he was a carpenter, Mark vi. 3: follow Paul's example, Acts xviii. 3, 4. He had been educated, at his own expense, in the best arts and disciplines but he did not, as ministers nowadays do, contend that the expenses of his education should be repaid from the proceeds of the gospel. (6:599–600)

In *The Likeliest Means* Milton looks to "those ancientest reformed churches of the *Waldenses*" as a model since they, uncorrupted by Constantine's pernicious wedding of church and state, "deni'd that tithes were to be given, or that they were ever given in the primitive church" (7:292).[13] This "ancient stock of our reformation" provides a solution to the problem of a minister's livelihood:

> Those preachers among the poor *Waldenses*, the ancient stock of our reformation . . . bread up themselves in trades, and especially in physic and surgery as well as in the study of scripture (which is the only true theologie) that they might be no burden to the church; and by the example of Christ; might cure both soul and bodie; through industry joining that to their ministerie, which he joind to his by gift of the spirit. Thus relates *Peter Gilles* in his histoire of the *Waldenses* in *Piemont*. (7:306–7)

The ministry, therefore, is not to be considered a trade, that is, the source of one's livelihood, as it was, by contrast, in England where ministers of the gospel have made it so because they either would or could perform no other trade: "Our ministers think scorn to use a trade, and count it the reproach of this age, that tradesmen preach the gospel. It were to be wishd they were all tradesmen; they would not then so many of them, for want of another trade, make a trade of thir preaching: and yet they clamor that tradesmen preach; and yet they preach, while they themselves are the worst tradesmen of all" (7:307). Taking hirelings at their word—that preaching is their trade— Milton reproves them for being "the worst tradesmen," yet they ironically "clamor that tradesmen preach." Embedded here is the ideal which would withdraw preaching from that "peculiar tribe of levites"—that "partie," that "distinct order"—and relocate it where it belonged—amidst all the people (7:320). Milton's strategy is remarkable: by denying preaching to be the sole basis for one's subsistence, he cleverly elicits the responsibility for teaching, preaching, and ministering from the entire ecclesia, including the most common believers. In other words, Milton begins by attacking the economics of preachers without another trade, thus, without income; proceeds by endorsing a ministry whose preachers have another trade; and concludes by promoting a spiritual truth—the right and responsibility for any and all (tradesmen) to preach.

Milton also cites the Waldenses as useful for their position on endowments from the state and their position on church revenues.

---

13. See Mohl, *Milton and* Commonplace Book, 80, 141. "From 1655 to 1658, the ancient Waldenses ('whom deservedly I cite so often,' Milton says) were the subject of some fifteen of his *Letters of State* and also of his famous Sonnet 18, 'On the Late Massacre in Piedmont'" (80).

> As for church-endowments and possessions, I meet with none
> considerable before *Constantine,* but the houses and gardens where
> they met, and thir places of burial: and I perswade me, that from
> them the ancient *Waldenses,* whom deservedly I cite so often, held,
> *that to endow churches is an evil thing;* and, that the church then fell
> off and turnd whore sitting on the beast in the *Revelation,* when
> under Pope *Sylvester* she receivd those temporal donations. (7:307)

Endowments from the state contaminate the church, just as church
revenues contaminate the magistrate, having him "take into his
own power the stipendiatie maintenance of church-ministers, or
compell it by law" (7:308). Such transaction "would suspend the
church wholly upon the state, and turn her ministers into state-
pensioners," but beyond this generic perversion is a particular one:

> And for the magistrate in person of a nursing father to make the
> church his meer ward, as alwaies in minoritie, the church, to
> whom he ought as a magistrate, *Esa.* 49.23 *To bow down with his face
> toward the earth, and lick up the dust of her feet,* her to subject to his
> political drifts or conceivd opinions by mastring her revenue, and
> so by his examinant committies to circumscribe her free election of
> ministers, is neither just nor pious. (7:308)

Using the Waldenses as an index again, Milton concludes:

> Whereby these pretended church-revenues, as they have bin ever,
> so are like to continue endles matter of dissention both between
> the church and magistrate, and the churches among themselves,
> there will be found no better remedie to these evils, otherwise
> incurable, then by the incorruptest councel of those *Waldenses,* our
> first reformers, to remove them as a pest, an apple of discord in
> the church, (for what els can be the effect of riches and the snare of
> monie in religion?). (7:309)

Finally, Milton turns to these ancient exemplars to observe "in
what manner God hath ordaind that recompence be given to ministers of the gospel":

> The *Waldenses,* our first reformers, both from the scripture and
> these primitive examples, maintaind those among them who bore
> the office of ministers, by almes only. . . . It [was] then by almes
> and benevolence, not by legal force, not by tenure of freehold or
> copyhold: for almes, though just, cannot be compelld; and benev-
> olence forc'd, is malevolence rather, violent and inconsistent with
> the gospel; and declares him no true minister therof, but a rapa-
> cious hireling rather. (7:312)

Thus both Scripture and history answer the question of how ministers are to live: as prophets, apostles, the Waldenses, and Christ himself—"by making use of your abilities, by some trade or some professions," certainly not by tithes or any other form of church revenue that would keep a peculiar party within the church elitist, ineffective, and idle (6:600).

Milton's most comprehensive, though quite compact, statement of his belief that the responsibility for speaking of things spiritual has been delegated to every single individual is recorded in the *Christian Doctrine*, where context, principle, clarification, practical directive, and precedents are provided:

> The modern method of holding meetings should not be retaind: instead that instituted by the apostles should be restored. Thus one man, and he with motives of gain, should not be stuck up in a pulpit and have the sole right of addressing the congregation. Instead each believer, according to his personal talents, should have a chance to address his fellows, or to prophesy, teach, or exhort. Even the weakest of the brethren should have an opportunity to interrogate or to ask advice from the older and more learned of those present. I Cor. xiv. 26, etc.: *whenever you meet together, each of you.* . . .
>
> The apostles imitated this custom from that of the Jewish Synagogue, and they retained it in the churches. . . . It is often recorded elsewhere that Christ taught in the synagogue and even in the temple. . . . The Jews allowed him to do this not because he was Christ but simply because he was a gifted individual. (6:608)[14]

Several chapters earlier Milton grants that "EXTRAORDINARY MINISTERS are sent and inspired by God to set up or to reform the church both by preaching and by writing" and that "to this class the prophets, apostles, evangelists and others of that kind belonged" (6:570). However, he exceeds this fundamental, middle-of-the-road ecclesiology as he takes up the topic of ordinary ministers to which he gives most of his attention. (Of the entire 119 lines on ministry, only

14. See *Areopagitica, CPW* 2:567. Milton urges people not to fear those "who appear to be the leading schismaticks" because they are lowly or have what some fear are "new and dangerous opinions." They should be given "gentle meetings and gentle dismissions. . . . As the dust and cinders of our feet . . . they may yet serve to polish and brighten the armoury of Truth." They may be "of those whom God hath fitted for the speciall use of these times with eminent and ample gifts, and those perhaps neither among the Priests, nor among the Pharisees, and we in the hast of a precipitant zeal shall make no distinction."

14 deal with extraordinary, whereas 90 deal with ordinary—not quite 4 of the 14 being Milton's *commentary* in contrast to half of the 90 being so.) "Any believer can be an ORDINARY MINISTER, whenever necessary, so long as he is provided with certain gifts (which constitute his mission)" (6:570–71).

Milton has increased the ministerial pool by stressing that the gospel has opened the ministry of preaching, prophesying, teaching, and exhorting (7:320; 6:570–72, 608). If Milton does not always use the terms *pastoring, teaching,* and *prophesying* interchangeably, he at least blurs their definitions to amalgamate their received distinct functions and to accommodate one of the major ideals of his church: universal opportunity in and responsibility for promoting the gospel, purifying worship, and governing the church. Thus, according to Milton's understanding of Scripture, "*pastors* are synonymous with *teachers,*" the second word added "as an explanation of the first, which is a figurative term." Since both teacher and pastor teach as well as exhort, Milton differentiates the twofold "function," because "one individual may be better than another at performing either task," "but the office and the agent are one" (6:570). And, as we have seen above, "the term *prophet* is applied not only to a man able to foretell the future but also to anyone endowed with exceptional piety and wisdom for the purpose of teaching" (6:572).[15]

15. See *CPW* 7:320.

11

"All Sorts and Degrees of Men"

Scripture's New Audience and Messengers

ilton believed that in Scripture alone he had all that he needed to take on that false visible church and its oppressive false prophets: "Then ought we to believe what in our conscience we apprehend the scripture to say, though the visible church with all her doctors gainsay" (7:251). Only on the basis of God's Word could Milton challenge the merely human word spoken by Prelates, Presbyterians, and even Independents in their customs, traditions, assemblies, and requirements. Only because he believed that God had impelled him to speak, as he had Isaiah and Paul, did Milton have the stamina to see himself as "separatist," "schismatic," and "heretic," and even as *speaking and writing prophet*, yet still see himself as one of the "unanimous multitude of good Protestants" constant to the Bridegroom and to the legacy of his gospel (1:787).

With Scripture as the ground, guide, and guardian of genuine and thorough Reform, Milton stands in the company of Wyclif, Hus, Savonarola, Luther, Calvin, Zwingli, Cartwright, Young, Perkins, Ames, Walwyn, Saltmarsh, Marshall, Dell, Williams, Reeve, and Muggleton. Armed with nothing but the Word of God, Milton, in good Reformist fashion, engages in warfare on (what he believes to be) God's side against the flesh of ceremony and tradition. As pointed out in *The Reason of Church Government*, Milton's Prelatical opponents, on the contrary, lack the very source of power and documented proof of having received that authority which alone can make one impregnable and truly secure:

> Mistrusting to find autority of their order in the immediat institu-
> tion of Christ, or his Apostles by cleer evidence of Scripture, they
> fly to the carnal supportment of tradition: when we appeal to the
> Bible, they to the unweildy volumes of tradition. And doe not
> shame to reject the ordinance of him that is eternal for the pervers
> iniquity of sixteen hunderd yeers; choosing rather to think truth it
> self a lyar, then that sixteen ages should be taxt with an error; not
> considering the general apostasy that was foretold, and the Churches
> flight into the wilderness. Nor is this anough, instead of shewing
> the reason of their lowly condition from divine example and com-
> mand, they seek to prove their high pre-eminence from humane
> consent and autority. (1:827)

Lacking Christ as the only real power and Scripture as the only
warrant of their commission, God's enemies, it appeared to the impassioned Reformer, could only be routed. Milton welcomes the
challenge of overthrowing God's opponents, as he makes the triply
iterative and elliptical pattern into the poetry of a battle cry: "But let
them chaunt while they will of prerogatives, we shall tell them of
Scripture; of custom, we of Scripture; of Acts and Statutes, stil
of Scripture, til the quick and pearcing word enter to the dividing of
their soules, & the mighty weaknes of the Gospel throw down the
weak mightines of mans reasoning" (1:827). Following the scriptural
tradition of Ephesians 6, Milton likewise metamorphoses Word into
sword before his readers' very eyes. In making that which is spoken
into that which cuts, Milton has read the signs of his times and
responded to them (just as Paul read those of his and acted). Seeing
himself as God's warrior in *The Reason of Church Government*, Milton
has counterproverbially turned ecclesiastical plowshares into
spiritual sword in an upside-down world where coercion, custom,
and convenience have had their way with peace. As Milton states
in *An Apology* the following year, human-made articulation of
religious tenets is superfluous: "We want no creed so long as we
want not the Scripture" (1:943). And in the *Christian Doctrine* (ca.
1658–1660) Milton paradoxically disclaims all doctrine, in a sense,
since "the rule and canon of faith . . . is scripture alone" (6:585).
James Thorpe reminds one that this treatise "in which Milton under-
took to set forth all that is essential to Christian theology . . . bears
as its subtitle 'Compiled from the Holy Scripture Alone.' "[1]
As Milton explains in *A Treatise of Civil Power* (1659), the very es-

---

1. Thorpe, *John Milton: The Inner Life*, 172.

sence of Protestantism is Scripture, which commands conscience and challenges the church:

> It is the general consent of all found protestant writers, that neither traditions, councels nor canons of any visible church, much less edicts of any magistrate or civil session, but the scripture only can be the final judge or rule in matters of religion, and that only in the conscience of every Christian to himself. Which protestation made by the first publick reformers of our religion against the imperial edicts of *Charls* the fifth, imposing church-traditions without scripture, gave first beginning to the name of *Protestant;* and with that name hath ever bin receivd this doctrine, which preferrs the scripture before the church, and acknowledges none but the Scripture sole interpreter of it self to the conscience. (7:247)

Milton, like many of the Reformers, believed that all believers themselves were capable of determining the meaning of Scripture along with making the appropriate application to their individual lives, even though sermons and public worship could provide worthwhile assistance. The original power of Scripture was available to all human beings; hence, the emphasized encouragement of every individual to read, ponder, and become united through it to the One who has spoken it. God has something to say to everyone—even to those biblical scholars who believe themselves to be so informed that they exclusively bear the commission, competency, and responsibility to tell the rest what God has said. Milton, however, in good Radical-Reformist fashion, reminds all his readers (multilingual, university-trained and unilingual, home-schooled) that God has universalized the educative potential of the Scriptures. As if to explain God's aesthetic and creative charity to his encyclopedic audience, Milton catalogs those whom "the whole divinely inspired scripture" benefits:

> It is *useful for teaching* . . . even those who are already learned and wise, I Cor. x. 15: *as I say this to intelligent men, consider what I say,* and even those who have arrived at full maturity, Phillip. iii. 15: *let as many of us as are adults think this*—such as Timothy himself and Titus, to whom Paul wrote. Also, that it is useful to the strong, I John ii. 14: *I have written to you, young men, because you are strong, and the word of God dwells in you* . . . ; Paul addressed his epistle to the Romans, i. 7, 15, but Peter here says that he wrote not only to them but to all believers: II Pet. iii. 1, 2. (6:577)

Milton interrupts the list of beneficiaries to enunciate the practical universalizing (distinctively Protestant) goal of this theological universalizing principle: "It is clear from all these texts that no one should be forbidden to read the scriptures. On the contrary, it is very proper that all sorts and conditions of men should read them or hear them read regularly" (6:577). Translating principle into particulars, he resumes the catalog: "This includes the king . . . ; magistrates . . . ; and every kind of person . . . ; that is, all the people. . . . If studied carefully and regularly, they are an ideal instrument for educating even unlearned readers in those matters which have most to do with salvation" (6:577–79). There is some need, therefore, on every person's part—learned and unlearned, strong and weak, young and old, ruler and subject—which God, through his Word, addresses and fulfills.

Milton's typically Protestant insistence for all people to read and ponder God's Word was a watermark evident in his writing to the very end. It was a position that meant the Scriptures would have to be available in English (and in every mother tongue) since most people could speak only their native language; it was a position that also meant the reverence attached to scriptural interpretation and understanding were no longer restricted to the few. Most of all, it was a position that thrived on the polemical, Reformist reaction to the exclusive, elitist reading tradition of Papists. Milton celebrates yet again that certain victory over his (and God's) opponents, merely from having gotten the Word out of a few designated hands and into most. He writes in his last tract, *Of True Religion*, in 1673:

> The Papal Antichristian Church permits not her Laity to read the Bible in their own tongue: Our Church on the contrary hath proposed it to all men, and to this end translated it into English, with profitable Notes on what is met with obscure, though what is most necessary to be known be still plainest: that all sorts and degrees of men, not understanding the Original, may read it in their Mother Tongue. Neither let the Countryman, the Tradesman, the Lawyer, the Physician, the Statesman, excuse himself by his much business from the studious reading thereof. (8:434)[2]

Thus, while the few have lost exclusive rights, all—even the disinterested or distracted—have inherited not only those rights, but the responsibility of "studious reading" as well.

2. See *Of Education*, CPW 2:370, for Milton's early (1644) emphasis on the adequacy of regarding as "learned" anyone "competently wise in his mother dialect only." In *Christian Doctrine* (1658–1660) and in *Of True Religion* (1673), Milton's purpose is to value the human being and to regard his natural and ordinary potential to learn as the basis for his educability, the fulfillment of which warrants his being regarded as "learned."

The Reformation's promotion of having Scripture accessible and available to everyone worried orthodox Puritans, lest dissemination of the Word mean rampant diversity of interpretation and, consequently, a divided and ultimately ruined church. Milton's response is the classically Reformist one: "The scriptures are, both in themselves and through God's illumination absolutely clear," "plain and sufficient in themselves" in revealing what God wishes us to know of him (6:578, 580).[3]

What Milton and others were to learn was that the Reformation had not unified the opposition to the Papist attitudes toward the interpretation of Scripture. An ever possible temptation to be "carried beyond the reach of human comprehension, and outside the written authority of scripture, into vague subtleties of speculation" was a spiritual affliction that could even strike Reformers, yielding a condition of relapse, which brings Milton to ask a series of questions (6:134):

> Through what madness is it, then, that even members of the reformed church persist in explaining and illustrating and interpreting the most holy truths of religion, as if they were conveyed obscurely in the Holy Scriptures? Why do they shroud them in the thick darkness of metaphysics? Why do they employ all their useless technicalities and meaningless distinctions and barbarous jargon in their attempt to make the scriptures plainer and easier to understand, when they themselves are continually claiming how supremely clear they are already? (6:580)

Having in mind those relapsed Reformers who once rightly maintained that distinctively Protestant position of scriptural clarity, Milton tries to shame them and bring them to see their error through mock postulates that, in negating or sullying Scripture, mirror their twistedness:

> As if scripture did not contain the clearest of all lights in itself: as if it were not in itself sufficient, especially in matters of faith and holiness: as if the sense of the divine truth, itself absolutely plain, needed to be brought out more clearly or more fully, or otherwise explained, by means of terms imported from the most abstruse of human sciences—which does not, in fact, deserve the name of a science at all! (6:580)

3. See Barker, *Puritan Dilemma*, 230.

Resisting rightful embarrassment and admission of error proves that they have already been lost. And their argument of scriptural obscurity unmistakably reveals their identity that, for Milton, is ironically clarified by Scripture: "The scriptures are difficult or obscure, at any rate in matters where salvation is concerned, only to those who perish: Luke viii. 10: *to you it is given to know the mysteries of the kingdom of God, but to others I speak through parables; so that they may look but not see, and hear but not understand*" (6:580).

The advantage to a belief in Scriptures that are "absolutely clear," "plain and sufficient in themselves," each passage of which "has only a single sense," was that experts, who reached "outside the written authority of scripture, into vague subtleties of speculation," were unnecessary. In the ordinary native language through frequent and regular reading and hearing (assisted with some instruction received in the "prophesyings" and sermons that taught or demonstrated simple exegesis), anyone and everyone could learn to perform the task of reading and understanding Scripture independently.

Milton acknowledges the need for thorough, scientific, and logical investigation of Scripture and provides the criteria and procedure for scriptural scholars and religious professionals:

> The right method of interpreting the scriptures has been laid down by theologians. This is certainly useful, but no very careful attention is paid to it. The requisites are linguistic ability, knowledge of the original sources, consideration of the overall intent, distinction between literal and figurative language, examination of the causes and circumstances, and of what comes before and after the passage in question, and comparison of one text with another. It must always be asked, too, how far the interpretation is in agreement with the analogy of faith. Finally, one often has to take into account the anomalies of syntax, as, for example, when a relative does not refer to its immediate antecedent but to the principal word in the sentence, although it is not so near to it. . . . Lastly, no inferences should be made from the text, unless they follow necessarily from what is written. This precaution is necessary, otherwise we may be forced to believe something which is not written instead of something which is, and to accept human reasoning, generally fallacious, instead of divine doctrine, thus mistaking the shadow for the substance. (6:582–83)

We are to take Milton at his word, and so, these are the "useful" principles to be followed. But this is his explicit, self-evident word. His forthcoming, more important, implicit word is signaled before the list by the disjunctive clause, "but no very careful attention is paid to it." His disappointing observation recalls the severe chiding several paragraphs before, when Milton wonders "through what madness . . . that even members of the reformed church persist in explaining and illustrating and interpreting the most holy truths of religion . . . , shroud[ing] them in thick darkness of metaphysics . . . [and employing] all their useless technicalities and meaningless distinctions and barbarous jargon." There, his queries climaxed in pointing to the inconsistency of these allegedly reformed church members who performed all sorts of interpretative machinations, yet claimed Scripture's clarity (6:580). Here, where the method is discussed, Milton is no less about scorning falsehood that results from the scholars' or professionals' having a practicable system but failing to use it, preferring instead to force others or themselves "to believe something which is not written instead of something which is, and to accept human reasoning, generally fallacious, instead of divine doctrine" (6:583). Milton, besides delineating "the right method of interpreting the scriptures," typically aims to expose the evil of following what is not written, of regarding human reason above divine doctrine, and of usurping the throne of others' religious intelligence, forcing them to believe what they may be ill-equipped to repudiate and correct without the same academic preparation.

It is ironic that at the outset of the very next paragraph—just after he has enumerated the nine requirements for interpreting correctly—Milton proclaims: "Every believer is entitled to interpret the scriptures" (6:583), a device to note that there is *interpreting*, and then there is *interpreting*. There is knowing how to read or lead as scholar or public minister (which does not automatically ensure adherence to divine doctrine), and there is knowing how to read as believer. Milton insists, "Indeed, no one else can usefully interpret them for him, unless that person's interpretation coincides with the one he makes for himself and his own conscience" (6:583–84).

By juxtaposing these two paragraphs, Milton corrects the presumed righteousness and ultimacy of a self-enclosed system without precaution against unfounded inferences and without recognition of another kind of interpreting that "every believer" is entitled to and is able to execute. Through this second paragraph Milton has the (perhaps) scripturally untutored (in one sense) show up the supposed expert scholars and preachers, for while the former may be unschooled in the procedure, they may read more ably and accurately than the others. It is important to note that Milton is certainly not renouncing "the right method" he delineates any more than he repudiates the university in *Of Education* or *The Likeliest Means.* His several purposes in all three cases are constant: he aims to dethrone the proud and presumptuous, to check sole reliance on human learning and skills, to reclaim the dignity and emphasize the potential of every human being, and to teach that learning and the concomitant wherewithal for knowing Scripture do not result *because* of a university system, or *because* of an interpretative system, but only *because* of the Spirit's illumination and tutelage. Milton's focus is broad and balanced: on Mother tongue and many languages, on unlearned and learned, on home and university. Here, too, as he considers the interpreter of Scripture, Milton's vision is dual. One eye is on the not necessarily systematic believer, the other on the well-trained exegete, warranting George N. Conklin's observation that "while the plain Scripture is adapted for the daily reading of all classes and orders of men, Milton's exegetical requisites for scholarly and professional interpretation reflect perfectly the new philology."[4] In Milton, though, where dualities are usually not final, the distinction between simple and sophisticated interpreter fades until what remains is the universal reading and believing human person. And, finally, as one ponders the actual interpretation of Scripture, Milton's double focus operates yet again, with one eye on this reading creature, and the other on the Holy Spirit—until that duality, too, eventually vanishes and creature is read by and reconciled into Creator.

4. Conklin, *Biblical Criticism and Heresy in Milton,* 34–35; see also Conklin 28–29 for the distinction between two kinds of readers. For extensive treatment of Milton and his use of the Bible, see also the following: Harris Fletcher, "The Use of the Bible in Milton's Prose"; Virginia R. Mollenkott, "The Pervasive Influence of the Apocrypha in Milton's Thought and Art," and Sims, "Milton, Literature as a Bible, and the Bible as Literature," in Sims and Ryken, eds., *Milton and Scriptural Tradition;* and James H. Sims, *The Bible in Milton's Epics.*

12

"If the Word Is Used Loosely"

Sacrament Revised

ne component of ministry for which this newly emphasized, broad-based lay ministry is also responsible is the
sacramental. Milton extends the privilege and duty of
this function as well: "If, then, any believer can preach
the gospel, so long as he is endowed with certain gifts, it
follows that any believer can administer baptism, because baptism
is less important than the preaching of the gospel" (6:573). Milton
has put first things first, namely, the preaching of the gospel. Furthermore, he has delayed discussion of the sacramental function of
ministry, making it the last point he considers with regard to ministers and the penultimate point of the entire chapter, "Of the Visible
Church." This placement is decidedly Nonconformist. The Conformist ministerial hierarchy (espoused by Prelates and clerics and
denounced by Milton throughout his prose) would surely not dis-
cuss the sacramental ministry last or almost last, since that particular function of the ministry is the one above all others that justifies
the Conformist ministers' necessity and preeminence and from
which the rest of the ministerial functions *in practice* derive. Milton's
intentional arrangement consequently gives a powerful Radical-
Reformist signal, reducing the exclusivity and importance of the
function without necessarily lessening the importance of sacramentality itself. Milton's positioning actually instigates a curiosity about
the definition and purpose of Sacrament, the implications of which I
shall begin discussing here, but complete only in the next chapter.

There is a change in the meaning of Sacrament that ensues from

Milton's repudiation of a special caste who are needed to deliver God's special goods. I am not so much concerned with the precise number of sacraments since Milton leaves room for debate. For him, Baptism and the Supper of the Lord are sacraments for certain (6:542). Matrimony he cannot regard "a sacred thing at all, let alone a sacrament." It is purely "a civil matter" (6:561) in the *Christian Doctrine*—likewise in *The Likeliest Means*: "A civil ordinance, a household contract, a thing indifferent and free to the whole race of mankinde, not as religious, but as men" (7:300). Confirmation or the Laying on of Hands should not "remain in the church as a sacrament" but "should be retained as a symbol of blessing" (6:560–61). Unction of the Sick, "merely the natural accompaniment of miracles . . . , ceased along with the gift of miracles" (6:561–62). And Penance and Holy Orders are not sacraments, in one sense: "It is quite clear to us, from the very definition of the word *sacrament*, that the other things which the Papists call sacraments—CONFIRMATION, PENANCE, EXTREME UNCTION, ORDINATION, and MATRIMONY—are not really sacraments at all. They are not divinely instituted, and they contain no sign appointed by God to seal the covenant of grace" (6:560). Yet, in another sense, Penance and Holy Orders *are* sacraments. Milton confesses he has "no objection to their being called sacraments if the word is used loosely, implying only that they represent sacred things, as did the old custom of washing the feet, and other customs of the same kind." One can hardly be concerned about a meticulous articulation of the criteria for rating a certain practice as Sacrament when Milton is not: "I do not see why much trouble should be taken to establish the precise meaning of the word when it does not even occur in the Bible" (6:561). So much for the clergy's raison d'etre. Papists have fashioned their sacramental system and matching self-important role to sustain it, both of which Milton reproves:

> Every sacrament is a seal of the covenant of grace. Thus it is clear that the Papists are wrong when they attribute to the outward sign the power of conferring salvation or grace. They think that this power is released whenever the rite is performed. But the sacraments cannot impart salvation or grace of themselves. They are merely seals or symbols of salvation and grace for believers. (6:556)

Milton, therefore, authorizes a certain lack of concern about the exact number and measurable criteria for calling certain religious customs "Sacrament."

It *is* important to notice, however, that which Milton himself expects one to notice (here and elsewhere), namely, attitudes of trust and flexibility, as well as tones of fluidity, which suggest a reliance on the Holy Spirit and an awareness that the age belongs to him. This Radical perspective on Word and Sacrament can be clearly distinguished from the received, Conformist view that requires absolute reliance on the visible church and an awareness that the age belongs to it. Also noteworthy is a new sort of power. For the Radical Nonconformist, power is released by Christ continuously through the Spirit so that this energy is ever accessible; it is not harnessed, then released through the sacramental rites themselves at designated moments. The sacraments are seals of the covenant that always exist. Third, one can observe a belief in renovation that is not just partial, so that special, clerical ministers are the sole performers of sacramental actions, but so universal and thorough that the laity can preach, prophesy, *and* offer sacraments. Finally, one discovers a radically Reformist hierarchy of authority: the sacramental system, even while Reformed according to the pristine apostolic arrangement based on God's Word, is subordinate to the preaching of that Word.

Discussing the antitypes within Christ and his Mystical Body, Barbara Lewalski points up the key difference between the two ages:

> In the Middle Ages such antitypes were found chiefly in the sacramental and institutional life of the Church, whereas the Reformers and especially the Puritans found them (often with the support of ingenious contemporary applications of the prophecies of Daniel, the Song of Songs, and the Book of Revelation) in the continuing historical experience of God's elect—most notably in the Reformation, the English Civil War, and the great Puritan adventure in the New World.[1]

Milton's treatises, however, as this book has aimed to show, did not reveal the break between those two worlds and their corresponding churches to be so clean. Throughout the 1640s, 1650s, and 1660s Milton found a "sacramental and institutional" mania that strove to return with seven times the strength it had when it had presumably been routed. Furthermore, during this period, England as type (like Israel waiting for perfecting) and antitype (unlike

---

1. Lewalski, *Protestant Poetics*, 129.

Israel having received the New Covenant of Grace) was in shift. The most recent historical experience was becoming less national and public than it had been previously. Developments—spurred on and climaxing during the middle decades because of Scripture's availability and instruction, lay leadership, and household churches—showed type and antitype at the common, domestic, even individual level. This was a trend of, perhaps, less significance to the new Presbyterian Puritan establishment (which replaced the old medieval, Papist one) than it was to the Radical Puritan individual whose foremost establishment was a spiritual communion with Christ and the members of his Body. The rather unifocal ecclesiology that was more national than it was anything else gave way to a trifocal ecclesiology—one that honored and fostered the individual, congregational (including household), and international dimensions of spiritual communion with Christ and his members.

The former notion of sacramentality, evident during Milton's lifetime in the Conformist church, suggests that the Sacrament is necessary as a vehicle for providing the spiritual reality and power of Christ. Aquinas and Milton represent Conformist and radically Nonconformist positions on the meaning of Sacrament, respectively. John Ulreich, Jr., explains that there is broad agreement between Aquinas and Milton on the question of sacramental participation: "The essence of a sacrament is *communion* with Christ. . . . Where Catholic and Protestant part company is over the question of sacramental efficacy." For Aquinas, sacraments *cause* grace whereas for Milton, they *signify* or represent grace. Therefore "this radical difference between an efficacious sign . . . and a mere outward sign . . . entails a very different conception of sacramental significance."[2]

The revised, Miltonic notion of sacramentality suggests that spiritually, by dint of Christ's having given his Spirit to all believers, the power of Christ and communion with the divine reality are always immediately and directly there, the sacraments simply standing for that truth. The outward instrument, that is, the *preached* Word (6:573) or administered Sacrament (6:556 and thereafter), only seals or expresses what, in fact, is already present for the Puritan. The former notion, on the other hand, would always have the believer arrive where the Radical Reformist believes he or she already is.

Also, there is gross inconsistency in the former Papist sacramen-

2. Ulreich, "Milton on the Eucharist," 44–45.

tal system, since on the one hand while agreeing in theory with the universal heritage (priesthood) of spiritual renovation, it prevents the enactment of that spiritual truth. Milton criticizes the self-claimed Papist right to determine the applicability of any "seal upon grace" which has been won by Christ for all: "Sacraments were chiefly instituted to set the seal upon grace and to confirm our faith. Therefore all sacraments should be distributed equally to all believers. But of these five papist sacraments, four are not available to all but only to particular men: penance to the lapsed, unction to the sick, orders to the clergy, and marriage to the laity" (6:562).

Thus, however much English Reformers aimed and claimed to have succeeded in routing Papacy by reducing the number of sacraments and eliminating the mutually exclusive matrimony and holy orders, many other Reformers found the Antichrist yet alive and well. Such changes and others were only superficial. Unless the sacral were thoroughly universalized and internalized, anti-Christian elitism, ceremonialism (however lessened), and custody of Scripture would remain, though rather dormant for twenty years, and would revive as an even greater force in the end. And unless the sacral were thoroughly universalized and internalized, there could never be the proper external ritualizing that, because of God's preference, must always conform to the internal.

Just as Milton has proclaimed the commission for all to preach and to baptize, he proclaims the liberation of every believer to celebrate the Sacrament of the Supper of the Lord:

> There is nothing in the Bible about the Lord's Supper being administered. The early Christians are said to have taken part in it regularly and in their own homes: Acts. ii. 42 . . . and ii. 46 . . . , and xx. 7, ... So I do not know why ministers should forbid anyone except themselves to celebrate the Lord's Supper. It might be said that Christ handed the bread and wine to his disciples, but he certainly did not give them to each individually, and besides he was acting as a founder of a new institution, not as a minister. (6:557)

In removing the Sacrament of the Lord's Supper from the church building and institutional control and in relocating this sacrament within the home for the ordinary believer to lead, Milton levels his most powerful blow to the entire current sacramental system, since the Supper was the Sacrament of sacraments for Papists and many Conformists—the epitome of ministerial privilege, prestige, and pride.

13

"A True and Living Faith"

The Ceremony of Works

orks are one very visible expression of the invisible church that is extremely important to, and very characteristic of, extreme Nonconformists like Milton. Before Milton's Michael ever gives Adam a final string of exhortations for possessing that inner, "happier" paradise, beginning with "add[ing] / Deeds to thy knowledge answerable" (*PL*, 12.581–87), Milton, in his budding theology beginning to be expressed in *The Reason of Church Government*, had as an aim the creation of "a fit person to do the noblest and godliest deeds" (1:842). As I discussed in chapter 9, the "wise and true valuation" of oneself is the prerequisite that will "stirre him up to walk worthy the honourable and grave imployment wherewith God and the Church hath dignifi'd him" (1:844). For Milton and all true Protestants, true piety issues forth in productivity. C. A. Patrides has remarked that the influence of the Cambridge Platonists can be noted in the age not by the enthymeme "I think, therefore I am," but, rather, "I act, therefore I am." The context has shifted, he claims, from the Cartesian philosophical one to the Whichcotian ethical one.[1] The point here is that deeds, works, honourable employment, virtuous action, or whatever one wishes to call the evidence of invisible holiness, has been a constant and predominant value for Milton's theology and ecclesiology and one that is typically empha-

---

1. Patrides, "The Experience of Otherness," in Patrides and Waddington, eds., *Age of Milton*, 191.

sized by other Radicals, too. Milton names "true evangelical charity, insofar as it can be distinguished by man" as the third of the four marks of the visible church (the other three being "pure doctrine, the true external worship of God . . . , and the correct administration of the seals" (6:563).

The former covenant required works as well, but the New was a "better Cov'nant," as Michael informed Adam, for the change in duty was from "works of Law to works of Faith" (*PL*, 12.302). Further instruction from the heavenly messenger reveals Milton's agreement with Luther's emphasis on the justification by faith, without robbing anything from the importance of works:

> . . . ere the third dawning light
> Return, the Stars of Morn shall see him rise
> Out of his grave, fresh as the dawning light,
> Thy ransom paid, which Man from death redeems,
> His death for Man, as many as offer'd Life
> Neglect not, and the benefit embrace
> By Faith not void of works . . .
>
> (*PL*, 12.421–27)

It is Christ who redeems not only all believers, but their works too, presenting both to the Father. Rescuing works from any Pelagian misinterpretation, Milton gives them their proper place within the entire eternal design and celebrates this doctrine in *Paradise Lost* as the Father discusses with the Son the process of redemption and what necessitated it. While Man must die for his sin, "Death becomes / His final remedy, and after Life / Tri'd in sharp tribulation, and refin'd / By Faith and faithful works, to second Life," Man will be "Wak't in the renovation of the just" (*PL*, 11.57–65).

Milton's position on works, which are the effect rather than the cause of sacredness, follows the doctrine as stated by Luther in *Concerning Christian Liberty*:

> Thus a Christian, being consecrated by his faith, does good works: but he is not by these works made a more sacred person, or more Christian. That is the effect of faith alone; nay, unless he were previously a believer and a Christian, none of his works would have any value at all; they would really be impious and damnable sins.
>
> True, then, are these two sayings: "Good works do not make a good man, but a good man does good works"; "Bad works do not make a bad man, but a bad man does bad works." Thus it is always necessary that the substance or person should be good before any

good works can be done, and that good works should follow and proceed from a good person.

Luther concludes his teaching on the matter with the scripturally based analogy of man as the fruit-bearing tree with either good or bad produce, depending on the health of the tree itself: "As then trees must exist before their fruit, and as the fruit does not make the tree either good or bad, but, on the contrary, a tree of either kind produces fruit of the same kind, so must first the person of the man be good or bad before he can do either a good or a bad work; and his works do not make him bad or good, but he himself makes his works either bad or good." Woodhouse explains, "The zeal for reformation results in part from the fact that the Puritan temper is, in general, active rather than contemplative. Though its official creed repudiates works as a means of salvation [as Luther surely would], it emphasizes them as a sign [also as Luther would]."[2] In explaining *how* our faith justifies us and our works, Calvin writes,

> Our doctrine . . . is that the good works of believers are always devoid of a spotless purity which can stand the inspection of God; nay, that when they are tried by the strict rule of justice, they are, to a certain extent, impure. But, when once God has graciously adopted believers, he not only accepts and loves their persons, but their works also, and condescends to honor them with a reward. In a word; as we said of man, so we may say of works,—they are justified not by our own desert, but by the merits of Christ alone. (*NRC*, 164)

Milton explicitly agrees with these founding fathers of Reform; however, he acknowledges the contemporary theological controversy over the *seemingly* incompatible positions, justification by faith (as found in Paul) and justification by works (as found in James) (6:489–90). James, Milton is certain, is "talking about justification, not in the sight of men," but in the sight of God:

> What [James] is saying is that we are not justified only by a useful, true and living faith, a faith which saves, but by works as well. . . . I cannot imagine what came into our theologians' heads to make them abridge the words of the apostles' conclusions. Had they not done so they would have seen that the two points of view, *that man is justified by faith without the works of the law,* and *that man is justified by works, not by faith alone,* are quite compatible. For Paul does not

2. *Luther's Primary Works,* 274–75; Woodhouse, *Puritanism and Liberty,* 44.

> say that man is justified simply through faith, without works, but *without the works of the law.* Nor does he say that he is justified by faith alone, but *by faith working through charity,* Gal. v. 6. Faith has its own works, which may be different from the works of the law. We are justified, then, by faith, but a living faith, not a dead one, and the only living faith is a faith which acts, James ii. 17, 20, 26. (6:490)

If "a true and living faith cannot exist without works," one needs to ask what these works of faith involved. This question is especially pressing since "works" were incorporated into the standard Lutheran, Reformist, justification-by-faith theology and were promoted very strenuously by the Radical church of the mid-seventeenth century in England, which one might automatically expect to stand at odds with the Lutheran doctrinal base because it was usually regarded as the conservative core of the Reformation. But, over the next century after Luther, the meaning and purpose of works became more and more refined, so that extreme Nonconformists during the reign of Charles believed that works according to the Old Law, and as manifested in the Laudian ritualism of the 1630s, referred to ceremonial worship. Works according to the New Law referred to works of charity that becomes the most perfect form of worship or, in other words, a renovated ceremonialism. Worship, in and through these ceremonies of charity, signals the liturgical move

> From shadowy Types to Truth, from Flesh to Spirit,
> From imposition of strict Laws to free
> Acceptance of large Grace, from servile fear
> To filial, works of Law to works of Faith.
> (*PL,* 12.303–6)

Understanding works of charity as worship is clarified in Milton's theological treatise: first, in the overall division of the entire work corresponding to the basic aspects of religion; second, in Milton's definition of "true worship." Modeled on Wolleb's division, Milton's *Christian Doctrine* consists of two main sections: "The PARTS of CHRISTIAN DOCTRINE are two: FAITH, or KNOWLEDGE OF GOD, and LOVE, or THE WORSHIP OF GOD" (6:128). His wording in the transition between books has even greater bearing on the point: "The first book dealt with FAITH and THE WORSHIP OF GOD. This second book is about THE WORSHIP OF GOD and CHARITY" (6:637). And Milton begins this second book by devoting the very first chapter to the doctrine "Of Good Works" (the title of the chapter).

Faith's purpose is not to give the believer abstract theological build-

ing material for a booth in which to dwell, removed from the awareness of the needs of the human community and the responsibility to
address those needs. The direction beyond self is to be the natural
outgrowth of "a living faith, not a dead one" (6:490). The association
of charity with worship is rather new. It generally characterizes the
Puritans, but especially the extremist segment of them. Christopher
Hill assesses this development: "Charitable works have value in so
far as they are directed towards the good of the community, of my
neighbors, and are not self-regarding as (in protestant eyes) the
formal works advocated by late medieval catholic theologians had
become."[3] Laudianism, Puritans felt, simply continued this religious self-absorption.

In his discussion of the *Christian Doctrine*, Arthur Sewell explains
the increasing importance Milton gave to works—a development
able to be monitored by the changes in his revision, changes that
reveal a correlative attention to the freedom of the will:

> When the treatise was first dictated, Milton seems to have laid
> insufficient emphasis on the freedom of the will and the renewal
> of that freedom through grace. We find him adding in a number of
> places the statement that the will as well as the mind is renewed. It
> was, indeed, necessary to Milton's thought that the renovation of
> man should not only involve enlightenment of the mind, but also a
> quickening of his will. For the end of faith is good works, freely
> willed out of an understanding of spiritual things.

Probing into Milton's personal motivation at an earlier period, while
he was writing *The Tenure of Kings and Magistrates*, Shawcross discovers the same concern and believes, "Milton recognized that one
has to do something to make what he wants actually come about."
Shawcross points out that the *doing*, in this case, is political:

> The future Milton sees therefore is one in need of "deeds in sub-
> stance" [3:194] from all who believe in justice for man. Surely one
> of the greatest sins is sloth, and of the slothful the worst is he who
> observes the need to do but does nothing. Too easily will there be
> those who will sit by doing nothing, or who will be persuaded . . .
> to berate the new leaders (the deliverers from the bondage of
> tyranny), some to the point of working for defeat of the new gov-
> ernment, internally or from forces without.[4]

3. Hill, *Society and Puritanism in Pre-Revolutionary England*, 495–96.
4. Sewell, *Milton's* Christian Doctrine, 20; Shawcross, "Higher Wisdom," in Lieb
and Shawcross, eds., *Achievements of the Left Hand*, 152, 154.

This attitude places Milton in the company of Radicals like many Levellers, Quakers, and Ranters who believed that faith must issue in works.[5] The place in Scripture that inflamed these Radicals' all-consuming devotion was the Epistle of James. As used by a Leveller like Walwyn, a mystical-political writer like Winstanley, a Ranter like Coppe, or, as we have observed above, a political-spiritual theologian like Milton, this epistle was a favorite among the Radicals for its denunciation of the rich, attention to the poor, and emphasis on works as the specific means to reset the balance of goods and extend charity to all.[6]

Especially noteworthy among this group, with whom Milton must have felt spiritual communion through practical works, is Gerrard Winstanley, claimed by Hill to be "the supreme exponent of the philosophy of action as opposed to contemplation." A typical Winstanleyan exhortation, whose rhetoric as well as message echoes a Jamesian or Pauline caricature of the supposed holy person's rebuff to the needy, shows why: "Thoughts run in me that words and writings were nothing and must die, for action is the life of all, and if thou dost not act, thou dost nothing."[7] This emphasis on action in Winstanley or in Milton cannot be taken to exclude the inner dimension, for the interior is always the starting point for conversion that Radicals believed could result in an external paradisal community. For them, there must always be the dialectic between the inner world and the outer world.

T. Wilson Hayes points out similarities between Winstanley and

---

5. See Hill, *World Turned Upside Down,* 338; and Hill, *Society and Puritanism,* 494.

6. See Morton, *World of the Ranters,* 69, 87, 147. See also Nelson, "Play, Ritual Inversion and Folly," 334; Ranters, eager to rail against social injustice, prophesied retribution for it (299). See *Christian Doctrine,* bk. 1, chap. 22, "Of Justification" (*CPW* 6:485–94).

7. Hill, *World Turned Upside Down,* 338. Also see Winstanley's discussion of the serpent in chap. 4 of *Fire in the Bush* (*Works*), where Winstanley remarks that the rich are getting richer, then advocates caring for the poor (463). Winstanley was able to transcend the dichotomy of individualism and collectivism "through his vision of a society based on communal cultivation and mutual support." Sabine observes in his introduction (*Works*) Winstanley's uniqueness among some other Radicals: he "differed from Fox and the Quakers chiefly in believing that this consciousness of human brotherhood must at once become the principles of a new form of community. For him true religion required the immediate creation of a society that substituted community and mutual aid for individualism and competition. He could not content himself with a religious experience that ended with a change of personal morality, nor imagine a moral reform that did not include the elimination and the removal of political oppression" (51).

John Everard, who holds that God planted an outward tree in paradise and an inward tree "in the heart of Adam." Hayes explains that the Garden is simultaneously an internal psychological existence and an external material existence, and the senses are the streams of communication between them. Particularly regarding Radical "inner light" thinking, which usually accompanied millennial expectations, there was a double directionality: both inward and outward—internalizing the imminent and urgent moment in order to externalize in the very near future.[8]

The link between the inner and outer worlds is imaged organically for Winstanley, as Hayes explains, "with the image of the seed of the sun of righteousness rising in the flesh." But, as in Milton, the organic outer religio-political growth transpires only if there has been true inner regeneration. One of the lessons of *Paradise Lost* is that descendants of Adam and Eve will become perfected by extending the inward Paradise outward, toward others. In Winstanley, too, the inward paradise should yield outward fruit, or love. Hayes charts the expected progress in Winstanley's reader of *Fire in the Bush* (1653) who is to be

> led through a process of microcosmic self-preservation that at all times has maintained contact with nature, the macrocosmic world of things. Now he draws near the final step when the inner image of his own transformation is projected back out onto nature. . . . the seed sprouts and flourishes until the Tree of Life reaches out from the individual and bears fruit in the world in the form of giving and receiving love.[9]

8. Hayes, *Winstanley, the Digger,* 179–80. See M. H. Abrams, *Natural Supernaturalism: Tradition and Revolution in Romantic Literature,* 58–67.
9. Hayes, *Winstanley, the Digger,* 196.

14

"Charity or Holiness of Life"

Spiritual Principle Linking the
Inner and Outer Worlds

ilton likewise focuses on the important intimacy between these inner and outer worlds. His device for doing so is the word *charity*, given the fullest semantic scope possible. At the outset of the second book of his *Christian Doctrine*, Milton is as pointed and terse about the heart of the important relationship between those two worlds as he is about the connection between worship and works. We have already observed that "this second book is about THE WORSHIP OF GOD and CHARITY," but we have not noted that for Milton "what chiefly constitutes the true worship of God is eagerness to do good works" (6:637).[1] In chapter 13 I have dealt with worship; here I shall turn to charity before drawing some conclusions about worship. While the two ideas for Milton are inseparable, they are clearly distinguishable for purposes of edification (then) and exposition (now). Milton explains this new sort of cultus: "GOOD WORKS are those which WE DO WHEN THE SPIRIT OF GOD WORKS WITHIN US THROUGH

---

1. On the Behmenist influence of works understood as worship circulating among the common folk, see Bailey, *Milton and Jakob Boehme:* "The virtue, civic as well as religious, upon which both Milton and Boehme lay most stress is that of 'brotherly love'. The true worship of God consists chiefly in the performance of good works; these include, with the observance of inner devotion and church rites, the duties of man to his neighbor" (168). For a thorough discussion of *cultus,* in general, and the difference between the old *cultus* and the new, in particular, see Lieb's *Poetics of the Holy* (on the new, see esp. 36).

TRUE FAITH, TO GOD'S GLORY, THE CERTAIN HOPE OF OUR SALVATION, AND THE INSTRUCTION OF OUR NEIGHBOR" (6:638). Milton elaborates on good works in *Colasterion* by discussing its equivalent term *charity* as the best way to keep "the holy rest of Sabbath":

> It is not the formal duty of worship, or the sitting still that keeps the holy rest of Sabbath; but *whosoever doth most according to charity,* whether he work, or work not; *hee breaks the holy rest of Sabbath least.* So Marriage being a civil Ordinance made for man, not man for it; he who doth that which most accords with charity, first to himself, next to whom hee next ows it, whether in marriage or divorce, hee breaks the ordinance of marriage contract least. (2:750)

If one is to keep "the holy rest of Sabbath," then doing charity outdoes refraining from doing other activity, presumably and traditionally forbidden on the Sabbath because it is considered work.

The new life that results from regeneration brings with it "an understanding of spiritual affairs and charity or holiness of life" (6:478). Unlike inadequate or imperfect forms of worship that were presumed to be acceptable but were not, charity enables the believer to achieve and express union with the divine as well as communion with other members of Christ's Body:

> CHARITY ARIS[ES] FROM A SENSE OF DIVINE LOVE WHICH IS POURED INTO THE HEARTS OF THE REGENERATE THROUGH THE SPIRIT. CHARITY AFFECTS THOSE WHO ARE IMPLANTED IN CHRIST, SO THAT THEY BECOME DEAD TO SIN AND ALIVE AGAIN TO GOD, AND BRING FORTH GOOD WORKS FREELY AND OF THEIR OWN ACCORD. This is also called HOLINESS. Eph. 1. 4 *that we may be holy and blameless in his sight, with charity.* (6:479)[2]

The closing synonym reinforces the connection between (acceptable) works and worship and announces the success of *these* works (in contrast to those under the Old Law) in accomplishing union with God, that is, "Holiness": "I am not talking about charity towards one's brother. The love I have in mind is love of God, and not only the love which we have for God, but a love which arises from the instinct and awareness of love which he has for us. . . . It is, as it were, the daughter of faith and the mother of good works" (6:479). These last two quotes come from the first book of the treatise that is devoted to faith or the knowledge of God. Each appears to present a discrepancy between two basic meanings of charity: on the one

2. See Lieb, *Poetics of the Holy,* 39.

hand, referring to divine love, that internal Christian ordering principle from which everything else derives; on the other, referring to good works, that external Christian ordering principle which is that "living faith" and which effects our return to the Father. (These two meanings, while certainly interlinked, receive separate focus in these two books, respectively.)

The problem is apparently compounded when within the first book we find a statement about charity that because of its deed-orientedness would seem to belong in the book not on faith (or divine love), but on charity (or good works): "So long, then, as charity, the greatest of gifts, exists, and wherever it exists, we should have no doubts about the truth of the visible church. John xii. 35: *by this all men shall know that you are my disciples, if you feel charity for one another*" (6:565–66). "Charity," here referring to works as a criterion for determining the "true" visible church, might seem to have been misplaced. However, Milton is neither confused nor self-contradictory. His two meanings of charity do not cancel each other out any more than Christian wisdom and classical learning mutually exclude each other on the basis of Milton's shifting concern for this or that body of knowledge, or on the basis of Christ's preference before Satan in the wilderness.

I began talking about works, deeds, and charity by referring to book 2 of the *Christian Doctrine* only to indicate one more trait that exemplifies visible harmony between Milton and other Radicals. The combined statements about charity from books 1 and 2 together, provide a comprehensive doctrine of works or charity. Milton here may appear to balk at or to question one definition then the other, just as he does the place of the classics and other fruits of university education in *Paradise Regained*. Yet here, as there, Milton is only interested in the right order of things. All proceeds from God and returns to him—all creation and all charity. That is Milton's point. Once one realizes that charity necessarily refers to both the divine and the human, to providence and community, one recognizes the modus operandi of charity that was in Milton's mind all along: charity begins with God, takes us to our neighbors, returns us to God, and is responsible for continuing and sustaining that eternal spiritual pattern by which God reforms and reconciles the church unto its complete glorification.[3] There is no clarity to be had if one expects a

3. See Charles M. Coffin, "Creation and Self in *Paradise Lost*," who talks of the

simplistic notion of charity. Milton is clear, however, about the double ordering inherent in and accomplished through charity and about the several functions of it. From the foregoing one can be certain about two things: first, the privileges and duties of charity never permit a cloistered dwelling in believers' heads to enjoy theological speculation or contemplation only privately; second, charity, both as the internal and as the external ordering principle, is the foundation of the new cultus. In dispensing with concern over whether or not any work is permitted on the day of rest, Milton, after the fashion of Scripture itself, promotes the spirit of the law over the letter of the law. Charity, therefore, is the word that binds the individual's interiorized renewed self-image with the externalized practical manifestation of that re-creation. It is not only "the soul / Of all" the virtues, but the soul of the invisible and the "true" visible church (*PL*, 12.584).

Charity becomes the linguistic knot tying the individual to Christ, the inner spiritual life to the outer world, and the individual to the community of members in Christ. Like love (*PL*, 12.583), it is a synonym for *Christ*, the internal redemptive principle, as well as for *labors of love*, the external effect of the renovated believer who is "alive again to God" (6:479). Because of Christ—the source, center, and goal of life—this individual and interior accent does not atomize and alienate. On the contrary, this individual and interior emphasis paradoxically links the spirit of the individual, correctly expressed in charity and through charity, more closely to the community of spiritual fellowship. Charity alone provides the only means for the Christian to reach from the inner spiritual realm to the outer societal realm where the Christian can contact other Christians through good deeds, and thereby bond with others' spirits. The bodily, fleshly dimension of personhood becomes the vehicle for genuine spiritual communication and a community of spirits. In understanding charity this way, one begins to appreciate "what chiefly constitutes the true worship of God," according to Milton: "Eagerness to do good works" (6:637). In terms of church, charity is thus the symbol for

---

tendency toward reconciliation embedded within the *separateness*, which characterizes man's and woman's relationship to each other, as well as the human relationship to God (14), as the "ideal" (16) that, like a magnet (4), summons us back to God where we belong.

both the invisible and visible church. It exhausts the explanation of the relationship of the church (individually and collectively) to Christ. It is causative, sustaining the status of the invisible mode of the church as Bride of Christ, and consequential, giving generous evidence of redemption's gratitude as an ongoing sign of the visible mode of the church. What is important to note is that Milton underscores his extreme Nonconformity by both meanings of charity. His use of the term in the first book conveys the typically Radical belief in the primacy of the spiritual relationship with God and with others (6:479). His use of the term in the second book demolishes a theology and a church dependent on external liturgical works and promulgates the typically leftist attention to brotherly love for all as the only sort of works desired by God to justify us and to be presented by Christ, in our behalf, as acceptable ceremony within the True Church (6:637).

In his *Christian Doctrine* Milton incorporates the contrast between "works of faith" and "works of the written law" (6:490), that is, between works required by the new dispensation as opposed to those required by the former, in terms of worship, in *Paradise Lost*. As Adam learns from Michael the inadequacy of the Old Law, he learns, as well, the power of the New.

> Law can discover sin, but not remove,
> Save by those shadowy expiations weak,
> The blood of Bulls and Goats. . . .
> Some blood more precious must be paid for Man,
> Just for unjust, that in such righteousness
> To them by Faith imputed, they may find
> Justification towards God, and peace
> Of Conscience which the Law by Ceremonies
> Cannot appease, nor Man the moral part
> Perform, and not performing cannot live.
> (*PL*, 12.290–99)

This "imperfet" Law (300) and the works that it demands must yield "to a better Cov'nant" (302) and its "works of Faith" (306). God uses this new arrangement, by which "works of Faith" (306) along with God's people of faith are redeemed, to bring all of creation to completion: "Tri'd in sharp tribulation, and refin'd / By Faith and faithful works, to second Life," Man will be "Wak't in the renovation of the just," and "Resign[ed] . . . up with Heav'n and Earth renew'd" (*PL*, 6.57–66). And at that time, as promised by the Father, and only because of charity, "God shall be All in All" (*PL*, 3.341).[4]

4. See also *PL*, 6.730, where the same eschatological idea, achieved through the same mounting and propelling force, is pointed with the identical phrase, and Col. 30:10. Echoes of both Bonaventure and Gerrard Winstanley can be heard in the lyrical and ecstatic "all in all" to express the ultimate reconciliation towards which all creation tends. Bonaventure revels in mystical prayer: "May my soul always rove around you, and seek you and find you! Let it turn to you and come to you! May you be the object of its thought and of its word. Let it sing your praise and the glory of your beloved name with humility and reserve, with love and delight, with ease and tenderness, with patience and peace, with success and perseverence unto the very end. You alone shall be all in all to me" (H. A. Rheinhold, ed., *The Soul Afire: Revelations of the Mystics*, 246). See Lieb, *Poetics of the Holy*, who cites John Gregory's Hermes-like God who is "All in All," whose circle is "everywhere" and circumference "no where" (130). For Winstanley's use of the term, see Christopher Hill, "The Religion of Gerrard Winstanley," in McGregor and Reay, eds., *Radical Religion*: "In the day of Christ, Winstanley had written in *Truth Lifting up Its Head*, all created flesh shall be made subject to Reason, 'so that the Spirit, which is the Father, may become all in all, the chief ruler in flesh' " (211).

15

"Written Records Pure"

Myth-Making the New External Scripture

f the Authorized Version was regarded by Milton as neither "sacred" nor "unalterable," but, instead, as Fletcher notes, "a convenient form of Scripture on which to depend in English," there were certainly other "convenient" (though perhaps less reliable and less preferred) forms: Coverdale's, Matthew's, the Geneva, and even the Douai Bible, depending on his purpose.[1] If the most convenient form (A.V.) were not sacred or unalterable, neither were the others. The Latin Vulgate, with its doctrine-influenced word choice, would be even less so. And, as we have already acknowledged, because of various kinds of human error, even the original Greek and Hebrew texts bore the condition of being flawed. How did Milton conceive of Scripture? And what was sacred about it for him?

Following the same union of opposite but integrated components that he presents in his discussions of church (invisible and visible), worship (internal and external), and man (inward and outward) examined thus far, Milton likewise conceives of Scripture as consisting of two divergent aspects, the internal and the external: "We have, particularly under the gospel, a double scripture. There is the external scrip-

---

1. On Bibles, see Conklin, *Biblical Criticism and Heresy*; Esther Cloudman Dunn, "The Bible in England in the Sixteenth Century," 234–61; Harris Fletcher, "Use of the Bible," 38; William B. Hunter, Jr., "The Theological Context of Milton's *Christian Doctrine*," in Lieb and Shawcross, eds., *Achievements of the Left Hand*, 269; Lewalski, "Biblical Genre Theory: Precepts and Models for the Religious Lyric," in *Protestant Poetics*, esp. 32–33; Sewell, *Milton's Christian Doctrine*; and Sims, *The Bible in Milton's Epics*, 97–102. (In Latin, Milton would have consulted the Protestant Latin Bible of Junius and Tremellius, and, depending on his intention, even the Vulgate.)

ture of the written word and the internal scripture of the Holy Spirit
which he, according to God's promise, has engraved upon the hearts
of believers, and which is certainly not to be neglected" (6:587). The
two, however, are not of equal power or weight: "The external authority for our faith . . . , the scriptures, is of very considerable importance
and . . . the authority of which we have first experience. The pre-emi-
nent and supreme authority, however, is the authority of the Spirit,
which is internal, and the individual possession of each man" (6:587).[2]

Georgia Christopher observes the very core of Protestant hermeneutics, which sets it apart from that tradition of reading Scripture that it seeks to overthrow and replace. About the origin and
scope of this new tradition Christopher writes: "For Luther, and
even more so for Protestants after him, the Holy Spirit provided the
experiential authentication for a reading of Scripture. This was the
most radical aspect of his hermeneutic, for Aquinas had discussed
the whole topic of revelation without mentioning the Holy Spirit."[3]
Calvin, too, teaches the necessity of the Spirit's ratification in the
believer's heart, an action apart from which Scripture cannot be
efficacious: "For as God alone is a fit witness of himself in his Word,
so also the Word will not find acceptance in men's hearts before it is
sealed by the inward testimony of the Spirit" (ICR, 79).

In Milton especially, emphasis on divine communication through
the internal Scripture seems to be the only effective way his doctrine can escape contradiction between, on the one hand, the expec-
tation that all people can know the doctrine and prophecy contained in Scripture and, on the other hand, the exhortation that only
those specially trained in the original texts, in the levels of language,
in syntax, and so forth can get at Scripture's truth. The internal
Scripture, authorized by the Spirit, is written and readable equally
for all, a fundamental tenet that allows Milton his radical invitation:
"Every believer is entitled to interpret the scriptures; and by that I
mean interpret them for himself. *He has the Spirit,* who guides truth,
and *he has the mind of Christ*" (6:583; emphasis added).[4]

---

2. See Schwartz, "Citation, Authority," for the political implications of Milton's
doctrine of "double scripture." Her recent discussion bolsters the ecclesial implications treated in this chapter, which was presented originally in my 1988 doctoral
dissertation ("Milton's House of God: Church, Scripture, Sacrament) and which, in
part, later appeared in my article, "The Mystical in Milton."
3. Christopher, *Milton and the Science of the Saints,* 6.
4. *CPW* 6:583–84 n. 23.

Two strains fuse here in Milton's scriptural schema: the prophetic (having the Spirit that directs one to God) and the mystical (having the mind of Christ—having "arrived at" or known that delightful harmonious union to which the Spirit continuously points).[5] A proof text for the Spirit's work in securing for believers the mind of Christ is 1 Corinthians 2. The text proclaims and revels in the accessibility of previously impossible things:

> Eye hath not seen, nor ear heard, neither have entered into the heart of man, the things which God hath prepared for them that love him.
> But God hath revealed *them* unto us by his Spirit: for the Spirit searcheth all things, yea, the deep things of God.
> Now we have received, not the spirit of the world, but the spirit which is of God; that we might know the things that are freely given to us of God.
> But the natural man receiveth not the things of the Spirit of God: for they are foolishness unto him: neither can he know *them*, because they are spiritually discerned.
> But he that is spiritual judgeth all things, yet he himself is judged of no man.
> For who hath known the mind of the Lord, that he may instruct him? But we have the mind of Christ. (9–16)

While the (almost concluding) question recalls the great gulf between God and humanity embedded in the awareness behind similar questions posed for Job and the Psalmist, the assertion in the final statement is a sort of ultimate reprise of the sudden, mysterious, and permanent bridging of that chasm. The swift simple retort linguistically enacts the same qualities about the theological truth contained in the chapter in particular, and in the gospel in general, for those to whom "God hath revealed [hidden things] by his Spirit." Here, as in Milton's treatise, the Spirit becomes the instrument for accomplishing that reclaimed dignity, lost since the Fall, and that

5. For another view that does not distinguish between having "the spirit" and having "the mind of Christ," see Thorpe, *John Milton:* "Fortunately, man does have this other source of guidance available to him, in addition to Scripture. He has the Spirit of God to guide him. Milton uses a number of different terms for this comforting idea. The Spirit of God most often, perhaps, but also the Holy Spirit, or the Comforter, or the mind of Christ in man, or Celestial Light, or inward light" (174). Not distinguishing, Thorpe argues, does not affect his argument of an increasing emphasis on the inner life. While this may be true for the *statement* of Thorpe's idea, his failing to distinguish between the two phrases leaves a nagging question about the *operation* of Thorpe's argument in reference to Miltonic interiority.

renovated capacity for knowing those "things" that, before Christ sent his Spirit to bring believers to himself, could not be known.

In trying to appreciate Milton's "double scripture," one should think of two distinct, genuine tablets on which God has written. One should not simply imagine one actual tablet and one meta-phoric, which resolve problems caused by the external Scripture, through some sort of redemption-heightened intelligence. Milton is talking here of two actual texts whose truth may be overlapping, intersecting, supportive, or conflicting. Each of these texts, that is, the external Scripture and the internal Scripture, is read most accu-rately and comprehensively with both "the spirit, who guides truth," and "the mind of Christ." Christ has come (and gone) that all might return to him in the end. Until that final victory, however, he has provided both that way to the end (through the Spirit's guidance) as well as periodic foretastes of it (through union with Christ's mind). And it is by virtue of so simple and ordinary a task as reading that these are made available.

One important trademark of the Reformation that Georgia Chris-topher observes is a shift in emphasis from the visual to the verbal—"from things to words." Commenting on the watershed of the Ref-ormation, she writes that in a piety that is anti-Catholic because it is antivisual, "Luther's exegesis makes a radical shift from physical to *verbal*, not simply from physical to mental, reference. In nearly every case, the referral of images to verbal matters calls in question the power of visual images to describe the motions of faith." Power was to be had, instead, in the new "word-based" piety, since, ac-cording to the commentaries of Luther and Calvin, Christ was pres-ent "in" the biblical narrative. In Christopher's view, this doctrine becomes "the core of Puritan experience for the next several cen-turies." And from that core, she explains, come two convictions that appear in Milton and most seventeenth-century Radicals: "That Scripture will become plain enough to anyone making a devoted study," and "that one encountered the Real Presence in biblical promise." Seventeenth-century Reformist practice diverged in its boldness to expand the means for conveying that promise, so long as that expansion began with Scripture's literal text and ended with confirmation by the Spirit's text in the heart. The important contri-bution that Christopher makes is showing what Milton shared with sixteenth-century continental Reformers: "Their attitude toward sacred texts and their belief in a 'verbal' sacrament," which distinguished them from their Papist enemies. "Of course the notion of *spiritually* ingesting a *physical* body that was located a cosmos away was never firmly grasped by the English Puritans, but the notion that a mental ascent was affected by divine 'figures' conferred a remarkable numinosity upon the tropes of Scripture, and in effect, turned reading the Bible and meditating upon it into a homemade sacrament."[6] The Papist leap in space, humane civility, and logic were more than Protestant sacramentality could bear. U. Milo Kaufmann ascertains a replacement, suitable to the Puritan aural orientation, for what Protestants regarded as a bizarre notion of sacrament among Papists. Protestants, he explains, retained the idea of transubstantiation; only for them, the mysterious change occurred not through the visible elements of bread and wine, but through the verbal elements of Scripture. Following Ambrose's and Baxter's emphasis on the importance of the spoken word, Kaufmann perceives that " 'sound' was continually being changed into substance as the divine Word, through preaching, hearing, and reading was transmuted into the flesh and bone of Christian life."[7] Calling upon *Paradise Lost* to exemplify this very important emphasis on the verbal, Christopher points out that the narrator's "flight to the upper reaches dramatizes the Protestant mystery of 'promissory possession'—the man of faith has verbal visiting rights to heaven but does not abide there yet."[8]

It is in the context of Sacrament that ideas on Church and Scripture come together, since for any believer—Presbyterian, Congregationalist, Anglican, Catholic, or Radical Puritan—there are always the outer structure and the inner business through both of which some sort of spiritual transaction between God and humanity occurs. Michael Lieb discusses the shift in the conception of cult as Old Testament ritual practices yield to New Testament ones, which the poet as hierophant inherits. God's Laws and Presence are contained in God's "Tabernacle." From God's specifications, "A Sanctuary is fram'd / Of Cedar, overlaid with Gold, therein / An Ark, and

6. Christopher, *Science of Saints*, 7–8, 12, 124. See chap. 13, "A True and Living Faith," for the distinction between the Catholic and Protestant meaning of *Sacrament*. According to Aquinas sacraments cause grace, whereas for Milton they signify it (Ulreich, "Milton on the Eucharist," 44–45).

7. See Milton's discussion of this doctrinal absurdity in his treatment of The Lord's Supper in *Christian Doctrine* (CPW 6:552–55). U. Milo Kaufmann, The Pilgrim's Progress *and Tradition in Puritan Meditation*, 244.

8. Christopher, *Science of Saints*, 125.

in the Ark his testimony, / The Records of his Cov'nant" (*PL*, 12.247–52). However, Lieb concludes: "In [Milton's] poetics of the holy, he fashions not tabernacles of 'Cedar overlaid with Gold,' but the temple of Christ with its truly 'spiritual architecture.' "[9]

Here is the spiritual twist asked for both by the New Covenant as well as by Milton's tracts, especially his *Christian Doctrine*. Yet this surely cannot be the final step required in the sacramental procedure that Milton's teaching on Gospel, Church, Renovation, Ingrafting, Conscience, Holy Spirit, and the Prophetic Function of Christ call for. Lacking still is the last step of *interiorization* of what has been fittingly spiritualized. Even spiritual *without* must become spiritual *within*. How does this sanctification occur? Does the reader inhabit the poem or does the poetic Word inhabit the reader? The poetic framework is that which the reader inhabits, but only initially, so that its inner meaning and center, namely Christ and his Spirit, can inhere within the reader and inscribe the internal Scripture in the heart, theoretically now in perfect fulfillment of the Father's prophetic promise to write one day upon fleshly tablets.[10]

Preceding Milton's doctrine by a few years, William Dell proclaims in *Trial of Spirits* (1653): "The believer is the only book in which God now writes his New Testament."[11] This statement expresses the Radical position on Church, Scripture, and Sacrament—a position that is so prophetic, so mystical, and so progressively revelational that it interfuses Church and Scripture, Tabernacle and Testament, architecture and function, sacramental vessel and sacred action, even while it simultaneously individualizes each believer as "house of God" and then interiorizes that status. The individual, then, transmuted to interfused Tabernacle and sanctifying action, becomes the most Radical and most perfect Sacrament—in Milton's terms, the suitable "external sealing of the covenant of grace" (6:542). With this understanding of worship space, worshiper, and worship, the poem, having been read and digested, dissolves till it is taken up *and in* again, going the way of other sacramental elements used in religious ritual. This is the logical outcome of an understanding of church that has developed from international Papist institution, to national English church, to loosely gathered congregations, to unaf-

---

9. Lieb, *Poetics of the Holy*, 58.
10. See Ezek. 36:26; and 2 Cor. 3:3.
11. Hill, *World Turned Upside Down*, 259.

filiated gathered assemblies, to household churches, then to the individual believer; the logical outcome of a concept of Scripture, whose emphasis has shifted from the external Word to the internal; and the logical outcome of the conflation of the ideas of church and Scripture with their respective changes. It is no longer parish church or home that functions as a domicile for God's dwelling.[12] The individual human being who has become one with Christ through Scripture and the Spirit now houses him. In this "church" the believer contacts not only Christ, but the members of his body, the "church," in the hope of recognizing and enjoying a definite ecclesial identity.

In his chapter "Of the Gospel, and Christian Liberty," Milton explains that this gospel is "THE NEW DISPENSATION OF THE COVENANT OF GRACE" that "HAS BEEN WRITTEN IN THE HEARTS OF BELIEVERS THROUGH THE HOLY SPIRIT, AND WILL LAST UNTIL THE END OF THE WORLD" (6:521). Milton's theological statement is in poetic agreement with Dell's description of the believer as book or sacred text. To give greater force to the trope, Milton cites a scriptural passage that itself uses the metaphor paradoxically recommending the dissolution of the entire literal text that provided Milton with metaphor and spiritual doctrine:

> And indeed all true believers either prophesy or have within them the Holy Spirit which is as good as having the gift of prophecy and dreams and visions. II Cor. iii. 3: *that you are the epistle of Christ ministered by us, written not with ink but with the Spirit of the living God; not on tablets of stone but on the fleshly tablets of the heart,* and iii, 6: *ministers of the new covenant, not of the letter but of the spirit: for the letter kills but the spirit gives life;* James i. 21: *receive with meekness the ingrafted word which can save your souls.* (6:523–24)

Milton allows the literal citing of Scripture to do the work of canceling its literal authority and viewpoint and, in the apparent vacuum, allows the Spirit, which has literally and truly made the believer into Scripture, to take its place. The believer is transfigured into sacred book, "*the epistle of* Christ . . . *written not with ink but with the Spirit of the living God.*" If he has known and been illuminated with

---

12. For discussion of the growth of the household or domestic church from gathered assemblies or *prophezei* as central in contributing to the atomization of the parish, see Hill, *Society and Puritanism,* 30–78 and 443–511; Davies, *Worship of English Puritans,* 30–32; Thompson, *Liturgies of Western Church,* 313–15; Nichols, *Corporate Worship,* 103; Nuttall, *Visible Saints,* 102; and Walzer, *Revolution of Saints,* 189, 197.

the fullness of the written scriptures, they have served their purpose. They can vanish (for now) since they were designed for self-destruction once they and believer have become ingrafted, and once believer has become ark of the ongoing covenant in the age of the Spirit. Believers are changed into the new architecture in which the holy writing reposes.

Here, in the Scripture Milton cites, one observes the typical iconoclastic spirit, which identified the more impassioned Reformers throughout the Reformation. Only here, that same spirit is in paradoxical artistic operation—concerned, as always, to shatter the concrete and tangible (in this case, the poem) in order to break and eliminate the false security of relying on any external; yet employing words, images, verbal patterns, and aesthetic structures to take away what is given. Michael Murrin discusses the iconoclasm evident in Milton's heaven where Murrin claims there is a biblical theophany modeled on that of Ezekiel's vision of the chariot. Analyzing the purposeful option of the artistic image-breaker, he explains, "The iconoclast could either multiply images or dispense with them altogether, opposite verbal techniques which have the same function." In either case the aim is to prevent idolatry. For the iconoclastic poet-prophet, "the rich proliferation of images makes impossible a single, clear image in our minds."[13] But this principle is true for more than the particular visions in Ezekiel's or Milton's heavens. What one discovers in miniature about the purposeful multiplicity of images here at the artistic-iconoclastic local level of the poem leads one to an awareness of Milton's attitude toward the poem as a whole. That is, at the artistic-iconoclastic global level of *Paradise Lost*, readings can become idolatrous. Just as "the rich proliferation of images makes impossible a single, clear image in our minds," so must rich multiple readings, guided by the same Spirit's light that was responsible for the poem's writing, make impossible a single, final interpretation.

Of course, one need not be inspired merely to read the poem. Milton, however, has designed a poem that will allow for and even foster inspiration and sanctification in addition to an informative and moving experience of reading. Ideally, one would approach Milton's "Word" time and again, just as one does any reading of Scripture or, in terms of the purest Protestant worship, just as one

13. Michael Murrin, "The Language of Milton's Heaven," 360, 362.

does any Sacrament to experience the seal of communion with Christ and the members of his Body. The Word thrives on a tentativeness that summons the reader to successive readings; otherwise, that "spiritual" utterance can become as fleshly and anti-Christian as have church buildings, ceremonial worship, hierarchical structures, and scriptural interpretations mandated by any visible church, all of which extreme Nonconformists time and again have insisted are idolatrous. Yet the believer needs to read—God's Word and Milton's poetic "Word" that, typical of any true prophet's message, is not to be differentiated from God's Word. The text contains the living God's commandment forbidding false gods and his essential direction of adhering to his revelation. Thus, the canceling process is not intended to rid the believer of necessary text to which one is to return in the future to remain faithful, but only to rid one of a kind of self-righteous and self-enclosed reading whose absolutism and finality will, in fact, enslave one by *literary* custom, ceremony, and superstition. Attitude is all—able to transform "all the sacred mysteries of Heav'n / . . . Left only in those written Records pure" into "written Records" *impure* (*PL*, 12.509–13). On the other hand, with the Spirit and the mind of Christ governing and guiding successive progressively revealing readings, these "written Records pure" can make readers themselves into living "written Records pure."

What happens through the course of the Reformation in England is that the individual becomes a domicile of God's living Word. In terms of worship, which for the Protestant is purest when it consists in the fullest sense of the Word explicated above, the individual becomes a sacred house for sacred action—a place where each believer expresses and celebrates communion with Christ and with the mystic "communion of members" (6:500). The proof texts which Milton cites, to ground his teaching that Christ is the only head of the visible church, make great use of the "house" trope and emphasize the potential of a church as particular as a single individual to enjoy that most universal of connections, mystical union with Christ and his mystic body:

> Just as Christ is the head of the mystical church, so no one is rightly or can possibly be at the head of the visible church, except Christ. Matt. xviii. 20: *there I am in their midst*, and xxviii. 20: *I am with you always, even to the end of the world;* I Cor. v. 4: *when you and my spirit are gathered together in the name of our Lord Jesus Christ with the power of our Lord Jesus Christ;* Heb. iii.6: *Christ is set over his own*

house; Rev. ii. 1: *who walks between the seven golden candlesticks.*
(6:566)

With Milton's doctrine and these biblical texts, one sees the power of
the particular and visible to convey the universal and invisible, the
opportunity of the individual to encounter the entire communion of
saints and angels, and the process whereby house, for a brief time,
conveys heaven.

Throughout the Reformation in England, which peaks at the time
of the Revolution, there has been increasing emphasis on individuality and interiority. These traits have produced a theology, ecclesiology, hermeneutic, sacramentality, and aesthetic that combine to
form and sustain a significant bipartite Radical myth very evident
in Milton's writing, namely, the myth of the single reading believer
as the most basic and adequate church and of the internal Word
(through all of the Spirit's external media) as the choicest sacramental food provided on the table in that House of God. There, the
invitation for pleasurable and nutritious consumption comes again
and again, providing that foretaste of those final "fruits Joy and
eternal Bliss" (*PL,* 12.551). This myth spiritually brought the individual (and Milton) into covenant and contact with God and his
people. As is evident in the prose writing examined in this study,
this myth was *in the works* even as it was *at work* throughout Milton's
preaching and prophetic communication. It was the concrete expression of a constant ecclesial impulse that moved Milton to speak
to and write for a Pure Church that he knew existed somehow, somewhere—even if that ecclesial communion were unable to make itself
as visible as Milton and others would have liked. For the time being,
the spiritual brotherhood he believed he enjoyed because of this
ecclesial impulse and its myth would have to be enough.

CONCLUSION

Kenosis: God's and Milton's Reforming Rhetorical Invention

The church in England during the mid-seventeenth century was in need of enormous assistance. Merely blaming believers for a truncated Reformation was neither a specific nor a constructive remedy for the problem. Any true, rigorous Reformer would find that kind of accusing far too mindless and cowardly and would, instead, need to tackle particular and precise basics like language—words and phrases that from long-term misuse or abuse, bolstered concepts and behavior that opposed the gospel. It was on these nuts and bolts that Milton concentrated his ecclesial impulse and verbal energy. Unperverting the language that camouflaged the falsehood, oppression, and self-service, Milton reasoned, was the strategy that would turn the world right side up, revealing Truth and completing Reform.

To him, terms that referred to ecclesiastical, scriptural, sacramental, or spiritual matters must have looked like the dry bones of Ezekiel's nightmare—especially when, in the course of the Revolutionary period, these phrases and concepts appeared eventually to be just as dead, as empty of godliness and gospel values for Presbyterians and Independents as they had been for Papists and even for supposedly reforming Prelates. Like Ezekiel, Milton believed he was ordered by God to prophesy. And prophesy he did—over ecclesiological bones, in an effort to assist his church during the 1640s in establishing and articulating its Radical ecclesial identity.

Thus, through the power of his prophetic spirit and mystical mind, Milton, time and again, believed he could work verbal miracles, making his recurring operative pattern a vehicle of spiritual power,

229

his "Word" a vehicle for God's. We can discover the process of verbal renovation at work throughout Milton's prose canon and with a variety of words and concepts, notably, *separation, schism, heresy, license, clergy, learning, trade, works, holiness, Sacrament, Scripture, house of God,* and *worship.*

Throughout his prose, Milton employed a certain verbal pattern with these doctrinal words: he would first empty the familiar terms of their accreted, expected meanings presumed to secure spiritual life; he would then allow these distorted or perverse notions to die; finally, with the aid of Scripture and the Spirit, he would raise the transfigured terms to new life and their original "true" meanings. But Milton's rhetorical invention was not new.

Kenosis is a traditional Christian theory to explain the mystery of the preexistent divine Christ's "condescension involved in the Incarnation." The scriptural source of the theory is Philippians 2:7 where the term is translated 'emptied himself'.[1] This action began the process of redemption that was completed only by his suffering, death, and resurrection. In other words, *kenosis* is God's rhetorical invention: his Divine Word—as Person and Utterance—discharges himself of all presumed status and premature glory, and is then informed with shocking and scandalous suffering-servanthood before he is exalted to a permanent, genuine, and effectual glory as Christ.

Kenosis is much more than an arbitrary analogical tool for packaging Milton's thoughts into a unified essay. I would argue that this christological tenet, articulated throughout chapter 16 of the first book of Milton's *Christian Doctrine,* is the very foundation of his theology and of all spiritual and ecclesial Reform in the view he shared with those in the Radical church communion.[2] Milton catechizes:

> Philipp. ii. 6–8: *he was in the form of God, he emptied himself, and took the form of a servant; he humbled himself, and was made obedient right up to his death;* I John iii. 16: *through this we know God's love, because he laid down his life for us;* Rev. i. 17, 18: *I am the first and the last, and I am alive and was dead. . . .* Of course, the fact that Christ became a

1. *The Oxford Dictionary of the Christian Church,* ed. F. L. Cross and E. A. Livingston, 777.

2. For a debate about the prominence of the theory of *kenosis* in Milton's theology, see William B. Hunter, "Milton on the Incarnation: Some More Heresies," and "Milton on the Exaltation of the Son: The War in Heaven in *Paradise Lost*"; and Lieb, chap. 4, "The Kenotic Christology," in his *Sinews of Ulysses,* 38–52.

sacrifice both in his divine and in his human nature, is questioned by no one. It is moreover, necessary for the whole of a sacrifice to be killed. So it follows that Christ, the sacrificial lamb, was totally killed. (6:440)

But this emptying (which includes Christ's death) is only the first half of the administration of redemption. The second completes, ratifies, and extends the victory: "Christ's humiliation is followed by his exaltation. By this it is meant that CHRIST, HAVING TRIUMPHED OVER DEATH AND LAID ASIDE THE FORM OF A SERVANT, WAS RAISED TO IMMORTALITY AND TO THE HIGHEST GLORY BY GOD THE FATHER, FOR OUR GOOD, BY VIRTUE PARTLY OF HIS OWN MERIT AND PARTLY OF THE FATHER'S GIFT, AND ROSE AGAIN, AND ASCENDED, AND SITS AT GOD'S RIGHT HAND" (6:440–41). Thus, Milton concludes: "Christ's exaltation, like his emptying of himself, applies to both his natures. It applies to his divine nature by virtue of that nature's restitution and manifestation, and it applies to his human nature by virtue of its accession" (6:443).

Like Christ, along with the corporate Church and individual believers who follow him, ecclesiastical words go through *kenosis* (emptying), then dying and burying, before they rise to a purposeful Reformist life. The entire process of redemption is, and must always be, both *personal* and *verbal*: Christ, 'the Word' of the Father, gives significance to his Church's words as the ongoing means for causing and sustaining its regenerate condition and ecclesial relationship to him.[3] Furthermore, like God's Word (Christ), Christ's ecclesial words (ecclesial terms) were those to be understood, not according to *human* concept, plan, and preference, but as God would have them. Now, to those words.

In *The Reason of Church Government*, Milton's teaching reevaluated and redefined the act of ecclesial separation and those to be identified as 'the separated'. Prelatical priests, in belonging to the false church, were the real, harmful separatists, whereas Milton and those in his spiritual company in belonging to the True Church had not ecclesiastically budged. And while Milton honestly and straightforwardly admitted that he and many "stand separated," that external

---

3. See Robert Entzminger's *Divine Word: Milton and the Redemption of Language,* wherein he too argues that "spiritual and verbal redemption are linked" (2), concluding that with the fall of language, "the agency for redeeming words is the Word which redeems humanity" (144).

condition is commanded by God in Scripture and necessitated by the ill health of the nation's church during the mid-seventeenth century (1:787–88). Milton punctures the concept of external ecclesiastical separation by mocking the Prelates (those whose purpose was to ensure church unity) for having alienated themselves spiritually from Christ and his True Church. In short, Milton has taken the received concept of separation, ridiculed and ruined it beyond usefulness, and reinvested it with other (inner) significance. Like all miracles, the new, Radical language of separation depends on paradox: here, separation means togetherness. To extreme Nonconformists, their literal separation became a rite of spiritual communion, whereas their opponents' imaginary and apparent union with the hierarchy and structures of the established church actually signaled spiritual disintegration and disaster.

Milton also takes the important concept of schism and grants the unique attribute with which the Prelates credit themselves (as being "the only mawls of schism") on the basis of what he means by mauling schism: "If to bring a num and chil stupidity of soul, an unactive blindnesse of minde upon the people by [the Prelates'] leaden doctrine, or no doctrine at all, if to persecute all knowing and zealous Christians by the violence of their courts, be to keep away schisme, they keep away schisme indeed" (1:983–85). Mauling schism, for Milton, means dulling the soul, blinding the mind, persecuting wise and zealous Christians. In short, it is to rend the very unity the Prelates presume to protect and promote. In turning the idea inside out, Milton has shown that the supposed "only mawls of schism" are really the masterful makers of it in its worst sense, and that those reputed to be "schismaticks" (1:786) or "sectaries" (2:555)— those labeled Brownists, Familists, and Anabaptists—are just harmlessly different members of the one Body—preservers of that soul, vision, and zeal associated with schism in its best sense.

In *Areopagitica,* having alluded to the living Temple trope of First Corinthians and Ephesians, Milton accepts the term *schism* and the identity of being schismatic as something honorable. Punning on the literal level (that schism means 'cutting'),[4] Milton deflates the literal meaning of the received ecclesiastical understanding of schism while directing our attention to the nonliteral, spiritual meaning and purpose: that all presumed church schisms are really unschis-

4. *CPMP,* 744 n. 242.

matic since the spiritual architecture requires that "there must be many schisms and many distinctions made in the quarry and in the timber, ere the house of God can be built"; he writes furthermore, "Neither can every peece of the building be of one form" (2:555). Milton removes the presumed sacredness of the literal prohibition against schism in order to instate and emphasize the required sacredness of the etymologically literal 'schism' if one is to be part of the spiritual building. The sin of spiritual schism occurs if one is not part of this spiritual edifice because one has tried to dismantle the varied "contiguous" stones—that is, eliminate the "many moderate varieties and brotherly dissimilitudes that are not vastly disproportionall." Such demolition is sinful, for out of these varied stones, in fact, "arises the goodly and the graceful symmetry that commends the whole pile and structure" (2:555).

It is in this ideological context of the wholesomeness and beauty of diversity within unity that Milton, in *Of Civil Power*, considers and redefines heresy. For him, heresy means "choice only of one opinion before another, which may be without discord" (7:250). Creating discord is "schisme . . . in the worst sense" and is far worse than heresy. But before Milton has finished, he returns to a notion of heresy that does refer to doctrinal violation. His concern here, however, is not directed to any particular tenet with its literal components and nuances, but to a general, mortal violation against the Spirit and conscience: "In apostolic times therefore ere the scripture was written, heresie was a doctrin maintaind against the doctrin by them deliverd: which in these times can be no otherwise defin'd then a doctrin maintained against the light, which we now only have, of the scripture" (7:250). If there is to be judgment of literal doctrine, Milton invites Scripture for the trial, at which the former accusers will become not only the spiritually accused, but the literally accused on the words of Scripture itself. Thus, Milton takes the received understanding of heresy as one kind of teaching, clears himself and those in spiritual communion, wrongly accused, by first redefining the exhibit for their presumed arraignment as mere harmless opinion, and next by calling upon the original and still preeminent literal instrument (Scripture) for testing the validity and acceptability of all heresy (that is, doctrinal opinion).

Milton transformed the word *license* as well. He was certainly aware that the word *liberty*, for which he and his Reformed church argued, could be mistranslated as 'license'. But even in Sonnet 12,

when reprimanding those who mean license "when they cry liberty" (11), his disgust is aimed at attackers of his prose who have
become part of the self-serving, self-protecting, and narrow-minded
new establishment. License refers to the pattern of ecclesiastical
self-will, doctrinal stubbornness, compromising hypocrisy, and unchecked use of force to support positions of power. For the Radical
Milton, who is bent on turning wrong things upside down and
inside out, license actually refers to all that stands opposed to internal and mystical ecclesial liberty. Milton begins with this term that,
according to things presumably right side up, describes those libertine Radicals whose social manners are looser than respectable society would like. Once he has emptied the word of its standard associations and has redefined it as irresponsibility through looseness
of speech and irresponsibility through self-serving tyrannical government, then this new definition implicates the political and religious establishment, without excusing the undisciplined antinomian sensuality of certain Ranterist assemblies or individuals. When
the renovated definition operates, the formerly supposed *un*licentious become the new guilty and are invited to be just as horrified of
their own form of license—one able to do much greater harm than
what they would regard as the license of the rabble's social improprieties. The irony here is that, spiritually speaking, some of these
ill-mannered may exemplify the converse of license in the usual
sense. Because they refrain from tyrannizing over others' consciences
as well as from impeding the free movement of the Spirit, these,
ostensibly guilty of license, may in fact be graced with the beginnings of "true" spiritual liberty and, consequently, may be at least
genuine initiates into real religious Reform.

As Milton deals with the more particular aspects of ecclesiology,
he turns to things more visible. The verbal cycle of emptying and
fulfilling can be seen here as well, in the interplay between the church's
visibility and its invisibility. In general, one can observe Milton's
renunciation of things visible, as defined by the established Prelatical religion, one by one, in favor of stressing the invisible, spiritual reality, which the respective external form only feebly adum-
brates. But, as always, this voiding of a concept's false meaning or
emphasis is not the end of it. There is an infusion of the concept
with new significance and an investiture of it with new visible characteristics. Examples of this process throughout Milton's tracts are
numerous. Representative selections follow.

With the typical Protestant emphasis on the Latin derivation of clergy (that *clerus* means 'heritage'),[5] Milton first acknowledges a special clerical caste, then dissolves it to allow for a leveling of humanity; again he takes up the idea of a special caste, but this time the group's summons comes from God, and its specialness is spiritual, gathering all who respond to universal grace. And so, an ordained ministry is renounced in favor of a lay ministry.

Learning, potentially valuable, is useless without those "solid things" that prove knowledge to be practical and rooted in experience. Consequently, in *Of Education* the multilingual university pedant, if inexperienced and impractical, is void of learning, whereas the worldly-wise unilingual "yeoman or tradesman" (2:369–70) is filled with learning. In Milton's schema, then, learning, presumed to be derived from formal training, is emptied of significance, yielding to another sort of learning obtained from the world, conveyed through one's "mother dialect only," and made available to anyone. In *The Reason of Church Government* Milton refers to learning exclusive of God's wisdom as "weak mightines" (1:827). This sort of learning he proceeds to obliterate, at the end of which action he reconstructs the kind of true learnedness that must be ever-submissive to the Divine wisdom of the gospel in its "mighty weaknes." This verbal flip-flop is a fitting index for the resurrected importance of learning, according to a world whose hierarchy of learning has been righted.

In *The Likeliest Means to Remove Hirelings* the concept of trade is overhauled (7:307). The spiritual enemies taken on in this treatise are supposed preachers (that is, traders) who rake in their subsistence—undeserved since their preaching is abysmal, not to mention unlegitimated since Scripture offers no apostolic models or directives. Yet Milton converses on their terms, initially granting the received (their) understanding of the term *trade*—a job with compensation owed for work delivered—before their cited unrendered service discredits their word and the overall integrity of their speech. They fall by this old, usual materialistic definition, just as they do by the new.

From the implosion of this vacuum of virtue the old elitist ineffective traders, along with their system of trade, ends. Out of this nothingness emerge those who can do the job well—and without pay for

---

5. For Huguelet's idea of "heritage" as a common Protestant translation for *clerus*, see *CPW* 6:572 n. 12.

it, even while they hold another job for hire—because the business of preaching is now open and potentially universal. Trade is now a metaphor for the task of leading people to spiritual commerce with God. With this verbal miracle, trade comes to mean nonwork in the material sense, as the spiritually topsy-turvy world sees things. To those in spiritual communion, however, it refers to a certain productive uselessness, affordable *practically*, through a trade (in the usual sense, but exclusive now of preaching) assuredly allowable in the material world by the spiritual realm and even recommended by Scripture. It is the materialistic entanglement with the ecclesial— the excuse for pay because of occupational laziness in exchange for evangelical incompetence—that previously posed the problem, not the understandable and necessary attention to survival in the world. With Milton's renovated definition, the metaphor trade now includes both the appropriate material and (the formerly absent) spiritual and ecclesial goods; the term *tradesmen* is correctly assigned to members of Milton's church by Milton himself and those within his ecclesia for whom he redeems words (7:307).

In the *Christian Doctrine* other ecclesiological terms likewise undergo a sort of death and resurrection. Holiness measured by ritual and purificational distinctiveness is rejected in favor of "charity or holiness of life" (6:478). Ceremonial works must be forsaken, for the believer must rely on nothing but faith; yet out of the ashes of that apparent liturgical nothingness is to proceed the phoenix of charitable works—the most acceptable ceremony.

Sacrament, too, undergoes a miraculous transformation. If Sacrament is taken in the Papist sense, to imply a release of power that confers salvation or grace, there is no such thing. In this case, for Milton's church, Sacrament has died. Yet, as "merely seals or symbols of salvation and grace," Sacrament lives indeed, and very prominently (6:556). In particular, Penance, and Holy Orders, taken to be sacrament by Papists, are not sacraments, Milton reminds us, in that they are "not divinely instituted," although they are Sacraments if the term *Sacrament* is understood "loosely, implying only that they represent sacred things" (6:560–61). Time and again Milton rescues for Protestants these visible manifestations of church that might otherwise have been lost.

Milton has transformed standard notions about Scripture, too. In this case, Milton begins not by dismissing the external written Word, but by having it reverenced as necessary—temporarily—as a starting point along the path that ultimately leads to the speaking Spirit and the primacy of what is revealed interiorly. The second step here is recognition of the primacy of the internal Scripture that is written by the Spirit in the heart of the believer and that provides the only truth to which God will hold the conscience responsible. The internal Scripture yields to a new external Scripture commissioned and inspired by the Spirit—an instructive, prophetic, and mystical Word—*Paradise Lost* being one example. Milton does the same thing with Scripture as he does with other religious components. God's spoken Word is considered visible and external, then ideally invisible and internal, and finally visible and external once again, but applied and adapted to current needs and by aesthetics that are as timely as they are timeless and that are, therefore, faithful to their reforming rhetorical source.

Similarly, the house of God, referring once to a designated place of worship set aside exclusively for that purpose, is renounced for its spatially-distinctive-based sanctity in favor of any place where an assembly congregates or an individual is privately summoned by God to worship. But it is not that place is unimportant in Milton, but place has become resignified so that person is now location. Milton details this new house of God as the absence of a designated physical structure that gives way to his scripturally alluded emphasis on the heart of each believer as the pillar and ground of truth (6:589).

We can additionally observe Milton's verbal transformation at work with regard to worship in and for his house of God or church. While external worship is "to go hand in hand with [the internal] . . . , never separated except by the viciousness of sinners" (6:666), Milton asserts which sort is preeminent and essential: "But internal worship, provided that it is sincere, is acceptable to God *even if the external forms are not strictly observed*" (6:668; emphasis added). Harmony results hierarchically: external devotion must conform to internal, not the reverse.

In discussing external worship, however, Milton provides guidelines of various kinds: some are promotive (cursing, fasting, vowing, covering or uncovering the head); some are dismissive (repeating the Lord's Prayer verbatim, raising voices in prayer, making lawful but wrongful vows); some are unitive (praying, which can be done at any time and in any place). Regardless of the type, though, while the enunciated principle argues the respective external form a certain place in the entire Miltonic scheme of worship, the principle's (sometimes many) qualifications deprive the external of the power of preemptive prescription. Milton's theology has no room for hard and fast rules about verbatim prayers, bareheaded believers, or hours for prayer because Scripture itself (cited often enough to document a practice and to signal a cohesiveness between God's Word and Milton's) is void of such prescriptions. It is as if rigid regulating would prevent the Spirit from blowing where it listeth—a horror to either writer.

The believer is free to use this or that acceptable external, but only as one optional, nonfixed rite presumably emptied of its superstition and rigidity. The renovating pattern here can be summarized as follows: external yields to solely internal that in turns yields to optional, nonfixed external. Yet, there is in Milton's ecclesiology a recognized need for liturgical space and action. But the only essential external is the individual reading believer—the most basic worship, book, and church—in sum, Milton's mythic vehicle for radical, thorough Reform.

Thus, in Milton's hands each of the terms, forms, or ideas considered in his ecclesiology follows a pattern of what might be called "verbal *kenosis*." Without exception Milton takes each one as received in its normal ecclesiastical or spiritual usage—a usage, according to Milton and the saints, which comes from a world that is upside down. Imitating God's rhetorical pattern of redemption (as recorded in Philippians 2), Milton empties each linguistic item of its regular, supposedly supernatural content, and allows that notion to die before he takes up the term again, resurrected with new, "truly spiritual" meaning. Out of this *kenosis* and *death*—out of this emptying, eventual disintegration and seeming formlessness—proceed renewed words, forms, and concepts that Milton and his church trusted would bear much fruit.

Time and again, in word and idea, Milton behaves as Jeremiah and any prophet always must: taking, tearing down, then building and planting (Jer. 1:9–10). Milton plants the pattern of renewal for his church and its ecclesiology through linguistic transubstantiation. But what was true even of Christ, the prophet of prophets, is no less true for those, like Milton, who participate in this prophetic pattern. The seed planted by the prophet may or may not survive and bear fruit, but if it does, often its growth will go unnoticed and its fruit untasted by him—at least for the present. Overwhelming evident success and tangible satisfaction were never guaranteed to the prophet in the Old or New Testament. After all, husbandry was not the job of the prophet alone. It was one he shared. His task was to tear down, to build, and to plant. Growing and harvesting were up to God—and the believer. By 1674 Milton had learned and come to love God's grandly justified providence—a truth with which Milton had wrestled all his life. While he clearly bore the scar from the struggle, Milton was not overcome, but, instead, knew an uncommon intimacy with the One who had sent that sinewy, strong angel to prepare him to gather and feed the Church with a formidable and functional ecclesiology.

BIBLIOGRAPHY

Abrams, M. H. *Natural Supernaturalism: Tradition and Revolution in Romantic Literature*. New York: W. W. Norton, 1971.

Adkins, Camille. "Adam's Room: Incarnation of the Divine Image in *Paradise Lost* and *Jerusalem*." Ph.D. diss., Texas Christian University, 1976.

Aland, Kurt. *Four Reformers*. Translated by James Schaff. Minneapolis: Augsburg, 1979.

Ames, William. *The Marrow of Theology*. Translated from the 3d Latin ed., 1629. Edited by John D. Eusden. Reprint. Boston: Pilgrim Press, 1968.

Bailey, Margaret Lewis. *Milton and Jakob Boehme: A Study of German Mysticism in Seventeenth-Century England*. New York: Oxford University Press, 1914.

Barker, Arthur. *Milton and the Puritan Dilemma: 1641–1660*. Toronto: University of Toronto, 1942.

Bennett, Joan S. *Reviving Liberty: Radical Christian Humanism in Milton's Great Poems*. Cambridge: Harvard University Press, 1989.

Berkhof, Lewis. *Principles of Biblical Interpretation*. Grand Rapids, 1950.

Berry, Boyd. *Process of Speech: Puritan Religion, Writings, and* Paradise Lost. Baltimore: Johns Hopkins University Press, 1976.

Blessington, Francis C. " 'That Undisturbed Song of Pure Concent': *Paradise Lost* and the Epic-Hymn." In *Renaissance Genres: Essays on Theory, History, and Interpretation*, edited by Barbara Kiefer Lewalski, 468–95. Cambridge: Harvard University Press, 1986.

Breslow, Marvin Arthur. *A Mirror of England*. Cambridge: Harvard University Press, 1970.

Bush, Douglas. *English Literature in the Earlier Seventeenth Century 1600–1660*. Oxford: Oxford University Press, 1946.

Calvin, Jean. "The Necessity of Reforming the Church. Presented to the Imperial Diet at Spires, 1544." In *Calvin's Tracts Relating to the Reformation*, translated by Henry Beveridge, 123–234. Edinburgh: Edinburgh Printing, for The Calvin Translation Society, 1844.

Calvin, John. *Institutes of the Christian Religion*. Edited by John T. McNeill.

241

2 vols. Library of Christian Classics. Philadelphia: Westminster Press, 1960.

Campbell, Gordon. "*De Doctrina Christiana:* Its Structural Principles and Its Unfinished State." *Milton Studies* 9 (1976): 243–60.

Christopher, Georgia. *Milton and the Science of the Saints.* Princeton: Princeton University Press, 1982.

Coffin, Charles M. "Creation and Self in *Paradise Lost.*" *ELH* 29 (1962): 1–19.

Cohen, Charles Lloyd. *God's Caress: The Psychology of Puritan Religious Experience.* New York: Oxford University Press, 1986.

Conklin, George N. *Biblical Criticism and Heresy in Milton.* New York: King's Crown Press, 1949.

Cosin, John. *Works.* 5 vols. Library of Anglo-Catholic Theology, vols. 31–35. Oxford: John Henry Parker, 1843–1855.

Crook, Margaret B., ed. *The Bible and Its Literary Associations.* New York: Abingdon Press, 1937.

Cross, F. L., and E. A. Livingstone, eds. *The Oxford Dictionary of the Christian Church.* 1958. Reprint. London: Oxford University Press, 1974.

Crump, Galbraith Miller. *The Mystical Design of* Paradise Lost. Lewisburg: Bucknell University Press, 1975.

Daiches, David. "The Opening of *Paradise Lost.*" In *The Living Milton*, edited by Frank Kermode, 55–69. London: Routledge and Kegan Paul, 1960.

Davies, Horton. *The Worship of the English Puritans.* Glasgow: Robert Marlehose, the University Press, 1948.

Desai, Rupin W. "Adam's Fall as a Prefiguration of Christ's Sacrificing Himself for the Church." *Milton Quarterly* 17 (December 1983): 121–25.

Dunn, Esther Cloudman. "The Bible in England in the Sixteenth Century." In *The Bible and Its Literary Traditions*, edited by Margaret B. Crook, 234–61. New York: Abingdon Press, 1937.

Entzminger, Robert L. *Divine Word: Milton and the Redemption of Language.* Pittsburgh: Duquesne University Press, 1985.

Fish, Stanley Eugene. "Discovery as Form in *Paradise Lost.*" In *New Essays on* Paradise Lost, edited by Thomas Kranidas, 1–14. Berkeley and Los Angeles: University of California Press, 1971.

———. "Driving from the Letter: Truth and Indeterminacy in Milton's *Areopagitica.*" In *Re-membering Milton: Essays on the Texts and Traditions*, edited by Mary Nyquist and Margaret W. Ferguson, 234–54. New York: Methuen, 1988.

Fixler, Michael. "The Apocalypse within *Paradise Lost.*" In *New Essays on*

Paradise Lost, edited by Thomas Kranidas, 131–78. Berkeley: University of California Press, 1971.

———. "Milton's Passionate Epic." *Milton Studies* 1 (1969): 167–92.

Fletcher, Harris. "The Use of the Bible in Milton's Prose." In *University of Illinois Studies in Language and Literature*, vol. 14, no. 3. Urbana: University of Illinois Press, 1929.

Greaves, Richard L. "The Puritan-Nonconformist Tradition in England, 1500–1700: Historiographical Reflections." *Albion* 17.4 (Winter 1985): 449–86.

———. *Saints and Rebels: Seven Nonconformists in Stuart England*. Macon: Mercer University Press, 1985.

Haller, William. *The Rise of Puritanism*. New York: Columbia University Press, 1938.

Hayes, T. Wilson. *Winstanley, the Digger*. Cambridge: Harvard University Press, 1979.

Hill, Christopher. *The Antichrist in Seventeenth-Century England*. The Riddell Memorial Lectures. Oxford: Oxford University Press, 1971.

———. *The Collected Essays of Christopher Hill*. Amherst: University of Massachusetts, 1986.

———. *The Experience of Defeat: Milton and Some Contemporaries*. 1984. Reprint. Harmondsworth, Middlesex: Penguin, 1985.

———. *Milton and the English Revolution*. New York: Viking, 1977.

———. *Puritanism and Revolution: Studies in Interpretation of the English Revolution of the Seventeenth Century*. New York: Schocken, 1958.

———. *Society and Puritanism in Pre-Revolutionary England*. 1964. Reprint. New York: Schocken, 1967.

———. *The World Turned Upside Down: Radical Ideas during the English Revolution*. Maurice Temple Smith, 1972.

———, Barry Reay, and William Lamont, eds. *The World of the Muggletonians*. London: Temple Smith, 1983.

Honeygosky, Stephen R. "*License* Reconsidered: Ecclesial Nuances." *Milton Quarterly* 25.2 (Spring 1991): 59–66.

———. "The Mystical in Milton: A Radical Protestant View." *Studia Mystica* 14.1 (Spring 1991): 45–59.

Hughes, Merritt Y., ed. *John Milton: Complete Poems and Major Prose*. Indianapolis: Odyssey-Bobbs-Merrill, 1957.

———. "Milton as a Revolutionary." *ELH* 10 (1943): 87–116.

Hunter, William B., Jr. "Forum: Milton's *Christian Doctrine*." *SEL* 32.1 (Winter 1992): 129–66.

———. "Milton on the Exaltation of the Son: The War in Heaven in *Paradise Lost*." *ELH* 36 (1969): 215–29.

————. "Milton on the Incarnation: Some More Heresies." *Journal of the History of Ideas* 21.3 (1960): 346–69.

Jackson, Samuel Macaulay, and Clarence Nevin Miller. *The Works of Huldreich Zwingli.* 1929. Reprint. Durham: Labyrinth Press, 1981.

Kaufmann, U. Milo. *The Pilgrim's Progress and Traditions in Puritan Meditation.* New Haven: Yale University Press, 1966.

Kelley, Maurice. *This Great Argument: A Study of Milton's* De Doctrina Christiana *as a Gloss Upon* Paradise Lost. 1941. Reprint. Gloucester: Peter Smith, 1962.

————, ed. Vol. 6 of *The Complete Prose Works of John Milton.* Edited by Don M. Wolfe. New Haven: Yale University Press, 1973.

————. "On the State of Milton's *De Doctrina Christiana.*" *English Language Notes* 27.2 (December 1989): 42–48.

Kenny, Robert W. Introduction. *The Law of Freedom in a Platform or, True Magistracy Restored,* by Gerrard Winstanley. 1941. Reprint. New York: Schocken, 1973.

Kent, Margo Anne. "Poetry as Liturgy: Poet as Priest in Some of Milton's Early Poetry." Ph.D. diss., York University, 1983.

Kermode, Frank, ed. *The Living Milton.* London: Routledge and Kegan Paul, 1960.

Kerrigan, William. *The Prophetic Milton.* Charlottesville: University Press of Virginia, 1974.

King, John N. *English Reformation Literature: The Tudor Origins of the Protestant Tradition.* Princeton: Princeton University Press, 1982.

Kranidas, Thomas. "Milton's *Of Reformation:* The Politics of Vision." *ELH* 49 (1982): 497–513.

————, ed. *New Essays on* Paradise Lost. Berkeley and Los Angeles: University of California Press, 1971.

————. "Style and Rectitude in Seventeenth-Century Prose: Hall, Smectymnuus, and Milton." *Huntington Library Quarterly* 46 (1983): 237–69.

Laud, William. *The Works of the Most Reverend Father in God, William Laud, D.D.* Edited by William Scott and James Bliss. Library of Anglo-Catholic Theology, vols. 51–57. Reprint (7 vols. in 9). Oxford: John Henry Parker, 1847–1860.

LeComte, Edward S. *A Milton Dictionary.* New York: Philosophical Library, 1961.

Lewalski, Barbara Kiefer. *Protestant Poetics and the Seventeenth-Century Religious Lyric.* Princeton: Princeton University Press, 1979.

Lieb, Michael. *Poetics of the Holy: A Reading of* Paradise Lost. Chapel Hill: University of North Carolina Press, 1981.

————. *The Sinews of Ulysses: Form and Convention in Milton's Works.* Pittsburgh: Duquesne University Press, 1980.

————, and John T. Shawcross, eds. *Achievements of the Left Hand: Essays on the Prose of John Milton.* Amherst: University of Massachusetts Press, 1974.

Luther, Martin. *Luther's Meditations on the Gospels.* Edited and Translated by Richard Bainton. Philadelphia: Westminster, 1962.

————. *Luther's Primary Works: Together with His Shorter and Larger Catechisms.* Edited by Henry Wace and C. A. Buchheim. London: Hodder and Stoughton, 1896.

————. *Works.* Edited by Jaroslav Pelikan and Helmut T. Lehmann. Vol. 53, *Liturgy and Hymns.* Edited by Ulrich S. Leupold. Philadelphia: Fortress Press, 1958–1967.

Lyle-Scoufos, Alice. "The Mysteries in Milton's *Masque.*" *Milton Studies* 6 (1976): 113–42.

McGiffert, Michael. "God's Controversy with Jacobean England." *American Historical Review* 88 (1983): 1151–74.

————. "Grace and Works: The Rise and Division of Covenant Divinity in Elizabethan Puritanism." *Harvard Theological Review* 75 (1982): 463–502.

McGregor, J. F., and B. Reay, eds. *Radical Religion in the English Revolution.* Oxford: Oxford University Press, 1984.

McNeill, John T. "Some Emphases in Wyclif's Teaching." *Journal of Religion* 7 (1927): 447–66.

Marcus, Leah S. *The Politics of Mirth: Jonson, Herrick, Milton, Marvell, and the Defense of Old Holiday Pastimes.* Chicago: University of Chicago Press, 1986.

Miller, Perry. *The New England Mind: The Seventeenth Century.* Cambridge: Harvard University Press, 1954.

Milner, Andrew. *John Milton and the English Revolution: A Study in the Sociology of Literature.* Totowa: Barnes & Noble, 1981.

Milton, John. *Complete Poems and Major Prose.* Edited by Merritt Y. Hughes. Indianapolis: Odyssey-Bobbs-Merrill, 1957.

————. *Complete Prose Works of John Milton.* Edited by Don M. Wolfe et al. 8 vols. New Haven: Yale University Press, 1953–1982.

Mohl, Ruth. *John Milton and His* Commonplace Book. New York: Frederick Ungar, 1968.

Mollenkott, Virginia R. "The Pervasive Influence of the Apocrypha in Milton's Thought and Art." In *Milton and the Art of Sacred Song,* edited by J. Max Patrick and Roger H. Sundell, 23–46. Madison: University of Wisconsin Press, 1979.

Möller, Jens G. "The Beginnings of Puritan Covenant Theology." *Journal of English History* 14 (1963): 46–67.

Morton, A. L. *The World of the Ranters: Religious Radicalism in the English Revolution.* London: Laurence & Wishart, 1970.

Mueller, J. A. *Stephen Gardiner and the Tudor Reaction.* New York: Macmillan, 1926.

Muggleton, Lodowick. *A True Interpretation of the Eleventh Chapter of the Revelation of St. John.* 1662. Reprint. St. John-Street, Clerkenwell: E. Brown, 1833.

Murrin, Michael. "The Language of Milton's Heaven." *Modern Philology* (May 1977): 55–65.

Nelson, Byron. "Play, Ritual Inversion and Folly among the Ranters in the English Revolution." Ph.D. diss., University of Wisconsin, 1985.

Nichols, James Hastings. *Corporate Worship in the Reformed Tradition.* Philadelphia: Westminster, 1968.

Nuttall, Geoffrey F. *Visible Saints.* Oxford: Oxford University Press, 1957.

Nyquist, Mary, and Margaret W. Ferguson, eds. *Re-membering Milton: Essays on the Texts and Traditions.* New York: Methuen, 1988.

Parker, William Riley. *Milton: A Biography.* 2 vols. London: Oxford University Press, 1968.

Patrick, J. Max, and Roger H. Sundell, eds. *Milton and the Art of Sacred Song.* Madison: University of Wisconsin Press, 1979.

Patrides, C. A., and Raymond B. Waddington, eds. *Age of Milton: Backgrounds to Seventeenth-Century Literature.* Manchester: Manchester University Press, 1980.

Paul, Robert S. *The Assembly of the Lord: Politics and Religion in the Westminster Assembly and the "Grand Debate."* Edinburgh: T. & T. Clark, 1985.

Pecheux, Mother Mary Christopher, O.S.U. "The Second Adam and the Church in *Paradise Lost.*" *ELH* 34 (1967): 173–87.

Pelikan, Jaroslav. "Some Uses of Apocalypse in the Magisterial Reformers." In *The Apocalypse in English Renaissance Thought and Literature,* edited by C. A. Patrides and Joseph Wittreich, 74–92. Manchester: Manchester University Press, 1984.

Perkins, William. *The Work of William Perkins.* Edited by Ian Breward. Appleford: Sutton Courterray Press, 1970.

Peters, Edward. Introduction. *Selected Works,* by Ulrich Zwingli. Edited by Samuel Macauley Jackson. Philadelphia: University of Pennsylvania Press, 1901.

Quint, David. "David's Census: Milton's Politics and *Paradise Regained.*" In *Re-membering Milton: Essays on the Texts and Traditions,* edited by Mary Nyquist and Margaret W. Ferguson, 128–47. New York: Methuen, 1988.

Radzinowicz, Mary Ann. *Toward Samson Agonistes: The Growth of a Poet's Mind.* Princeton: Princeton University Press, 1978.

Reeve, John. *A General Treatise on the Three Records.* In *A General Epistle to Ministers.* 4th ed. London: Printed for Joseph Frost by Luke James Hansard, 1854.

Reeve, John, and Lodowick Muggleton. *A Remonstrance from the Eternal God to the Parliament and Commonwealth of England.* In vol. 1 of *The Third and Last Testament of Our Lord Jesus Christ.* 4th ed. London: Printed for Jospeh Frost by Luke James Hansard, 1854.

Rheinhold, H. A., ed. *The Soul Afire: Revelations of the Mystics.* Garden City: Image Books, 1973.

Ross, Malcolm MacKenzie. *Poetry and Dogma: The Transfiguration of Eucharistic Symbols in Seventeenth-Century English Poetry.* New Brunswick: Rutgers University Press, 1954.

Schultz, Howard. "A Fairer Paradise? Some Recent Studies of *Paradise Regained.*" *ELH* 32 (1965): 275–302.

Schwartz, Regina M. "Citation, Authority, and *De Doctrina Christiana.*" In *Politics, Poetics, and Hermeneutics in Milton's Prose,* edited by David Loewenstein and James Grantham, 227–40. Cambridge: Cambridge University Press, 1990.

————. *Remembering and Repeating Biblical Creation in* Paradise Lost. Cambridge: Cambridge University Press, 1988.

Sewell, Arthur. *A Study in Milton's* Christian Doctrine. Oxford: Oxford University Press, 1967.

Sims, James H. *The Bible in Milton's Epics.* Gainesville: University of Florida Press, 1962.

————. "Milton, Literature as a Bible, and the Bible as Literature." In *Milton and the Art of Sacred Song,* edited by J. Max Patrick and Roger H. Sundell, 3–21. Madison: University of Wisconsin Press, 1979.

————, and Leland Ryken, eds. *Milton and Scriptural Tradition: The Bible into Poetry.* Columbia: University of Missouri Press, 1984.

Thompson, Bard, ed. *Liturgies of the Western Church.* 1961. Reprint. Philadelphia: Fortress Press, 1985.

Thorpe, James. *John Milton: The Inner Life.* San Marino: Huntington Library, 1983.

Ulreich, John C., Jr. "Milton on the Eucharist: Some Second Thoughts about Sacramentalism." In *Milton and the Middle Ages,* edited by John Mulryan, 32–56. Lewisburg: Bucknell University Press; London: Associated University Press, 1982.

Walzer, Michael. *The Revolution of the Saints: A Study in the Origins of Radical Politics.* 8th ed. New York: Atheneum, 1976.

Wilding, Michael. "Regaining the Radical Milton." In *The Radical Reader,* edited by Stephen Knight and Michael Wilding, 119–43. Sydney: Wild and Wooley, 1977.

Williams, George H. *The Radical Reformation.* Philadelphia: Westminster, 1962.

Winstanley, Gerrard. *The Law of Freedom in a Platform, or True Magistracy Restored.* Edited by Robert W. Kenny. 1941. Reprint. New York: Schocken, 1973.

———. *The Works of Gerrard Winstanley.* Edited by George H. Sabine. Ithaca: Cornell University Press, 1941.

Woodhouse, A. S. P. *Puritanism and Liberty.* Chicago: University of Chicago Press, 1965.

Zwingli, Huldreich. "The Church: A Reply to Jerome Emser." In *The Works of Huldreich Zwingli,* edited by Samuel Macaulay Jackson and Clarence Nevin Miller. 1929. Reprint. Durham: Labyrinth Press, 1981.

Zwingli, Huldrych. *Writings.* Edited by Dikran Y. Hadidian. Vol. 1, *In Defense of the Reformed Faith.* Translated by Edward J. Furcha. Allison Park: Pickwick, 1984.

INDEX

While the core of Milton's church doctrine is given its own subdivision, delineations and applications of his doctrine are indexed under *Church* because of explicit and implicit ecclesiological and ecclesial overlapping and interinvolvement with other Reformers and because of easier manageability of what would otherwise have been, for reader and writer, a burdensome list of modifications for three subentries under *Milton* (*doctrine*, *works*, and *church*) instead of two.

Law (Old *v.* New Testament), 115, 176, 176*n10*, 177, 209, 214, 217, 223
LeComte, Edward S., 81*n1*
Leftist(s), 84, 129, 163; ecclesial identity of, 1, 137–38; political implications of church identity, 93. *See also* Radical(s)(-ism)
Levellers, 11–12, 48, 93–94, 137, 185*n7*, 211
Lewalski, Barbara K., 10*n14*, 96*n25*, 203, 219*n1*
Libertarian policy, 130*n7*
Liberty, 61, 72, 105, 118, 121, 128–29, 131, 140, 207–8
Lieb, Michael, 1, 4–5, 122*n9*, 175*n9*, 213*n1*, 214*n2*, 218*n4*, 223–24, 230*n2*
Lilburne, John, 92–93
Liturgy(-ical), 1, 10, 11, 23–27, 64, 71, 110, 173–79, 182, 222–25, 232, 236–38
Lollards, 82*n2*, 110, 163, 170*n3*
Lord's Supper, 202, 205, 223*n7*
Luke, St., 158
Luther, Martin, 13, 19–29, 32, 52, 62, 75, 81, 82, 86, 90*n18*, 163, 169, 171*n5*, 172, 176*n10*, 179, 193, 207–8, 209, 220, 222
Lyle-Scoufos, Alice, 4, 5

McGiffert, Michael, 56–57*n9*
McGregory, J. F., 11, 69*n2*, 85, 183*n4*
McNeill, John T., 53*n6*
Magistrates, 155, 156. *See also* Milton: doctrine: magistrates
Manning, Brian, 93, 185*n7*
Marcus, Leah S., 3–4
Marshall, Stephen, 82, 118, 193
Mary (Tudor), Queen, 32, 82*n2*, 146
Mather, Richard, 32
Miller, Perry, 46*n1*, 56*n9*, 71, 74, 127–28, 135, 183*n4*
Milner, Andrew, 11–12, 137
Milton, John: church identity of, 107, 112, 118–19, 126, 135–38, 154, 163, 168, 169, 184, 229; church membership of, 15–16, 27–29, 70, 106, 108, 112, 125–26, 135–38, 139, 153, 154–55, 159, 166–67, 184, 230, 233, 236; disputed church orthodoxy of, 10–11*n15*; ecclesial impulse of, 1, 13, 228; Independents and, 15, 72, 107, 126, 127, 137–38, 139, 144–45, 156, 157, 159, 181, 193, 229; Papist(s) and, 35, 84, 92, 124, 158, 196, 197, 202, 204–5, 223, 224, 229; Prelates and, 97–98, 104, 106, 107, 108–19, 123–24, 126,

127, 130, 140, 172–74, 178, 181, 193, 229; Presbyterians and, 15, 72, 84, 106, 107, 119–23, 126, 127, 133–34, 144–45, 150, 156, 159, 181, 193, 229; Protestant church and, 15, 19, 97, 110, 128, 143, 193, 204, 206, 236; Radicals and, 11–16, 68–69, 82, 92, 94–95, 120, 126, 128, 129–30, 134, 141, 146, 147, 163, 179–80, 185*n9*, 187, 194, 201, 203, 206–7, 211, 215, 222, 230; recurring verbal pattern, 13, 16, 108, 135, 158–59, 229–30; Restored Anglicans and, 107; rhetorical style of, 47*n2*, 64–71, 73, 104–5, 109–18, 120–22, 124, 134–35, 174–76, 184–85, 187–89, 191–92, 194, 198–200, 225
—doctrine: adoption, 60, 171, 175, 177, 178; Antichrist, 14, 79–80, 104–5; assurance of salvation, 60–61; ceremony(-ialism), 61, 105, 110, 141, 150, 171, 172–79, 183, 191, 209, 217, 223–24, 236–38; charity (or holiness of life), 5, 15, 35, 61, 62, 121, 128, 141, 141*n4*, 144, 167, 171, 195, 207, 209–10, 213–18; church, 1, 2, 3, 5–16, 30–44, 45–61, 140, 159, 166, 169–77 (*see also* Church for delineation and application of Milton's church doctrine in Reformational context); clergy, 15, 91, 159, 173–79, 182, 185, 189, 201–2, 234; complete *v.* incomplete glorification, 9, 60, 215; conscience, 14, 72, 84, 104, 105, 115, 139–60, 181, 217; dignity and sanctity of all believers, 15, 84–85, 105, 154, 167, 169–80, 183, 200, 221; double scripture (external *v.* internal), 164–65, 219–28; education, 183–87, 195–96; heresie, 108, 109, 128, 133, 144–45, 150, 158, 159, 233; holiness, 91, 159, 171–79, 206, 236 (*see also* charity); Holy Spirit, 114, 121, 122, 141, 147, 149, 165, 170, 171, 184, 200, 203, 220–22, 225, 226, 227, 238; House of God, 16, 30, 122, 164, 228, 237; illumination of Scripture through the Spirit, 84, 139*n2*, 142–43; indifferency, 140; indwelling Spirit, 14, 70, 134, 140, 142–43; ingrafting, 9, 42*n8*, 58–59, 123, 127, 170, 225–26; inner light, 84, 146, 182*n3*, 187, 221*n5*, 226; internal *v.* external man (or inward *v.* outward man), 90–94, 142–60, 170–72, 219; justification, 177, 206–12, 217; laick *v.* rightful clergy of Christ, 15, 91, 167, 173–79; learned *v.* un-